Giving Voice to Bear

Hidatsa shield cover.
*Photo courtesy of the Buffalo
Bill Historical Center, Cody,
Wyoming.*

GIVING VOICE TO
BEAR

*North American Indian
Rituals, Myths, and
Images of the Bear*

David Rockwell
Illustrations by Janet McGahan

ROBERTS RINEHART PUBLISHERS

For My Parents and Addy

Published in the United States by Roberts Rinehart Publishers
Post Office Box 666, Niwot, Colorado 80544

Published in Ireland by Roberts Rinehart International
3 Bayview Terrace, Schull, West Cork, Republic of Ireland

Published in Canada by Key Porter Books
70 The Esplanade
Toronto, Ontario, Canada M5E 1R2

Designed by Polly Christensen

Cover photograph: "Bear's Belly, Arikara"
from *The North American Indian* by Edward S. Curtis
(Norwood, Massachusetts: Plimpton Press, 1908).
Reprinted with the permission of the Boston Public Library.
Calligraphic letters by Arthur Baker.

International Standard Book Number 0-911797-97-1
Library of Congress Catalog Card Number 91-60437
Printed in the United States of America

CONTENTS

Acknowledgments   vii

Introduction   ix

Prologue   xv

1. "Bears Are Half Human"   1

2. "That is the Way They Are Born, in the Form of a Bear"   9

3. "Grandfather, I Am Sorry I Must Kill You"   25

4. "It May Change into Anything"   47

5. "A Bear Will Devour Your Flesh"   63

6. Digging for Medicine   75

7. "Ah Bear, We Are the Same Person"   91

8. Giving Voice to Bear   113

9. Moving Like a Bear   147

10. "I Know Where the Bear Is Living"   163

11. Honey-Paws in the Old World   179

12. Beneath is a Bear   195

Notes   203

Bibliography   211

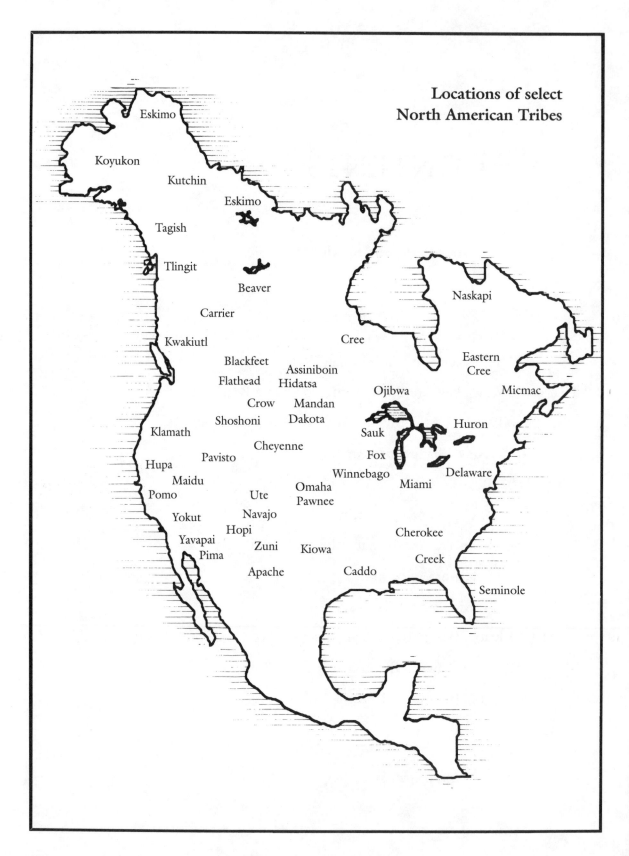

Locations of select
North American Tribes

Eskimo

Koyukon

Kutchin

Eskimo

Tagish

Tlingit

Beaver

Carrier

Kwakiutl

Naskapi

Cree

Eastern
Cree

Blackfeet

Flathead

Assiniboin

Hidatsa

Micmac

Crow

Mandan

Ojibwa

Shoshoni

Dakota

Huron

Klamath

Cheyenne

Sauk

Fox

Pavisto

Winnebago

Delaware

Hupa

Miami

Maidu

Pomo

Ute

Omaha

Pawnee

Yokut

Navajo

Hopi

Cherokee

Yavapai

Zuni

Kiowa

Creek

Pima

Apache

Caddo

Seminole

ACKNOWLEDGMENTS

I OWE A PARTICULAR DEBT of gratitude to Mary Stranahan for her belief in this project from its inception, and for her patient support. I am indebted also to Doug Baty for his unfailing loyalty and generosity, and for the cabin. I wish to thank Jerry McGahan for his painstaking editing of the manuscript, for his ideas, and most of all for his remarkable enthusiasm. I am grateful to Dorothy Patent for valuable comments on the book outline and work on early chapter drafts, to Harvey and Emmalou Baty for their support and counsel, and to Tom Roy for his encouragement and help. Several others read the manuscript and offered constructive suggestions. I would especially like to thank Mike Dolson for his careful readings. Beth Farris, Charles Jonkel, Roy Bigcrane, Tom Smith, Steve and Marilynn French, and Joseph Epes Brown also reviewed all or parts of the manuscript and provided helpful comments. I owe a special thank you to Johnny Arlee for his early encouragement. Marianne Farr and others at the Mansfield Library in Missoula and Bob Bigart at the Salish Kootenai College Library generously assisted me with hundreds of requests. Marianne and Antje Baty translated several letters and articles. I also wish to thank Deborah Broaddus, the book's copy-editor at Roberts Rinehart, for her many contributions to the manuscript, and Rick Rinehart and Carrie Jenkins for their help with various aspects of the book. I am grateful to Janet McGahan for the charcoal sketches that appear throughout the book. Finally, I wish to thank my wife, Nancy, for her ideas, for her help with editing and proofreading, and for her support and understanding.

Grateful acknowledgment is hereby made to the following publishers for use of material under copyright:

Chapter One
To Yale University's Peabody Museum of Natural History for the story "The Man Who Slept in a Bear's Hole," which appeared in the article "Ingalik Mental Culture" by Cornelius Osgood in the *Yale University Publications in Anthropology*, Number 56. To Crossroad Press for the quote

from *The Spiritual Legacy of the American Indian* by Joseph Epes Brown. Copyright 1982 by Joseph Epes Brown. Reprinted by permission of the Crossroad Publishing Company.

Chapter Two

To the University of Chicago Press for the quote from *Pueblo Indian Religion* by Elsie Clews Parsons. Copyright 1939 by the University of Chicago Press. Reprinted with permission.

Chapter Four

To the University of Chicago Press for Chief Henry's quote from *Make Prayers to the Raven* by Richard Nelson. Copyright 1983 by the University of Chicago Press. To the American Folklore Society for the Athapaskan riddles from the *Journal of American Folklore* 97(Jan-March 1984):383. Not for sale or further reproduction. To the Canadian Museum of Civilization for the Inland Tlingit description of how one discovers if a bear is inside a den.

Chapter Six

To the University of Oklahoma Press for the vision of the Lakota bear medicine man from *Sioux Indian Religion: Tradition and Innovation*, edited and with an introduction by Raymond J. DeMallie and Douglas R. Parks. Copyright 1987 by the University of Oklahoma Press. To the University of California *Publications in American Archaeology and Ethnology*, 1(2), for the Hupa tale "Bear Discovers Medicine for Women," which appeared in the article "Hupa Texts" by P. E. Goddard. To the University of Nebraska Press for the Thomas Tyon quote reprinted from *Lakota Belief and Ritual* by James R. Walker, edited by Raymond J. De Mallie and Elaine Jahner. Copyright 1980 by the University of Nebraska Press. To the American Folklore Society for the tale about Bear Old Man from *Journal of American Folklore*, Volume 34. Not for sale or further reproduction.

Chapter Seven

To the Canadian Museum of Civilization for the tale "The Girl Who Married the Bear." To the University of Chicago Press for Richard Nelson's journal entry from *Make Prayers to the Raven*. Copyright 1983 by the University of Chicago Press. To the American Folklore Society for the Yavapai tale about the toothed vagina from *Journal of American Folklore*, Volume 34. Not for sale or further reproduction. To Columbia University for the grizzly-bear woman tale from Archie Phinney's 1934 article "Nez Perce Texts" in Columbia University *Contributions to Anthropology*, Volume 25. To St. Martin's Press for the tale "The Boy Who was Kept by a Bear" from Adrian Tanner's book *Bringing Home the Animals: Religious Ideology and Mode of Production of the Mistassini Cree Hunters*. Copyright 1979 by Adrian Tanner. To the University of Nebraska Press for the Thomas Tyon quote reprinted from *Lakota Belief and Ritual* by James R. Walker, edited by Raymond J. De Mallie and Elaine Jahner. Copyright 1980 by the University of Nebraska Press.

INTRODUCTION

IN THE EARLY 1980s I worked as a wilderness ranger for an Indian tribe in Montana. One spring morning I sat in the tribal council chambers and listened to Patrick Big Horse*, a tribal game warden and spiritual leader, ask the council to close the reservation to grizzly bear hunting. He had brought a small group of tribal elders with him.

Patrick told the council that few Indians hunted grizzly bears, that the elders did not think Indian people should kill them for sport or meat, that they believed it was important to have grizzly bears in the mountains. "We want you to protect the few bears that are left," he said.

He sat down, and two federal biologists presented the results of a research study to the council. They warned that the grizzly bear population on the reservation was seriously threatened. A brief discussion followed and the council voted unanimously to prohibit all grizzly bear hunting on the reservation. It would take one month for that ordinance to become law.

Three weeks later, an Indian man named Louie Joseph killed an eight-hundred-pound, nineteen-year-old grizzly bear thought to have been killing calves. The death of that bear, and what happened after, motivated me to write this book.

I had just arrived at work when Jim Middleton, the Bureau of Indian Affairs biologist on the reservation, called me on the radio. "I need your help," he said. "I'm at Bob Page's. Louie's killed a bear. Bring the blue tool box and a radio."

Zuni bear fetish. *Smithsonian Institution.*

Page, a dairy farmer, had been having bear problems. He had lost two calves the week before. His farm sat against the mountains and bordered a shallow swale dense with willow, alder, and birch. In the spring the bears frequented the thicket because a multitude of bear foods sprouted there long before they appeared in the mountains. A

---

* To protect the privacy of those involved, the names of individuals in this introduction have been changed.

few years before, a researcher had counted nine radio-collared grizzly bears within a quarter of a mile of the Page house.

After the first calf was killed, tribal game wardens and Middleton had set several snare traps and a culvert trap near the house. They baited two of them with the remains of the calf and the others with rotten fish from a nearby trout farm. Within three days they had caught two young male grizzlies, and the Indian wardens hauled the bears to Canada and released them in a river bottom, miles from the nearest human habitation.

Middleton and the wardens had decided that the chances were good that at least one of the bears was the nuisance, and they removed the traps. But two days later, Page lost a second calf. They found the carcass in the thicket where the first calf had been left, and Middleton decided that the same bear had probably killed both animals. The wardens set the traps again.

Page was worried. He could not afford to lose another calf, and his three kids could not stay in the house all the time. To ease Page's mind, Middleton spent the next two days and nights there, watching the traps in the swale from the loft in Page's barn and sleeping with a rifle and sawed-off shotgun at his side. But the bear did not show itself, so Middleton abandoned his lookout. He went back to his original routine and visited Page's farm twice a day to check the traps. Page felt that he had been abandoned. He called Louie Joseph, a tribal member who had let it be known that he wanted to kill a grizzly bear.

Louie camped at the Page farm the night before he shot the bear. At first morning light he stood at the fence behind the house. He heard a noise, looked into the swale, and saw a grizzly rear up above the brush thirty yards from the house. He shot it once in the chest. His bullet hit both lungs and the bear collapsed.

By the time I arrived, the bear lay on its belly with a gut pile beside it. Louie had his knife out and was cutting the heart free from the lungs. Perhaps a dozen of Page's neighbors, the biologist, and five or six tribal wardens, including Patrick Big Horse, stood in a half circle around him and the bear.

The bear was enormous. It appeared that Louie, crouching near the animal, could easily have curled up inside the head and neck alone. Its fur, a rusty brown on the back, darkened to chocolate on the legs and belly, and, except for a ring of blood and dirt that matted the hair around the neck, it appeared clean and soft. The face seemed passive. The eyes, dark and small, stared beyond.

Two men, neighboring ranchers, came forward and kneeled next to the bear. One of them picked up a front paw and put his hand

Above and opposite: Two examples of bear effigy pipes from the southeast. Cherokee. *Photos courtesy of the University Museum, University of Pennsylvania.*

against the pad to measure its size. The other held the paw against his chest. The five inch claws touched the man's collar bone, the lowest part of the pad rested against his belly, the width of the paw hid all but an inch on either side of his chest. He put the paw down, remarking about what it could have done to a person, then reverently touched the long copper-colored claws.

Louie moved excitedly between the bear and the crowd. He talked and laughed with the ranchers and spoke briefly and seriously with Middleton and Patrick Big Horse about how he had killed the bear. He reluctantly allowed Middleton to take some measurements and pull a tooth from the bear, but he helped to hold the jaw open while Middleton worked. (We later learned from the tooth that the bear was nineteen years old.)

The onlookers stood in two groups. One group, composed of ranchers and neighbors, none of whom were Indian, gathered close to Louie and the bear. They sipped coffee as they talked and approached and touched the dead animal, and they joked about it. "Now its a good bear," I heard a woman say. One man put his cap on the bear's head. Others laughed about all the law enforcement vehicles on the road and the measurements Middleton made. One man told Page, "If it had been me, I would have shot and shoveled. Now the tribe, the state, and the feds are gonna be on your ass."

The uniformed Indian wardens stood farther back. Middleton, who, as a biologist, had handled many bears, was cordial in his dealings with Page and Louie, but the wardens were quiet and dispirited. Several of them left the crowd and waited by their trucks. Patrick Big Horse was openly angry. He is a big man with braids that hang to his waist. I have seen him smile only rarely. When he is angry, he looks mean, even dangerous.

Page brought out a chainsaw and cut and limbed a small tree. He and Louie tied a rope from it to the bear, and seven or eight of the men held the log against their chests and drug the bear out of the thicket and into Page's driveway. Page then attached a rope to a rear leg and hoisted it with the bucket of his tractor. The bear hung upside down while Page and his neighbors took pictures.

I turned to look back toward the thicket and saw Patrick Big Horse standing alone in the knee high grass at the edge of Page's yard, his eyes fixed on the bear. He was praying. He spoke in his native language, his voice a kind of murmur, almost a whisper. I don't think anyone else heard him.

Eventually, Page lowered the bear into the back of a red pickup truck and Louie hauled it away. Three days later Page called to report the loss of another calf. "You better bring your traps back," he said. "I think Louie got the wrong damn bear. This calf is lying in the same place as the other two."

I was depressed and angered by the death of this bear. There were few grizzly bears left on the reservation. I felt ashamed of the disrespect shown toward such an awesome creature. I was intrigued by Patrick's reaction and wanted to know more about Indian spirituality and about the Indian's traditional relations with animals. Specifically, I wanted to know about Indians and bears and how they lived together before Europeans arrived in North America.

That is the principal topic of this book. The first ten chapters explore, in some depth, the role of the bear in American Indian initiation and healing ceremonies, in shamanic rites, in the quest for guardian spirits, and in various dances. They describe bear hunting methods and rituals and include a number of myths and tales about bears.

Early on in my research, I came across Irving Hallowell's 1926 crosscultural study, *Bear Ceremonialism in the Northern Hemisphere*. That monograph, famous among anthropologists, examined in great detail the bear hunting traditions of boreal peoples from around the world. Hallowell found a remarkable correspondence: native North Americans, Europeans, and Asians possessed strikingly similar bear-hunting rituals—they used the same circumlocutions to address bears before and during their hunts, they used the same weapons to kill the animals, they decorated the carcasses in similar ways, they observed similar restrictions when they ate bear meat, and they disposed of bones in the same way. As I read more about bears and people, I learned about many other traditions, traditions that had nothing to do with hunting, that Europeans shared with American Indians. I wanted to know why these correspondences among cultures existed. What is it about bears that would lead people with such different backgrounds to create the same rituals?

The last two chapters of the book attempt to answer this question of origins. Chapter eleven describes European traditions that are analogous to each of the American Indian traditions discussed in the earlier chapters. Chapter twelve considers the bear dreams of contemporary Europeans collected by Carl Jung in the 1940s, and explores why the bear has the power it does over the human imagination and spirit.

This book is about people more than it is about bears. It is about human traditions perhaps twenty-thousand years old, about rituals in which men and women imitate bears, indeed are believed to change into bears. It is about hunters' dreams and shamans' travels into the spirit world. It is about magic and myth and dance and things sacred.

It is a book about how we, as humans, for most of our history, have lived with and thought about animals.

An Inuit carving depicts a person and a bear seated back to back. The bodies come together so that one merges with the other. The person appears to be singing. Perhaps the bear is too. It is this relation between humans and animals that the traditions described in this book convey.

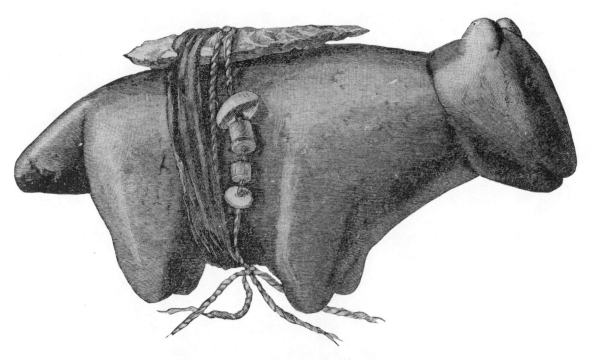

Black bear fetish. Zuni. Ethnologist Frank Cushing wrote that among the Zuni, Black Bear is "Master of the West…The coat is the color of the land of night." *Smithsonian Institution.*

PROLOGUE

IT IS EARLY SPRING, but the land is cold and all but invisible through blowing snow. The evenness of the snow and light take away all perception of depth and hide gentle rises and coulies. The hills, white as the air, have disappeared. Only the dark rolling waters of the river stand out.

Through this storm a Northern Cheyenne family follows the river to their spring camp. They are bundled and moving on foot, the wind at their backs—a man, two women, two children, and three dogs. They pass a stand of cottonwoods. The dogs begin to bark and growl, then whimper and act afraid. The family pauses. The man points at the grove. "They are frightened by the trees," he shouts over the wind. "In this storm they look like ghosts."

But then they see a shadow-like form moving through the squall against the gray trees. Through gusts of snow the shape becomes more defined. It is a grizzly bear and it crosses their path not far from where they stand. The bear carries its head low, close to the ground, and moves with purpose. Its shoulders are humped. Its fur is a rich brown. A thin blanket of snow covers its back. In a moment it appears shadow-like again and disappears into the whiteness. It is the first bear any of them have seen in seven moons.

The family reaches their camp later that day. The days that follow are clear and warm. The snow melts and buttercups bloom. Their spring camp grows muddy. Birds return. Cottonwood buds swell. It is spring.

"Bears are Half Human"

ONCE A MAN WENT OUT in the fall just before the first snow to hunt for a bear. The weather was cold. He found a bear hole at last, killing the bear and skinning it. Then because it was so cold he crawled into the bear hole which seemed like a nice place to stay overnight. He piled grass over the opening to keep out the air and went to sleep. When he woke up from time to time, he turned over. At last he woke up, but he felt strange. The flesh of his face was drawn tightly over his cheekbones. He listened for a moment and could hear flies at the door. It was spring.

"Did I sleep all winter?" he asked himself.

Then he went out. He found the remnants of his bear meat with flies all over it. He felt very weak and it took him a long time to walk home. The people were surprised to see him. They had hunted for him all winter.

Someone asked, "Didn't your father tell you not to sleep in a bear hole?"

That is why people do not go into bear holes.[1]

BEARS AND INDIANS have lived together on the continent of North America for thousands of years. Both walked the same trails, fished the same salmon streams, dug camas roots from the same fields, and, year after year, harvested the same berries, seeds, and nuts. Indians came face to face with bears when both coveted the same berry patch, for instance, or when a hunter, bringing help to pack home an elk he had killed, discovered that a bear had buried the carcass and was lying on the mound. Sometimes the hunter fled, sometimes the bear. The relationship was one of mutual respect. But it went well beyond that.

Bear headdress belonging to Bear Head, a western Sioux. *Photo courtesy of the Smithsonian Institution, National Anthropological Archives.*

1

Bears were often central to the most basic rites of many tribes: the initiation of youths into adulthood, the sacred practices of shamanism, the healing of the sick and injured, the rites surrounding the hunt. For many Indians, simply speaking about bears required the observance of specific taboos.

All across North America, Indians have honored bears. When northern hunting tribes killed one, they spoke to its spirit, asking for its forgiveness. They treated the carcass reverently; among these tribes the ritual for a slain bear was more elaborate than that for any other food animal.

Why was the bear significant to these peoples? Partly because Indians feared bears, feared being mauled and maimed or even killed. Bears were dangerous, one of the few animals that posed much of a threat to Indians. Indian ritual practices, myths and tales, and attitudes reflect this fear. Immediately after slaying a bear, the hunters of some northern Athapaskan tribes would cut off its forepaws and poke out its eyes so the dead animal could not hurt them or see who killed it.[2] The Kootenai of southern British Columbia sang, prayed, and danced every spring to avoid being killed or mauled by a bear that year.[3]

But fear alone does not account for the rich and varied traditions linked to bears in native North America. An Indian's deepest feelings about bears transcended fear. They felt a kinship with bears, for the two shared many basic physical characteristics.

Bears are built somewhat like people. Unlike other large animals familiar to the Indians, bears often stand on their hind legs and, from time to time, walk upright. Their tracks—imprints of heel, arch and toes—suggest the passing of some large, wild, forest person. When a bear rises up on its hind legs, or when it sits, its front legs hang like arms. A bear often stands and reaches, as a person would, for berries it cannot grasp with its mouth. And bears display considerable dexterity with their paws—in captivity they have been known to peel peaches. The Blackfeet word *o-kits-iks*, refers to both the human hand and a bear's paw.[4] A skinned bear carcass looks human.

These physical resemblances were especially meaningful to the Indians, who tended to anthropomorphize the world around them. They constantly looked for similarities between animals and people. Indians talked about animals in human terms and assigned them human motives. Their myths and tales told of a time when animals acted and lived as Indians lived: in lodges, hunting for their food, making fire to cook with and keep warm. In the Yukon, the Tlingit said, "Grizzlies are half human."[5] The Ojibwa often referred to bears as *anijinabe*, their word for Indian.[6] Likewise, the Yavapai of Arizona

Fool Bull, a Sioux medicine man. His bear-claw necklace is typical of that worn by warriors of the Great Plains tribes. *Photo courtesy of the Nebraska Historical Society.*

"Bears Are Half Human"

3

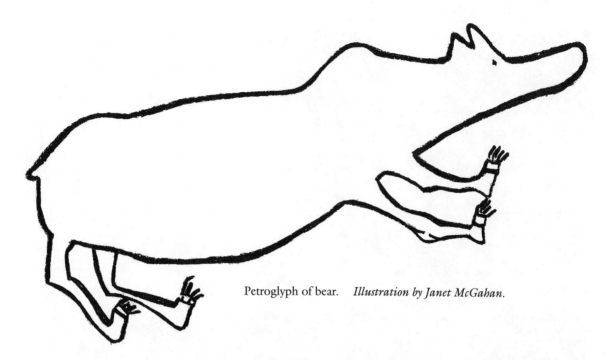

Petroglyph of bear. *Illustration by Janet McGahan.*

said, "Bears are like people except that they can't make fire."[7] Many plains and southwestern tribes, including the Yavapai, would not eat bear meat because they believed it was like eating a person, a relative.

There are other correspondences, too. Bears are famous for their fierce maternal devotion. Getting between a mother bear and her cubs can be a fatal mistake. Most human-bear encounters where someone is hurt involve a sow with cubs. Humans admire good mothers. Joseph Henderson, in his book *Thresholds of Initiation*, tells us that bears, because they are so protective and such careful nurses, symbolize for us the ethics of maternity.[8] This is fitting, for few young animals depend on their mothers as much as bear cubs. Black bear and grizzly cubs are born in the winter den, blind, helpless, and nearly hairless, weighing only about ten to fourteen ounces each. The world they are born into is another womb, an earth womb, a safe place of nurture and protection where they can continue to grow and develop as they did inside their mothers' bodies. Until they emerge from this second womb, they are still one with their mothers. In the first few minutes after birth, the mother helps her cub find its way to a nipple, and it begins to suckle the fat-rich milk. For the next several months, it clings to her, nursing and sleeping, beneath the earth. The only smell it knows is the scent of her, mingled with that of the earth. The only sounds it hears are the constant rhythms of her heart and breath. In spring, mother bear and cubs crawl out of their earthen womb into the daylight. After leaving the den the family stays together—in the case of grizzlies, for up to two

GIVING VOICE TO BEAR

or even three summers. They sleep through the intervening winters together in the same den. Bear cubs stay tied to their mothers twice as long as other North American mammals of comparable size. This protracted juvenile period is essential because so much of what a bear does is probably learned.

As with bears, our long infancy and childhood gives us time to interact with our parents and siblings; safe time to play, learn, experiment, observe. As a consequence we form strong emotional bonds, especially with our mothers. The analytical psychologist Erich Neumann suggested that this bonding is "at the very foundation of our social life and hence human culture." He writes, "The human species is the only one in which the infant, during the first year of life, may be regarded as an 'embryo outside the womb'. This implies that it completes its extrauterine embryonic life in a social environment essentially determined by the mother. The circumstance enhances the importance of the mother for the child and strengthens the mother's attachment to the child, whose embryonic dependency becomes a basis for her unconscious and conscious maternal solicitude."[9]

Indians saw other resemblances between bears and humans—diet, for instance. Bears and Indians ate the same foods and, in some instances, in the same relative proportions. About 80 percent of what a bear eats is vegetable, while around 70 percent of the food consumed by many gathering-hunting tribes came from plants.[10] Berries, of course, were consumed in large quantities by both, but bears and Indians also shared a variety of other vegetable foods. Both visited the same mountain prairies in mid-summer to dig starchy roots and bulbs. Both harvested pine nuts from the wooded ridge tops. Both ate the same seeds, leafy plants, and mushrooms.

It is probable that Indians ate more meat only because they were better at obtaining it. But bears were as familiar as Indians with the winter ranges of deer, elk, and buffalo. Indians went there to hunt, bears to find winter-killed carrion. It is likely that bears, like Indians, knew and hunted the fawning and calving grounds and the places where bucks and rams, injured or exhausted by the effort of the fall rut, might be found. And wherever salmon spawned, Indians and bears alike gathered to harvest the bounty. Both had the flexibility to take advantage of the highest quality foods available at any given time.

These similarities in lifeway did not escape the Indian. For them, every animal—bear, eagle, wolf, prairie dog—had its own way of living in the world. Each animal represented a different aspect of life, and Indians looked to each as a model to be understood and emulated and as a source of wisdom. Among the plains tribes the wolf, as a hunter, presided spiritually over the hunt and war parties. The buffa-

Mimbres images of bears from New Mexico (from the tenth to the twelfth century). *Illustration by Janet McGahan.*

lo represented fecundity and virtue. The bear knew the secrets of the plants. The bear appears again and again in native American myth and lore as plant gatherer, as master forager, and as bestower of the secrets and mysteries of plants. For the Indian, the bear was the shaggy berry picker, the shambling nut gatherer asleep under the piñon tree, the mysterious herbalist collecting medicines in the dense undergrowth of the wet bottomlands. Using its claws instead of a digging stick, the bear was that wise old animal person digging roots on the sun-baked hillsides.

Because Indians identified with the bear in all these ways, they imitated it in ritual. When the Yokuts of California had finished gathering and storing their fall acorn crop, Bear Clan members danced a bear dance. No one could eat any acorns before the dance was finished. The dancers wore loose bear-skin robes, bear-claw necklaces, and bear-paw skins pulled over their hands like mittens. They mimicked bears gathering nuts.[11] In their annual feast, the Bear Clan of the Prairie Potawatomi, a Great Lakes tribe, ate maple sugar, meat, walnuts, and berries, known favorites of bears.[12] Clan members carved acorns, the emblem of the bear, on their war clubs.

But spiritual traditions were not simply imitations. The bear was a religious symbol for American Indians, and religious symbols transcend objective reality. They emerge spontaneously and reveal something of the mystery of the world. In his book *The Spiritual Legacy of the American Indian*, Joseph Epes Brown writes that, for plains Indians, animals and other natural forms reflected aspects of God:

> Animals were created before human beings, so that in their anteriority and divine origin they have a certain proximity to the Great Spirit . . . which demands respect and veneration. In them the Indian sees actual reflections of the qualities of the Great Spirit, which serve the same function as revealed scriptures in other religions. They are intermediaries or links between human beings and God. This explains not only why religious devotions may be directed to the deity through the animals, but it also helps us to understand why contact with or from the Great Spirit, comes almost exclusively through visions involving animal or other natural forms.[13]

Every year bears disappear with the first heavy snow of fall, the snow that marks the beginning of winter. They crawl into the earth, the source of all life and the place where all life must one day return. For half the year they lie underground in a death-like sleep, while outside the world sleeps with them. In the spring, they awaken and emerge from their dens into a fresh new world, a world in which the earth itself is being reborn.

Black bear mask. The human face represents the spirit of the bear. From the lower Yukon. *Photo courtesy of the Smithsonian Institution, National Anthropological Archives.*

Some tribes, such as the Delaware, tied bears directly to the springtime rebirth of the earth and honored them in new year ceremonies. Because bears periodically disappeared and reappeared, northern hunting tribes such as the Cree connected them with the renewal of game animals. Other tribes incorporated bears into their healing and initiation rituals because those traditions, too, were fundamentally rites of renewal, or of death and rebirth.

Bears were important to Indian people because they hibernated *and* because they resembled humans, both in their physical appearance and in the way they lived. A bear is a furry person, a relative, that goes underground when the earth sleeps and emerges when it wakes.

Bear and neophyte.
Kwakiutl. *Photo courtesy of
the National Museums of
Canada, Ottawa.*

2

"That is the Way They are Born, in the Form of a Bear"

I N [AN] INITIATORY CEREMONIAL the initiate is brought into close contact with any fear-inspiring object like yucca switches or with any fearful being the group is associated with, with Bear or Mountain Lion or Snake or the Dead. He is frightened so he will no longer be afraid, a kind of inoculation against fear. He receives the paraphernalia proper to membership. He goes through the indispensable rite of head-washing and naming. He may be treated ritually as an infant, for he is "reborn," into another circle, a world-wide theory of initiation. At Zuñi the annual ceremony at which initiation takes place will be held in a waxing moon, a time propitious to rebirth; the preliminary retreat will be held four days before the full moon. When the Fathers of Isleta initiate, they dramatize the birth by covering the novice and his "mother," the senior woman of the society, with the same blanket. From under the blanket as they sit near the altar the "mother" draws the corn-ear fetish which "through the power of the chief has been born from her." The chief embraces "mother" and novice under this blanket from which the novice emerges as a bear. "That is the way they are born, in the form of a bear."[1]

IN THE FALL OF THE YEAR, as shorter days and changing weather signals the approach of winter, bears begin searching for den sites. Grizzly bears look for isolated locations, usually high on timbered slopes near fall foraging areas. Black bears, too, generally search out denning areas away from human activity. Remoteness is important to both species in den selection because they are vulnerable during hibernation.

A grizzly bear often digs its den at the base of a large tree or stump, the roots of which serve as a protective ceiling. The bear works for days and sometimes weeks. After shaping the cavern, it covers the floor with twelve to eighteen inches of conifer boughs or soft mosses and grasses. Once the den is prepared, the bear returns to its fall feeding. By then there is often a skiff of snow on the ground and a bite to the air, even on bright sunny days. The bear continues to forage for roots and berries to satisfy an obvious appetite and to build fat stores as high as possible. It finally returns to its den sometime after the first substantial winter storm.

Black bears occasionally dig dens, but more often they find hollowed out trees, natural caves, or dense brushy thickets to sleep in. Biologist Stuart Free, working in New York State, has documented behavior apparently designed to frustrate hunters attempting to track black bears to their dens. He found that, just before denning, black bears investigate several possible sites. "They will walk up to a den site, go in, then back out, stepping in their own tracks for twenty yards or more, then leap perhaps fifteen to twenty feet to the side and continue on to find another site and then do the same thing."[2]

Inside its den, a bear, whether it is a black bear or a grizzly, curls up and falls into a deep sleep. Outside, the relentless snowfall seals out the light and cold and conceals the bear from the world. It will not eat, drink, urinate, or defecate for the next five to seven months. Its temperature will fall as much as five degrees centigrade, its heart will slow from the summer rate of forty to fifty beats per minute to only eight or ten. With its body functions slowed and suspended, a bear might lie without moving for up to a month at a time. But if disturbed, it can awaken with surprising celerity.

Many Native American initiation ceremonies suggest that Indians associated initiation with hibernation. Initiation was one of the most widespread of all American Indian spiritual traditions. The ceremonies, which encompassed puberty rites, the initiation of shamans, and the initiation of men and women into secret societies, were practiced by every tribe on the continent. Rituals varied, as did the myths supporting them, but a common pattern underlay the differences, and that pattern—prolonged isolation, fasting, symbolic death and rebirth—paralleled a bear in hibernation.

The first step in many initiations was the withdrawal of the novice from his or her family and village. The individual was guided or went alone to a special place, sometimes deep within the forest or desert, sometimes as close as the edge of the encampment. He or she might enter a secluded hut or cave or might simply lie beneath a blanket.[3]

In their isolation, which lasted anywhere from days to months, candidates faced arduous restrictions—going without food and water, for example—or were forced to refrain from certain kinds of normal behavior. Sometimes they endured tortures. Typically, the rites included a visit from an elder, who taught them secrets of the tribe or society—myths and traditions only the initiated were allowed to know.

The isolation, the darkness of the hut or cave, the fasting and tortures, and other elements of the rites symbolized the candidate's ritual death. Often initiates imagined themselves devoured by an animal

Bear with eagle plumes and rattle. This image was painted on the wall of a society chamber when a boy was initiated into one of the societies. Acoma Pueblo. *Smithsonian Institution.*

such as a bear, cougar, or mythic monster. Some tribes dramatized an actual "killing." The rites ended with the novice awakening from his or her "death," born into a new life and a new status in the tribe.[4]

There are obvious reasons why the rites of initiation were associated with hibernation. Hibernation began with the bear's fall retreat to an isolated den site; initiation commenced with the neophyte's separation from the tribe or band and a retreat into the forest or some secluded place. Bears hibernated in earth dens or hollowed trees; initiation often included seclusion in a special hut or cave. Like a hibernating bear, the candidate often went without food and sometimes without water. Like the bear, the candidate "died" and was reborn.

The Dakota, a Sioux-speaking tribe of southern Minnesota, described a boy's initiation into manhood as "making a bear." Before the rite could be performed, the boy had to have a significant dream, one which indicated his readiness to become a man. Then he and a group of elders readied the ceremonial grounds, a large cleared area away from the village. There, the boy, who had fasted for days, erected a pole from which he hung a pipe offered as a sacrifice, and a fawn skin painted with images from his dream. At the base of the pole he drove two arrows into the ground and scattered painted feathers. Two- to three-hundred yards from the pole, the boy dug a hole about two-feet deep into the ground. The Dakota called it the bear's hole. He made two paths cutting across it, the ends pointing toward the four cardinal directions. Around this "den" he built a brush enclosure.

For the next two days the boy stayed in or around the den and acted like a bear. He walked on all fours, dug in the earth, snapped his teeth, and made bear noises. He used two hoops, one in each hand, to extend the reach of his arms so he could walk on four legs. Like a spoked wheel, the inside of each hoop was crisscrossed with leather thongs decorated with eagle feathers.

On the last day of the retreat, young men from the village gathered together. With their faces and bodies painted, and carrying guns loaded only with powder, they came to "kill" the "bear." They circled around the hole while the bear watched from the safety of his den. He growled as they moved around him. Some of the men taunted him by yelling and kicking dirt into the circle. The yelling grew louder, and the hunters moved faster and faster. Then, shouting and firing their guns directly at the bear, they rushed down the paths leading into the den. The boy charged out wildly, alternately using his hoops as forelegs and jabbing a wooden lance at anyone within reach. He escaped, racing past the hunters into the surrounding trees. They pursued him, shooting repeatedly with their rifles. Then he turned and charged back at them. He struggled until he was able to fight his way back into the den, where he could rest until the hunters attacked again. (According to a non-Indian who witnessed the ritual, the bear was able to "use any violence he pleased with impunity against his assailants...even to taking the life of any of them."[5])

Three times the hunters charged the den, and three times the bear dashed out, each time taking a different path. Each time, he escaped to the trees and then fought his way back to the den. The fourth time the hunters charged, the bear rushed out of the den onto the only path he had not yet taken. This time he could not return. Wildly, desperately, he tried to fight his way free, to escape to the trees, but the hunters chased him and finally "killed" him with their guns or knives.

They carried him like a corpse into a lodge erected for the ritual and left him there, isolated from the rest of the camp. Later, an elder joined him, and the two smoked and prayed for the remainder of the day. At sunset the young man emerged from the lodge. His tribe now considered him an adult, qualified to do all those things reserved only for men. The hunter who had "killed" him earned the honor of leading the next war party.[6]

Over one thousand miles away, in California, an Eastern Pomo initiation for boys began with an all-night dance.[7] The following morning a man impersonating a female grizzly bear came running into the village. He wore a full bearskin. Raccoon skins, on each side of the costume, represented cubs. This she-bear charged back and forth in front of a subterranean dance house. Older men gathered up the young initiates and pushed them toward her and then shoved one of the terrified boys into her path. The bear knocked him down. The boy struggled to get to his feet several times, and each time the bear threw him back to the ground. The bear then ran into the dance house. It circled and climbed the center post. At the top of the post it flipped over backward and came down head first, turning four somersaults on the way. It went to the rear of the dance house and took off the bearskin. With his costume removed, the bear-impersonator smoked tobacco and prayed for the people, then he put the female bearskin back on, danced again, and left.

The older men sent the boys outside to play. As they ran about, one or more tall black figures called *Kuksu* approached them. (In Pomo mythology, the *Kuksu* is the first man.) Frightened, the boys ran, but the *Kuksu* chased them and herded them toward a hut in the forest. There, the *Kuksu* blindfolded them and made them lie face down on the ground, where he scratched their backs enough to make them bleed.

The boys stayed in the hut that night. They woke in the morning to the sounds of a group of people approaching their hut. The men in the group planted a long pole in front of the entrance, which the boys climbed, imitating bears. They hung from the top while female relatives threw beads and grain at them. Later, when they returned to the village, their female relatives bathed them. There were more dances, and the ceremony finished with a feast.[8]

Unlike the Eastern Pomo, the Coast Pomo initiated both boys and girls in their *Kuksu* ceremony. After a dance, the children were taken into the bush where they were surrounded by a group of adults standing in a circle. The *Kuksu* and a grizzly bear impersonator then appeared. With terrifying grunts the grizzly came up just behind the initiates and dug a hole (a grave or den). In the meantime, the *Kuksu* charged the initiates from the front with a flint-pointed spear and pretended to stab them. One by one, the children collapsed into the bear's hole.

Several adults picked up the "dead" children and carried them to the dance house. There, each mother undressed and bathed her child and provided him or her with new clothes. The children then returned to the bush and remained there for four days and nights. During this time they learned to use sacred instruments, to name and use medicinal plants, and to sing secret dance songs. All the while, the bear prowled close by. When the neophytes finally returned to their village, their mothers washed them and gave them gifts.

The bear played a different role in the initiation of Ojibwa girls. The girls did not imitate bears as did Dakota and Pomo boys, nor did a bear appear during their initiation rites. Instead, the community identified them with bears. Specifically, they associated girls undergoing initiatory rites with the dangerous aspect of the bear, because initiation for girls came with first menstruation. Most tribes considered women to be dangerous during their menstrual periods, and the first period was the worst. Mountain Wolf Woman, a Winnebago, remembered that as a girl her mother told her what to do at the time of her first menses: "When that happens to you," she said, "run to the woods and hide some place. You should not look at anyone, not even a glance. If you look at a man you will contaminate his blood. Even a glance will cause you to become an evil person."[9] It was the Winnebago tradition that a girl should isolate herself and fast until her bleeding stopped.

Standing bear figurine. Adams Lake
Indian Band, Chase, British Columbia.
Photo courtesy of the Kamloops Museum.

Many tribes immediately isolated girls at the initial signs of their first menses, so that they would not injure or contaminate others with their strong and potentially dangerous powers. In most Indian societies the bulk of a girl's and a woman's life was spent in group activities—gathering, child rearing, fishing, or doing an assortment of other domestic, but collective activities. Her seclusion at the time of her first menses was often the only time in her entire life when she was alone and isolated from family and community for any length of time.[10]

Usually girls remained isolated in small huts set apart from their village for anywhere from four days to a month or even longer. A Tlingit girl could remain isolated for an entire year. During her seclusion, she observed a number of taboos: she fasted or ate only certain foods; she drank water through a reed or hollow bone; and, often, she was not permitted to scratch herself with her fingernails. Elder women of her village visited her and taught her secret stories and ceremonies.[11]

An Ojibwa girl about to start her first menstrual period was called *wemukowe*, which means "going to be a bear." At the first sign of her blood she smeared soot around her eyes and put on her poorest clothes. Her mother or grandmother rushed her out of the village to a tiny hut hidden in the forest. As they slipped away along a path where they were unlikely to meet anyone, the girl looked only at the ground and touched nothing. The Ojibwa believed her powers to be so great that her glance or touch could bring paralysis to another, death to a child, or the destruction of the year's berry crop. At the hut, the girl crawled inside. Her mother closed the entrance and returned to the family's lodge. During her seclusion, the girl's relatives called her *mukowe*—literally "she is a bear."[12]

She sat quietly within her hut. When she went outside to stretch her legs or relieve herself, she scattered leaves along her path to warn others of her presence. At some point, an elder woman from camp, who was past menopause and no longer susceptible to the girl's power, came to visit, bringing buckskin, quills, and sewing materials. Together, the two sewed and talked. The woman revealed mysteries and told stories that only women knew. She spoke about what it meant to be a woman, about child-bearing, and about men.

After her bleeding stopped, the girl went to a stream and washed herself. Then she returned to her hut and remained in seclusion until an appointed time. When, finally, she went back to her family, her initiation continued with a series of less dramatic ceremonies. These seasonal rituals, conducted by her mother and grandmother, took place over the course of a year and were often attended by aunts and other elder women of the village. At their conclusion, dietary and other taboos were lifted and the girl resumed a normal life. She was considered a woman now and eligible for marriage.[13] (Some tribes allowed girls to marry before puberty. Among these tribes, initiation could take place after marriage.)

In this initiation rite, and others like it, the people associated girls with bears even though there was no direct imitation. Relatives and others identified them with bears partly because their initiation ritual resembled hibernation: they disappeared alone into a den-like hut. But the association went beyond that. For the Ojibwa and most other American Indians, menstruating women represented a serious danger to the community, as did bears. The bear in this case was not only a symbol of initiation but also a symbol of the maleficent powers of the menstruating woman.

Many of the tribes of the Pacific Northwest told a tale that warned of the dangerous forces unleashed if the power of a girl undergoing initiation was not properly contained. Southwestern tribes told a similar tale. The version that follows is from the Coos Indians of Oregon:

Once there was a girl who was lazy. She refused to work. At first the people were angry and ridiculed her but as time went on they simply ignored her. She had no friends except for her younger brother. He did whatever she asked.

On the day when her first menstrual period came her family closed her up in a hut away from the village and did not give her anything to eat or drink for five days. All the people stayed clear of the hut, so no one noticed her younger brother smuggling her food and water.

On her second day in the hut she began to feel strange. Something was happening to her. Coarse black hair grew on her arms and shoulders. On the third day it covered her body. After four days her fingernails turned to long copper-colored claws and her canines grew long and sharp. She moved around on all fours. She had turned into a bear.

On the fifth day her brother came in the morning as usual. He pushed dried salmon under the door. She grabbed his hand and pulled him into the hut. It was dark inside, but he knew a bear had grabbed him.

"Younger brother," she said. "It is me. Do not be afraid. I will not hurt you, because you are my only friend. Stay here. Do not go out until I come back."

Her brother sat down in a corner of the hut while she slipped out and went to her parent's lodge, where her mother and father sat. When they saw her come in, they tried to escape, but she stopped them.

"You have always treated me badly," she said. "Now I am going to kill you!" She attacked them and tore them to pieces. Then she went from lodge to lodge until she had killed everyone in the village. She gathered up all their clothes and other possessions and put them in a pile outside the hut where her brother was sitting. He came out. "Stay here," she said, "I am going down to the creek to get a drink."

She went into the woods and did not come back. Her brother waited a long time. Finally, he gathered up all his relatives' possessions and went to live at his brother-in-law's village.[14]

As with puberty rites, the initiation of an adult into a secret society centered on the symbolism of death and birth, and the bear played a role there too. Initiations into the Midewiwin or Medicine Lodge Society of the Ojibwa provide examples of secret society initiatory rituals involving the bear.[15] The Midewiwin Society, whose membership included both men and women, was principally a healing society that relied on herbal remedies. Its members adhered to the teaching that after death they would be born into a new life in another realm. The bear was the society's principal patron, and all Midewiwin initiates were said to "follow the bear path."

Each of the Midewiwin's four progressively higher degrees or levels required a new initiation involving more complex teachings. A year or more of instruction preceded each initiation, during which the candidates learned secret society songs, myths, and traditions, as well as the medicinal properties of specific plants.

Ojibwa bands held Midewiwin initiations twice a year—in the spring, when families gathered together to harvest maple sugar, and in the fall, during the harvest of wild rice. The rites took place in a large rectangular lodge located in a clearing away from the main encampment. The walls, composed of pine poles and hardwood saplings intertwined with short leafy branches, were eight to ten feet high. Saplings thrown over the top provided shade, though most of the roof area was left open. The main entrance faced east, toward the rising sun, and another entrance faced west. A small dome-shaped sweat lodge sat about one hundred yards to the east of the main entrance.

In some communities the Midewiwin society built special lodges for candidates entering the fourth or highest degree. They added two additional entrances and constructed a small brush hut, which was called a bear nest, opposite each. Just inside the lodge, on either side of the east and west entrances, they set posts, painted red and

Midewiwin Lodge. *Photo courtesy of the Smithsonian Institution, National Anthropological Archives.*

black, and placed a rock at the base of each. The posts represented the four limbs and feet of the bear spirit who, in the ceremony's origin myth, created the four lodge entrances to expel the malevolent beings who opposed him. The bear rested in the nests after his struggles with these spirits.

Midewiwin initiation ceremonies differed slightly from band to band, but, in general, five or six days before the start of a formal initiation ceremony, the candidate traveled, sometimes for several days, to the encampment where the rites were to take place. He built himself a birch bark wigwam near the ceremonial lodge, apart from the other dwellings, so he could be alone until the society priests came to him. Except for the time he spent walking to and from the sweat lodge for a daily sweat, he spent the next four days isolated in his lodge, where he fasted and prayed.

On the day before the initiation, his tutor and a group of Midewiwin priests came to see him. They smoked together, and the priests revealed the meanings of magic objects, instructed him in the preparation of ceremonial effigies, and recited the society's origin myth. Toward dusk, after the priests had gone, the candidate sweated again, in final preparation for the next day's ceremony.

Bear-paw medicine bag
used in Ojibwa Midewiwin
Ceremony.   *Photo courtesy*
of the Smithsonian
Institution, National
Anthropological Archives.

In the morning, he dressed in his best buckskin, decorated with quillwork especially for the occasion. He went first to the sweat lodge, where he again joined his tutor and the priests. They sat together, chanting songs and prayers and smoking. The candidate prayed and made offerings of tobacco to the bear spirit. He asked it to compel the dangerous spirits to draw away from the entrance of the ceremonial lodge so he could enter safely. After the prayers and singing had ceased, the group left the sweat lodge and walked solemnly to the large ceremonial lodge, the candidate leading the way, and the priests chanting as they walked behind. When the group reached the main entrance, they stopped. The candidate's sponsor and one of the priests stepped forward and took positions on either side of the candidate. The other priests entered the lodge and sat down. A drummer began to drum and sing. Starting to the south, the candidate and his escorts walked around the lodge four times. His relatives and people from the encampment watched. Sometimes, four people, representing four benevolent bear spirits, accompanied the three as they circled the lodge. Four evil bear spirits challenged them during their circuit, but the benevolent bears always overpowered the evil ones and allowed the candidate to complete his journey.

When the group reached the entrance on the fourth round, they stopped. The candidate asked to enter. "Let me come in!" he shouted. "I come for death, I come for life!" The priests said prayers. The candidate entered and the priests led him around the inside four times. He shuffled slowly with the beat of the drum, his body and knees bent forward. Others fell in behind until everyone was dancing. After four circuits the dancing stopped, the priests returned to their places, and the candidate moved to the west end of the lodge. Four priests approached him. The drumming slowed, and the priests prayed. The drumming stopped altogether. In the silence, the chief priest stepped forward, holding a bear-paw medicine bag. A cowrie shell shot out of the bag and hit the candidate. He collapsed as if he had been shot with an arrow. The priests danced around him, each holding a medicine bag and taking a turn touching the apparently lifeless body. At last the chief priest commanded the man to stand. He stood and began singing. Again, the priests chanted prayers and made offerings. They gave a medicine bag to the man, now a newly initiated member. He carried it as he circled the lodge and thanked the priests.

The origin myth for this ritual taught that the bear had originally carried the Midewiwin doctrine "of everlasting life" to the Ojibwa,

One version of the "evil" bear who challenges the Midewiwin candidate during his or her initiation. After a drawing in Dewdney, *Sacred Scrolls of the Ojibway. Illustration by Janet McGahan.*

and when a candidate started his instruction, he or she offered feasts and chants to *Makwa Manido*, the bear spirit. He believed that *Makwa Manido* and the other bear spirits, both good and bad, would be present throughout the rites. Among some bands, candidates imitated bears during their initiations into the third and fourth degrees, crawling on their hands and knees and making bear-like sounds as they approached the ceremonial lodge. Candidates being initiated into the fourth degree moved bear-like up to each of the four entrances and shot the evil spirits inside with their bows and arrows. Then they hurried back outside to hide in one of the small brush bear nests. Sometimes the medicine bags of fourth-degree initiates were made from bear paws or the skins of bear cubs.

Throughout the ceremony, the Midewiwin Society stressed that death was simply a transition, a passing from one world to another. In each initiatory death and new birth the candidate moved to a new level of spiritual knowledge, preparing, in the end, for true death. By symbolically dying over and over again, initiates prepared themselves for the final transition, the passage from this world to the next. The bear symbolized this kind of passage. Its annual autumn descent into

Painted Kiowa tepee cover depicting a bear emerging from its den. Photo courtesy of the Smithsonian Institution, National Anthropological Archives.

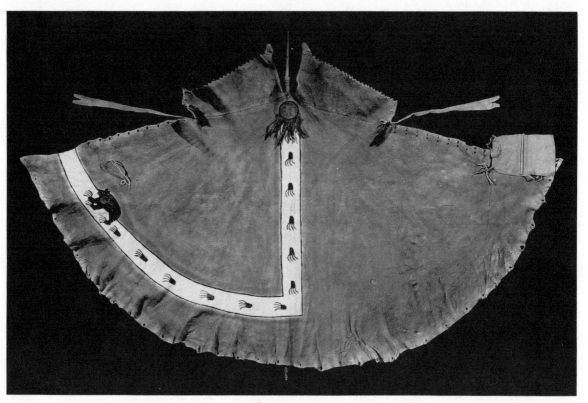

GIVING VOICE TO BEAR

the den, its long heavy sleep suggestive of death, its spring emergence from the earth analogous to a birth, matched exactly the journey of the initiate. Midewiwin candidates imitated bears during their initiations. Ojibwa girls and Pueblo boys were called bears. Pomo youth were helped by men dressed as bears, and Dakota boys "died" as bears. In each instance, initiates "died" without fear of annihilation because they shared the bear's power of resurrection.

Painted bear skull from the
eastern subarctic. Naskapi.
*Photo courtesy of the Royal
Ontario Museum, Toronto.*

"*Grandfather, I am Sorry I Must Kill You*"

OUTSIDE HER FAMILY'S winter hunting lodge, a lone Eastern Cree woman sits, legs crossed, on a birch bark mat. A small black bear skull rests in her lap. Her right thumb is covered with vermilion. She draws it twice across the top of the skull and makes two neat, broad lines.

"See how handsome you are now?" she says in a low voice, speaking to the skull. "Bring my husband a good dream."

Turning the skull, she makes two red circles on the back with a twisting motion, then two more circles on the upper part of the mandible. She turns the skull to face her again and makes a broad short line across the end of the snout. After wiping the dye from her hands, the woman ties ribbons of caribou hide through the eye sockets. The ribbons are elaborately decorated with quillwork.

"Short Tail," she tells the bear, "you have been treated well here. Tell your relatives what it is like to be killed my husband." She stands, holding the skull carefully with both hands and steps into the lodge where her husband sits. She hands it to him. "I am finished." she says.

Her husband places a plug of tobacco in the skull's jaw. Using leather thongs, he ties it to the frame of the lodge just above the place where he rests his head when he sleeps. Two other painted bones are also tied there. The Cree call this place *taawpwaataakan*, "that which brings dreams."

From a birch bark cup he scoops out a small amount of warmed bear grease, and, asking the bear to bring him a dream, he smears the soft white fat all around the dream place. He pauses for several moments, as if recalling a hunt or a dream. Then he rubs the grease left on his hand into his hair and, speaking to the skull again, he says, "Bring me a good dream, Grandfather. Bring me a dream of your relatives, that they may lie down as you have."

INDIANS HUNTED BEARS in various ways. The method used by the Eastern Cree, an Algonquian-speaking group of northeastern Canada, is representative of a ritual hunt found across a large part of North America. The hunt began with divination rites. Hunters used these rites and their own dreams to predict the outcome of their hunts, a matter of enormous significance to the Cree. Some Cree men would not hunt without first divining the outcome.

Both divination rites and dreams involved communication with the spirits that "owned" the animals. Like other northern peoples, the Cree believed that an "owner" or "spirit boss" controlled every species of animal. *Okiciko*, the Keeper of the Geese, looked after the blue, snow, and Canada geese, *Cicenapew* took care of the caribou, and *Memekwesiw*, was the bear spirit.[1] Some Cree bands believed the bear spirit controlled the supply of all the animals that were hunted for food.

The Cree believed that if they respected the animals they killed and observed all the taboos, the owners or keepers of the animals would be pleased and inclined to release more animals. Once free, the animals themselves could choose to be killed. But if the people insulted the animals or somehow proved unworthy, the animals would not give themselves, or their keeper would withhold them. The people would starve.

In fall divination rites, hunters hoped to learn the locations of bear dens and whether they would kill bears in the coming year. A shaman or hunter sent out a message to *Memekwesiw*, Spirit Boss of the Bears. If the hunters were worthy, *Memekwesiw* answered by telling the hunters that they would kill some bears and where they might find dens.

In a divination ceremony called the Shaking Tent, the shaman (or conjurer, as he was sometimes called) entered a small tepee and summoned his spirit helpers. As the spirits arrived, singing their songs in strange voices, the tepee swayed. Speaking through the shaman, the spirits answered questions about relatives far away, about sick people, and about the weather. They told some where to find things they had lost, and they told hunters about future hunts.

In these rites, the shaman often called *Memekwesiw* into his tent. When *Memekwesiw* arrived, those outside saw the shape of a bear claw press against the wall of the tepee. *Memekwesiw* would say to the shaman, "If you can throw me flat, that's good, I'll like it, and then those men out there will get some bears. But if you can't, if your spirits aren't strong enough, those men won't be able to kill any bears."[2] The shaman and the bear spirit fought and the tent shook violently. After a time, the fighting stopped and *Memekwesiw*

GIVING VOICE TO BEAR

Hunter's birch bark comb case with etched
bear figures from a dream experience. From a
photo in Speck, *Naskapi*. *Illustration by
Janet McGahan.*

"Grandfather, I am Sorry I Must Kill You"   **27**

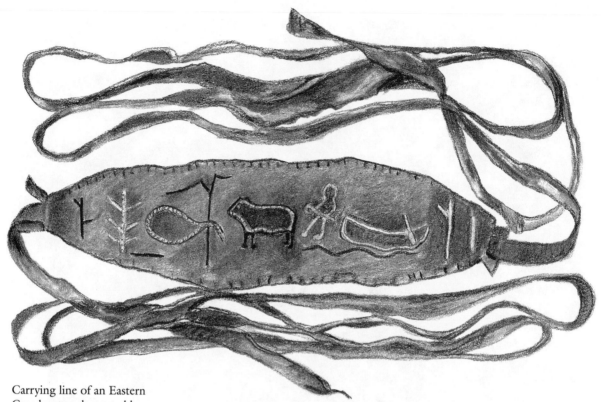

Carrying line of an Eastern Cree hunter, decorated by his wife with dream images. The images are, from left to right: trees, the bear's den, the bear, the hunter with ax, and canoe. From a photo in Speck and Heye, "Hunting Charms of the Montagnais." *Illustration by Janet McGahan.*

announced the winner. If he won, the hunters would have no luck with bears. But when the shaman and his helping spirits won, the men in camp knew they were going to kill some bears that season. *Memekwesiw* was not embittered when he lost. He just wanted to fight with the shaman to see if the shaman's powers were strong enough, to see if the people deserved to kill any bears.

In another rite to divine the future, a Cree hunter put a bear's knee cap on a hot rock. If the bone wobbled around it was a good sign—the hunter might kill as many as six bears. If the bone did not move or moved only slightly, it meant no bears would die. On another occasion, the hunter put the bone on the floor of the lodge and, blindfolded, tried to pick it up. Success meant he would kill one bear, and failure, no bears.[3]

Dreaming also played a vital role in the hunt. Cree hunters believed that dreams were one of the best ways to divine the outcome of a future hunt. They would say, *nto'pwata'm mack`*, "I dream hunt a bear."[4]

Many Native American cultures held that when people dreamed, their souls (or one of their souls, often called the traveling soul) left their bodies and traveled about in the spirit realm. In dreams, they believed, one saw things otherwise invisible, for example the spirit

GIVING VOICE TO BEAR

home of the bears. Or a dreamer might see the Spirit Boss of the Geese and be shown a good place to hunt geese. On his dream journey, the hunter might learn a design for his knife sheath that pleased the animals or a song that called caribou. This was sacred knowledge because it came from a spirit realm. It contributed enormously to the hunter's confidence.

A hunter did several things to bring the kinds of dreams he sought. He put bear grease in his hair at night and tied dream charms such as bear patellas and porcupine scapulas above where he laid his head when he slept. He called this place *taawpwaataakan*, "that which brings dreams," and he smeared it with bear grease each fall, upon first entering the lodge for the winter season.[5]

A dream's symbols had to be interpreted. When a hunter dreamt of a woman, it meant he was going kill something—the woman signified a game animal. If he dreamt of killing a small animal such as a rabbit, it meant that he was going to kill a large animal, maybe a caribou. If he dreamt of a baby, he was soon to kill a bear. Sometimes a man or his wife might have a very specific dream that did not immediately reveal its meaning. But the dream was not to be forgotten, for it foretold something.[6]

Such a dream came to Charlie Kanatiwat, an old Cree of James Bay, Quebec, early one January in the 1950s. The dream, and the account of the hunt that followed it, were recorded by anthropologist Richard Preston.[7] The story does not depict a traditional Cree bear hunt, but it tells us much about how a Cree hunter incorporated dreams into his waking reality.

Charlie came home tired to his wigwam after a day of hunting and went to sleep. That night he dreamt he was out hunting again, wandering through the woods looking for partridges. Before long he came upon a wigwam hidden in the trees. A woman sat inside. She was old, very old, and she had two children with her. Charlie felt sad because she was so old. He grew uncomfortable standing there. He wanted to say something, to help her somehow, but he could not. Next he dreamt about one of his daughters who had died. She sat with her mother, Charlie's wife.

When Charlie awoke, he said nothing of the dreams to his wife. Contemplating them, he decided that they were significant. He was sure the first dream meant he was going to make a big kill. He was unsure about the second dream.

A month later, Charlie and his grown son, Albert, were out hunting partridges. Charlie shot one, and he and Albert sat down to rest. They made a fire and ate some of the food they carried. While they were resting, Charlie got a strange feeling that told him to start

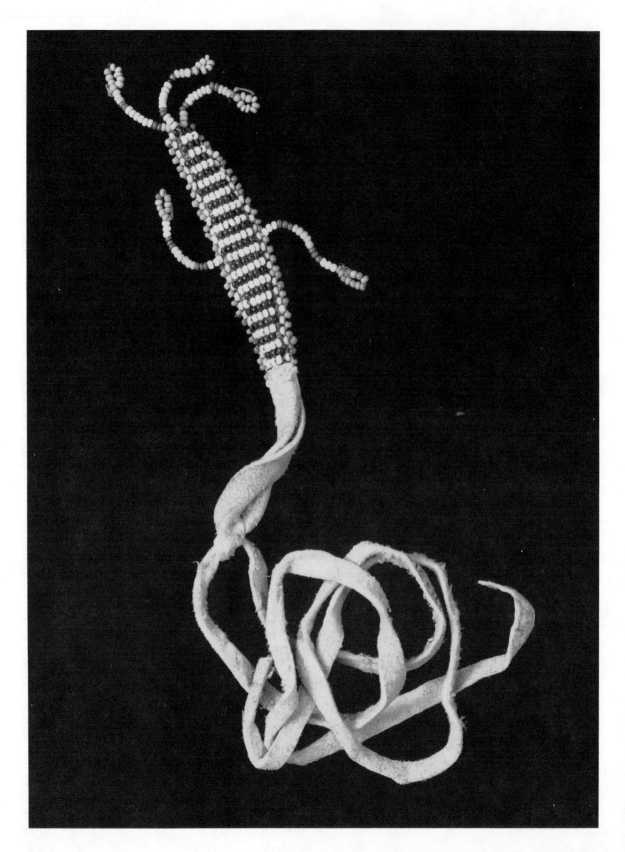

walking. He quickly packed his things and left. His son stayed behind to finish his lunch.

Before long, Charlie came to a lake and started across it. It had snowed the night before, so he could see that someone had recently walked across the lake. He wondered who it was so far away from any camp. Perhaps his wife. Maybe she was looking for him. Then he saw that the tracks were not human but polar bear. He followed them. They led in the direction that Albert would be traveling. Maybe the bear would reach his son before he caught up. When he found Albert's tracks, they went in a different direction than he had expected. The bear had turned and followed the same bearing as his son's. Charlie thought the bear was following Albert, and he followed the tracks. Soon he saw the bear, with two cubs following behind her, cutting across another lake. They moved fast, but paused now and then to look back at Charlie.

The bears ran into the woods toward some trees that had blown down. Afraid she would escape, Charlie shot. The bullet struck the mother bear in the eye. He called to her, saying, "What are you trying to do?" The bear stood and after a moment walked again. He shot her once more. She rose again, limping. She reminded Charlie of how his son had moved through the snow when he was very young. He called, "Albert, my son, why are you leaving me behind?" The bear sat down and Charlie approached her. As he recalled, "I was very close to her, and she was hardly moving. All of a sudden, I felt sorry for her."

Beaded hunting charm. Part of a bear's tongue is sewn into the decorated pendant. Naskapi. *Photo courtesy of the National Museums of Canada, Ottawa.*

He stood there for a while, looking at her, then he shot her one last time. She died, and he buried her in the snow and covered the pile with boughs. He then went to look for Albert. The two dragged the bear home. Charlie gave it to his father and told him of his dream. "There was a woman with two children. I dreamt that I was walking among the trees when I reached her and her children. She had two children. She acted very strange. I felt very uneasy with her. Then I started to dream about my wife. Then I woke up."

His father told him that the dream meant he would kill the bear. Later that same month, Charlie's wife died. "When she died," he said, "my other dream came back to me."

Charlie found his dream. That is what the Cree would say when a person's dream came true. Even though the dream's message was concealed in metaphor, Charlie was able to anticipate an important kill. And after his wife died, he realized that her death had been foretold in his second dream.

Dreams were often more explicit: they could tell the hunter where to find an animal and whether he would kill it. William

Katebetuk, a Cree who spent his life hunting the spruce forests along the eastern shore of James Bay, often had such dreams. He dreamt about every animal he had ever killed. When he got older he quit hunting altogether. "I can't hunt anymore," he said. "Even though I dream, I can't remember them when I get up in the morning."

He did remember a dream he had had as a young man, his first dream of *Memekwesiw*, the Spirit Boss of the Bears.

> I thought I went to Memekwesiw's place, and I thought the door was of stone. He had a hairy face and hair hanging down all over. He came and got hold of my hand. There were lots of trees standing in a bunch and he said to me, "That is where my little pup is," and he gave me that [the pup].
>
> I didn't tell my dream, but the next day I put on my new mittens and went out hunting. At the place I had been shown, I found a bear and killed it.[8]

Two phases comprised the traditional Cree bear hunt. The first involved locating the den in advance of the actual hunt. The second was the hunt itself, when the hunter returned to the den and killed the bear.[9] There were several ways a hunter could find a den. After the first autumn snow, he might track a bear directly to its den. He checked old den sites where he had killed bears in years past. He looked in the places where he knew bears liked to den—brushy thickets, hollowed trees, natural caves. Sometimes while out hunting caribou in mid-winter he happened upon a den. And sometimes he learned of a den's location in a dream, as William Katebetuk did. The Spirit Boss of the Bears would say, "That is where you are going to find him." The next day he would search for the place shown to him in his dream.

Whenever he found a den, he checked to see if it was occupied by looking at the breathing hole: if the bear was in the den, the snow around the hole was frosted yellow-brown from the bear's breath. Or he poked a forked stick inside to see if he could feel the bear or catch some of its hair.

Usually he waited until early spring to go after the bear. This was the second phase of the hunt, and it took place in spring because that was often when food stores were lowest. The Cree also said that bears were best for eating in the spring. Because the hunter knew the location of a bear in advance, a bear hunt was considerably more predictable than a hunt for caribou or moose.

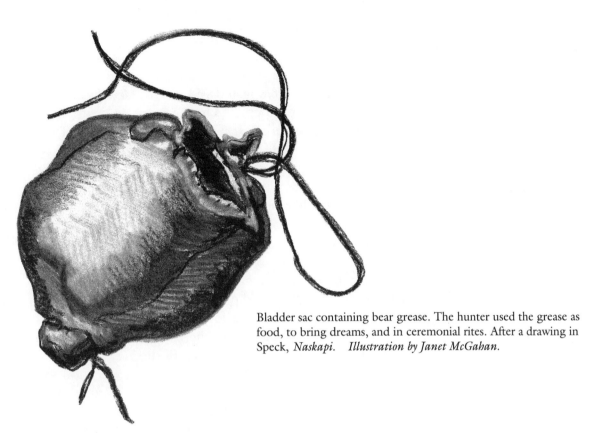

Bladder sac containing bear grease. The hunter used the grease as food, to bring dreams, and in ceremonial rites. After a drawing in Speck, *Naskapi*. *Illustration by Janet McGahan.*

One night several days before a Cree set out to kill a bear, he sat alone with his drum or rattle and sang a bear hunt song that had come to him in his dreams. The words were simple, perhaps: "He wants me."[10] He sang it over and over, and he sang as if the bear were listening, as if he were communicating directly with the animal. As he sang, he could see the hunt unfold in his mind. He could see the den with the bear emerging. He sang because it helped him see these things in advance and because his dream songs gave him power. The songs came to him in his dreams. They were gifts from *Memekwesiw*, and they pleased the animal he was about to kill.

Cree hunters never said the word bear when they prepared for a hunt. Instead they might refer to the animal as "Grandmother" or "Cousin." Or they might use a metaphorical expression such as "Black Food" or "The One who Owns the Chin." Other names used were "*Memekwesiw's* Little Pup," "Chief's Son," "Four-Legged Human," and "Food of the Fire." They said that it angered the bear if a hunter did not call it by one of these names. The bear liked to be called something special.[11]

Hunters sweated before a bear hunt.[12] A sweat bath cleansed. The forest, unlike the camp, was spiritually clean, as was everything that came from it. If a man was going to go into the forest to hunt, he had to be clean. Otherwise the helpful spirits might ignore him, or the bear might leave its den before he got there.

The night before a Cree hunted a bear, he threw a pinch of tobacco into the fire as an offering and said, "Here *Memekwesiw*, this is in exchange for your little pup."[13] On the morning of the hunt, the hunter unwrapped his very best hunting clothes: his special skin coat, his leggings, garters, and moccasins, his mittens and cap. Like his body, his clothes had to be clean. All but the skin coat were heavily embroidered and beaded by his wife, with designs that he had dreamed. The designs, like his songs, gave him power and pleased the animal. He carefully unfolded his *tapiskakan* (roughly translated as "chest-hanging cloth"), a richly beaded kerchief, and strung it across his chest. The image on the cloth, which had come in a dream, was of a bear, either symbolically or realistically depicted. When he killed the bear, he would put the cloth on its chest and the bear would wear it as it was carried into camp.

Next, he took out his knife sheath, the bear's carrying line, and the club, ax, or spear that he would use to kill the bear.[14] Each had been decorated according to bear-hunt dreams, for it was known to the Cree that "everything a man uses in hunting, he has to dream it first."[15] The carrying line recreated the hunted animal's spirit. His wife made it from woven strips of caribou or bear hide. She made a head (a knot at one end) and a tail, and she decorated it with quills, beads, ribbons, and feathers. Unlike a carrying line for caribou, beaver, or geese, the bear's was not actually used to carry the bear home—its function was purely ceremonial. As with the *tapiskakan*, the hunter placed it upon the dead bear to please its spirit.

If his clothes were new, the hunter had to prepare them. He cleansed them by placing them in the forest before sunrise on a "fine morning." After a few hours in the fresh cold air and first sunlight they could be used.[16] Everything had to be clean and handsome so the bear and its spirit boss would look favorably upon the hunter.

If a piece of equipment, such as a knife sheath, was newly made and had never been on a hunt before, it had to be initiated before it could be used. After he had killed the bear, the hunter would place the item on the carcass for a short time. It could then be used on future hunts.

When everything was ready, the hunter left for the den. While he was gone, his wife kept the camp clean and well ordered. A bear would not allow itself to be killed if it was going to be taken to a dirty camp.[17]

The hunter was silent on his way to the den. He did not whistle, because whistling brought strong winds that could force him back to camp before he reached his goal. Taking the most direct route to the den, he moved quickly and quietly on his snowshoes. If, on the way, he saw caribou or moose tracks in the snow, he did not follow them, even if the tracks were very fresh. It was taboo to go after another animal when hunting a bear—that would be unfaithful. The bear waited to be taken.

When he reached the den, he carefully positioned himself to one side of the snow-covered entrance. With club readied he addressed the bear saying, "Grandfather, it is already warm! Time for you to come out now." If the bear did not come out, he called to it again, "Grandfather, I've found you so show me your head!"

If the bear did not answer to Grandfather, he called it Grandmother. He prodded it with a pole. Inside the den, the bear came to life and began to growl. The hunter kept calling, "Grandmother, Chief's Daughter, allow yourself to be killed!" Finally, the bear charged out. The hunter quickly stabbed it with his spear or struck it hard on the head with his club or ax. The bear went down. The goal was to kill it with one sharp blow, but often the bear got up, and the hunter had to hit it over and over until it was dead.[18]

The Cree believed that it was proper to kill a bear only with a club, ax, or spear. It was taboo to use a bow and arrow or a gun to hunt them. The Cree said that these weapons "were not strong enough" for a bear—arrows and bullets were not powerful enough for the bear's spirit. And the bear's spirit, as much as its physical body, was the object of the hunt. When a hunter used striking or thrusting weapons, he and the bear were more evenly matched. He had to be perilously close to the bear—close enough to strike it soundly on the head or run it through with a spear. His hands were jolted by the impact of his club or stone ax against the bear's skull. His entire body felt the penetration of his spear into the bear's chest. These archaic weapons allowed the hunter to feel the animal's death in a way he could not with a bow and arrow or a gun.

Once he was sure the bear was dead, the hunter dragged the carcass out, turned it on its back, and put some tobacco on its chest. He removed his chest-hanging cloth and tied it around the bear's neck, fixing it so that it hung neatly over the animal's chest. Then he draped the bear's carrying line around its neck.

He sat down on the snow and spoke solemnly to the bear. "Black Food, do not be angry. Do not let the other bear spirits be angry. I killed you only because I am poor and hungry. I need your skin for my coat and your meat so my family can eat. We have nothing to eat. See how fine you look now? It is a good thing to be killed by me.

When you go back to *Memekwesiw*, tell him how I have treated you." He smoked his stone pipe and put the pipe into the bear's mouth saying, "Grandfather, I will light your pipe."[19]

He did not dress the carcass in the forest. Other animals, yes, but bears were dressed in camp. In the woods the hunter simply made two short slits in opposing directions along the ventral line from the breast bone, one toward the rear and one toward the head; removed the stomach, small intestine, and some fat; placed them in his hunting bag; and sewed the slits tightly back together. He cut off a single claw from one of the front paws and added it to the fat and organs already in his bag. All the time he was careful not to spill any blood—the Cree had a taboo against leaving the blood of animals on the snow. Finally, the hunter buried the bear with snow and spruce boughs and went home.[20]

When he reached camp he did not speak to anyone. It was taboo even to shout greetings. Children might peek at the returning hunter, but they were not allowed to run out and greet him. He went straight to his lodge, where he sat quietly and smoked. It was the Cree custom to be silent when returning from a successful hunt.[21] They believed it was dishonorable to boast about killing an animal. The animal made a gift of its life. For a hunter to openly take credit denied that gift and violated his union with the animal's spirit.

After a time, the hunter silently gave the claw he had removed from the bear to someone he had chosen to haul the animal back to camp. Usually this was his wife or sometimes his father, son, or brother. Whoever took the claw did so in silence. Usually he or she recruited someone else to help, and together they headed off with a toboggan and retrieved the slain bear.

As they pulled the bear into camp, women and children chased dogs away. Young women, because they were believed to possess potentially dangerous powers, were not allowed to look at the animal. They covered their eyes and left camp.[22] Several men carried the bear into the hunter's lodge, which had been carefully cleaned. They laid it belly-up on a mat of newly cut spruce boughs with its head towards the rear of the lodge, the area where the men slept and sat. Its hind legs stretched toward the door, into the woman's half of the lodge.[23] The bear still wore the hunter's decorated carrying line and his beaded *tapiskakan*.

Relatives and people from other families crowded into the lodge to see and admire the bear. A tense silence, even among the children, belied an undercurrent of excitement and satisfaction. Some of the visitors stroked the bear's fur. The hunter put a plug of tobacco in its mouth and smoked his pipe with the other men. Still there was no conversation—nothing was said until the hunter, the man who killed bear, spoke. Humbly, he gave the bear to the oldest man in the camp. Called the feast-giver, he was now the owner of the bear, and he took charge of preparing and hosting the feast.[24]

At the old man's request, two or three of the older, married women skinned the bear. They removed the stitches sewn by the hunter and extended the lower cut downward toward the tail, opposite the direction used for cutting other animals—bears liked to be treated differently. When the women finished skinning, the men cut up the carcass. The man who had killed the bear made an offering by cutting a piece of meat from the bear's heart and throwing it into the fire, saying, "Come *Memekwesiw*, be pleased. Send us another one of your little pups."[25]

Under the old man's direction, the men set up a feast lodge in the forest, away from camp. There the men divided the meat into two piles: The bear's head and front legs, man's food, were laid together to be prepared and eaten by men. The hind legs, woman's food, were cooked, along with whatever other meat was left, by the older married women in camp. During the feast, women could eat only from the hind legs. Among some Cree bands, women did not participate in the bear feast at all. Among others, women ate during a second sitting.

Just after sunset, people from camp, dressed in their best clothes, gathered around the feast lodge. When everyone had arrived, the feast-giver beckoned them to enter. Inside the lodge, those preparing the feast had arranged the various dishes of bear meat on a clean birch bark sheet in the center of the floor. The rest of the floor was covered with newly cut spruce and balsam boughs. As the men and boys came in amidst the smell of cooked meat and evergreen, they moved around the food and found seats in the rear of the lodge. The women came in and sat in the front by the door. Together the men and women formed a near circle around the bear meat and the fire. With everyone inside, the feast-giver sealed the lodge, covering every opening and every crack with birch bark or skins. No one could open the lodge until dawn, when the feast was finished.

The feast-giver sang to begin the feast. He made offerings to *Memekwesiw* by dropping pieces of meat from each of the dishes into the fire. He offered prayers, asking the bear's spirit to ask *Memekwesiw* to send more bears to be hunted. He poured some tobacco on the fire and then some bear grease. Finally, he drank some of the grease and smeared a bit on his forehead "to feed his soul." He passed the container of grease clockwise around the lodge, and others did the same.[26]

The Cree considered fat the most important part of any animal. One reason they valued bears above other animals was because of their body fat and because the fat rendered down into a high-quality grease. During the preparation of the bear feast, bear fat was rendered apart from the meat, as it had special symbolic value. Before the people entered the feast lodge, the feast-giver smeared it on the poles of the lodge and rubbed some of it into his hair.

The first part of the bear to be eaten was the head. The feast-giver served it on a large wooden platter, which acted as a communal dish. Several men might eat from the platter at the same time. The oldest men ate first, the youngest last. When they had eaten all the meat from the head, they set the skull aside and placed the two front legs, one at a time, on the platter. Again, only men ate from them. The atmosphere was reverent. Children were told to speak quietly, food was eaten slowly, nothing was wasted. Otherwise, the spirit boss of the bears would be angered. Food animals would disappear. The bear's spirit might take revenge on the disrespectful.[27] The Cree considered the meal an integral part of the hunt, a crucial clause in the hunter's agreement with the bear and its spirit boss. In the words of a Cree, starvation "was due to things that happened while people were having a feast. If someone did something wrong at a feast, things might go badly for him in the future. And if nobody did anything wrong at a feast, then they would kill plenty of game, even if they were almost out of food."[28]

After the men had eaten the sacred parts of the bear—the head and the forelegs—the feast-giver wiped the platter clean, wrapped it, and set it aside. From then on, the rest of the food passed in a clockwise direction as the men served, and everyone, including the children, ate. Gradually the mood lightened. The excitement that had built throughout the day started to show. People talked and laughed. Tobacco made the rounds, and men smoked. As the night wore on, the feast-giver sang and drummed. Later, others drummed and sang their songs. In the early morning hours, after most of the food had been consumed, people danced. Both men and women moved in single file around the fire, the women wearing their beaded dance caps. Everyone danced until just before sunrise. The feast had to end before the sun came up.

Finally, with all the meat eaten, the feast-giver wiped clean each plate with his fingers and then licked clean each finger. He collected all the crumbs from the birch-bark mat and ate them or threw them into the fire for *Memekwesiw*. When he was certain that no morsel had been wasted, he said a prayer and smeared some charcoal below his lower lip to "seal his mouth."[29] This was the sign that the feast was over. Everyone else did the same, and the feast-giver unsealed and opened the lodge.

The unsealing of the feast lodge recalls an important Cree myth in which a young Cree hero saved the people from starvation. In the myth, a powerful man called Nenimis captured all the animal spirits and locked them away inside a tightly sealed box within his lodge. The people, not knowing what Nenimis had done, searched in vain for the animals. For many days they hunted. In the winter they began to starve. Some died. A young man came forward and said he would find the animals and return them to the forest. After traveling far, he came upon Nenimis's lodge. Nenimis invited the young man in and offered him food but warned that unless he ate everything he was offered, he would be killed. The young man said he would eat everything. Nenimis then proceeded to give him one of every kind of animal, each cooked whole. The young man managed to eat them all. Nothing was left. Defeated, Nenimis left the lodge and walked into the forest. The young man immediately broke open the box, and the spirits of all the animals flooded out. He cut a giant hole in the side of the lodge, and the spirits escaped into the forest. He returned to his people. From that day forth, they hunted and killed game.[30]

The Cree called this young man "The One Who Owns The Feast." When they opened the feast lodge at the end of their ritual meal, the spirit of the bear, like the animal spirits in the myth, escaped into the forest and returned to *Memekwesiw*. If in *Memekwesiw's* eyes, everything had been done right, the bear was returned to its animal form so it could be killed again by the people.

Sometimes, if the bear was large or the group was especially small, meat might be left uneaten. The Indians wrapped these leftover pieces carefully at the end of the feast and left the sealed bundles behind after the lodge was opened. Bear meat entering the feast lodge did not come back out. The people returned on another night to finish it, and no hunting was allowed until all of the bear had been eaten.

Cree ritual also involved inedible parts of the bear such as the bones and the skull. They did not allow dogs near them because dogs are unclean, and they protected them from other kinds of abuse. Carelessness invited retribution. For example, a Cree man named Anderson Jolly once killed a bear by clubbing it on the head, hitting it so hard that he cracked the skull. This offended the bear's spirit, and Anderson went five years without seeing another.[31]

A "bear's chin," decorated with beadwork and used as a hunting charm. James Bay Cree. *Photo courtesy National Museums of Canada, Ottawa.*

Opposite: Bear pole of the Eastern Cree. After a hunter killed a bear, he lashed the skull, ears, and skin of the muzzle to a tree. He also decorated the tree as an offering to the bear; at certain intervals he peeled away the bark and rubbed the wood with red ocher. After a drawing in Skinner, *Notes on the Eastern Cree.* *Illustration by Janet McGahan.*

After the feast, the Cree cut down a tree fifteen or twenty feet tall and stripped it of most of its bark and branches so only a small tuft of new growth was left at the very top. They painted it from the bottom up with horizontal red stripes and stuck it in the ground at the edge of camp. They made circle and bar designs with vermillion on the bear's skull, stuck tobacco in the jaw, tied ribbons of hide and cloth to it, and then lashed it to the pole about ten feet above the ground so that it faced east, toward the rising sun. They bundled the other bones and hung them from the pole about six feet above the ground. The Cree did this for every bear they killed "so the bear would return to life and come back to be killed again." If they killed many bears during any one winter, a long column of painted and decorated skulls hung from the pole.[32]

Sometimes, before the bear skull went to the pole, the hunter who had killed the bear placed its skull in his lodge above where he slept, in "the place that brings dreams."[33] The spirit of the slain bear helped him dream more bear dreams.

The hunter stretched the bear's skin on a rack and let it dry for a few days. He painted the neck, eyebrow, a spot in the center of the hide, and a spot just above the tail with a red dye. Then, to show respect for the bear, he put it away for one year. Later he might use it for charms or clothing.[34]

40

The Cree focused special attention on the skin under the bear's chin. The wife of a successful hunter decorated it with beads, quills, and little tassels of cloth, and gave it to her husband. He carried it as a hunting charm that would help him kill more bears. One of their many names for bear was "The One Who Owns the Chin." The custom relates to a Cree narrative about a giant bear that would eat only the head, forearms, and meat from under the chin of the animals it killed. For a Cree, these parts of the bear were sacred.[35]

Nearly all the northern and northeastern Algonquian-speaking tribes and bands hunted bears in a manner similar to that of the Cree. Variations on major elements of the ritual occurred elsewhere in North America too, especially among the hunting tribes of Alaska and western Canada.

Anthropologist Irving Hallowell, in his classic monograph entitled *Bear Ceremonialism in the Northern Hemisphere*,[36] compared the bear hunting techniques of natives throughout northern Europe, Asia, and North America. Hallowell found amazing parallels between the bear hunt of certain North American Indians and bear hunts in Scandinavia, Siberia, and Japan. His monograph revealed an ancient circumpolar bear hunting tradition among subarctic peoples. Throughout the regions of North America, Europe, and Asia where the bear hunting ceremonies were performed, Hallowell found that hunters and others involved in the rites believed that the bear represented "a supernatural being or power," which governed either the supply of game animals or the supply of bears alone.[37] He also identified common elements of the hunting ritual. First, the hunt took place in early spring while the bear was still sleeping in its den. Second, no one could refer to the bear except by metaphorical expressions or kinship or deferential terms such as "The One Going Around in the Woods," "Grandfather," or "Great One." Third, hunters called the bear from its den ("Grandfather, Come out! I am sorry I must kill you!") and killed it at close quarters with an archaic weapon—a club, an ax, a spear, or a knife. Fourth, the hunters made conciliatory speeches to the bear's spirit after its death. Fifth, the carcass became the focus of elaborate ceremonial attention in which it was dressed up in borrowed finery and offered food, tobacco, or decorated objects. Sixth, there was a communal, often eat-all feast of bear meat governed by numerous prescriptions and taboos and emphasizing sexual differences. Finally, the people respectfully disposed of the bones, especially the skull, by placing them in a tree or returning them to the den. Hallowell concluded that the tradition may have originated in Eurasia during the paleolithic and migrated

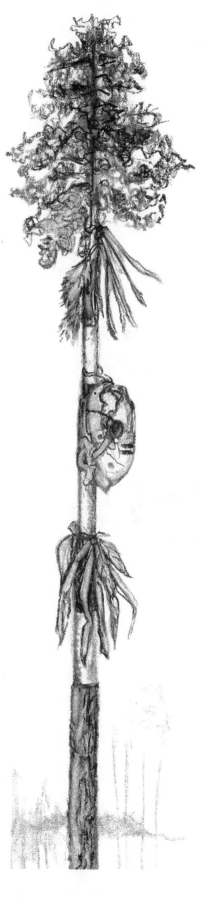

"Grandfather, I am Sorry I Must Kill You"

into the New World by way of hunters pursuing caribou herds across the Bering land-bridge.

When asked about the meaning of their bear hunting rites, the Cree have said things like, "We do [the rites] to keep from starving...we do them because it pleases the bears, it makes them want to be killed by us. And we do them because *Memekwesiw*, the spirit that watches over the bears, would be offended otherwise and would stop sending his children to us. We do these things because it is the proper way to behave toward an animal that is making a gift of its life."

From the Cree perspective, a bear killed by a hunter wanted to give its life. It wanted its flesh to be consumed, its skull to be painted and put in a place of honor. When the hunter stood before a den and asked a bear for its life—"Grandfather, show me your head!"—and the bear came out, it was presenting itself to be killed. It gave its body willingly, sacrificing its physical self so the hunter and his family might eat.

A misconception about traditional hunting societies is the assumption that hunters felt no regret when they killed food animals. On the contrary, the people of most Indian cultures strongly sympathized with game animals. The Cree viewed the animals they hunted in terms of fervent respect, the kind of respect they felt for members of their own families. They expressed this attitude in the lyrics of their songs, in their conversations with food animals, and in their myths and tales about the hunt. The hunter might sing or talk about the caribou as he would about his wife, or the bear as he would his son or grandmother.[38]

Bear skull with ceremonial markings. The skull is cleaned, dried, and painted with vermilion before being hung in a tree with tobacco and other offerings. Eastern Cree. After a drawing in Skinner, *Notes on the Eastern Cree. Illustration by Janet McGahan.*

Just as their feelings varied for each family member, hunters felt differently about each of the animals. Caribou, for example, were often represented in songs, dreams, and rituals as the female lover of the hunter. Caribou were lustful, eager to be killed. In the words of one Cree, the hunter "believes the caribou love him because they are waiting for him to kill them, just like a young wife waiting for her husband."[39]

Bears, on the other hand, the Cree viewed with an affection usually reserved for one's children or grandparents. After killing a bear the hunter felt honored, as if rewarded by a respected elder. He felt the bear cared for him as a grandparent cares for a grandchild. The animal wanted to be killed by him.

For his part, the Cree hunter empathized with the animals he killed and with the spirits that sent the animals to him, and he wished to return something of value. He did this with his rituals, with the beautiful quillwork designs he wore, with the songs he sang and drummed, and with his offerings of tobacco and food. Even his manner of communicating about the bear was a gesture of respect, a way of saying, "You are a great animal. Your gift is one of true value to me. I honor you. I want to please you." For the Cree, hunting food animals was as much an act of giving on the part of the hunter as it was of receiving.

The hunter also knew that there was grave spiritual danger involved in hunting, and that killing an animal, any animal, implied responsibility. If a man failed to show the proper respect, he risked offending not only the animal's spirit, but also its spirit boss, who would then withhold other animals of the same kind. The consequences of a disrespectful act could be fatal for the hunter and his family. The hunter avoided doing anything to offend the spirits.

The Cree honored all the animals they killed. The rites conducted for other species—caribou, moose, beaver, waterfowl, and even fish—differed in degree but not in kind from those performed for bears. The chief difference was that in the bear hunt, the rites coalesced into a ceremony, more so than for any other animal. And the attitude was different. The Cree were much more circumspect in the rites they directed toward a slain bear.

The Cree had an image of the ideal hunt. In the perfect hunt, the outcome was known in advance. Before a man left camp, he knew, by virtue of his dreams or sacred rites of divination, what he would kill and exactly where he would kill it. In the real Cree world, however, a man hunting caribou or moose might not find his animal. He might roam tens of miles in a single day without success. Even if he found a caribou herd, he might not get close enough to make a kill.

Bear hunting charms of the Eastern Cree. A claw, a ring of claws, and a string of bear "chins," each painted red and with a piece of the bear's tongue fastened to the inside. After a drawing in Skinner, *Notes on the Eastern Cree*. *Illustration by Janet McGahan.*

All was in question. But when a man hunted a bear, the prophesy that he would make a kill almost always came true, for he located a den first and returned later to kill the bear. He knew the bear would be there when he returned. A bear in its den was cached meat.

The element of certainty associated with the bear hunt was important in a hunting society such as the Cree, where so much depended upon the hunters' success. If the men consistently failed at hunting over a long period of time, life became more difficult. The people grew uneasy. They ate less and turned to their stores of dried meat and berries. They brooded more over the outcome of future hunts. When hunters were unsuccessful for weeks or longer, they tried to encourage their dreams. They asked elders to perform divination rites that they—the hunters—would have performed themselves in times of plenty. They asked shamans to make shaking tents. Everyone became more careful in their observance of taboos.

The bear hunt was a paradigm. It came closest to matching the image of the ideal hunt.[40] For this reason, it tells us as much about the Cree's relationship with food animals in general as it does about their relationship with bears. Anthropologists Regina Flannery and Mary Chambers wrote of the East Cree, "While due respect was paid to all food animals, special ritual attention was given to every bear, to the first of each species taken in season, and to the first of each species killed by a young hunter. Rites of these 'firsts' seem to be more or less patterned after the bear ceremonial."[41]

Two other elements unique to bear hunting supported Cree religious beliefs about the hunt. The first dealt with the conviction that animals killed in the hunt wanted to die, that they gave their physical bodies to the hunter because they loved him and wanted him to have enough food to eat. A bear, especially an angry one, could easily kill or maim a man. The weapons the Cree used to attack bears—clubs and spears—put the hunter at greater risk than would a bow and arrow. Yet men were seldom injured when they killed bears at their dens. Most of the time the bears did not attack. Nor did the bears, who were assumed by the Cree to know their fate in advance, try to escape. A bear waited in its den for the hunter. When the hunter called it to come out and be killed, the bear came out. It was clear to the hunter that the bear wanted to die. Although the Cree believed that every animal they killed died willingly, only bears gave themselves so predictably, so obviously.

The Cree also believed that all beings, food animals included, are immortal. In an insightful paper published in 1928, anthropologist Erna Gunther, then a doctoral candidate at Columbia University, compared the first salmon ceremony of the North Pacific Coast with the bear-hunt ritual of the northern Algonquians and Athapaskans and found them much the same. Like the bear, salmon were believed to be immortal and wanted to be caught and eaten by the people.[42] Although these concepts were extended to all food animals, they were most vivid with animals, such as salmon and bears, that made a periodic appearance. Both salmon and bears represented renewal and immortality: the salmon swimming upriver, returning every year in numbers so great a person could not see the bottoms of the streams; the fat bear crawling into the earth every fall and coming out again every spring.

In the bear-hunt ritual the people intervened in the bear's winter sleep. That intervention enabled them to participate in the realm of the animals and it gave them access to the Owner of the Animals. The bear was a messenger carrying a plea for game.

Petroglyph depicting a bear and two hunters. Utah.   *Illustration by Janet McGahan.*

4

"It May Change into Anything"

ALONE, THE OLD MAN STANDS above the carcass in silence. Surrounding him are timbered hills, lightly dusted with snow from a sudden morning storm. The air is cold and fine, and the old man's breath makes small clouds that quickly dissipate. It is mid-January, and for miles all seems still.

In his arms he cradles a club of piñon wood smeared with red ocher and sprinkled with pollen. The bear that killed a dozen of his people's sheep last summer now lies at his feet. He found it sleeping in its den, called to it, and when it came out he struck it hard on the head just above the nose, knocking it to the ground where he clubbed it until it was dead.

Having caught his breath, the old man kneels and begins to talk to the bear. He speaks gently, as if he were talking to a friend. He calls it *atco naxeti*, which in Navajo means, "it may change into anything." "*Atco naxeti*," he says, "understand me, I am not doing this because I have bad feelings toward you. I am doing it because you have done a great deal of damage among The People. What you have done—stealing food—The People cannot forgive. But hear me, *atco naxeti*. You are not killed. The only reason I do this is because I want you to realize what it is to steal. The den is still yours. You still rule the mountains."

The old man repeats these words several times to the bear, then turns it over onto its back, and with effort positions it so the head is facing the entrance. Pausing now, he begins to sing one of his family's bear songs. As he sings, he takes out a small bag of pollen, the Navajo symbol of harmony, and sprinkles a line of it up the bear's belly and then along the inside of each leg to the paw. With his knife, he cuts along these lines of pollen and then skins the bear. After laying the pelt carefully aside, he opens the belly and cuts through a thick layer of fat. Reaching in, he pulls out the steaming intestines. They are slippery and hot, and he pauses for a moment to warm his cold hands in them. He cuts the mass free and lays it in a loose pile beside the carcass. He removes the gall but leaves the heart, lungs, liver, bladder, and windpipe in place. Holding the belly open with his foot, he slides the intestines back into the carcass.

Still singing, the hunter removes a white shell from a small bag and places it at the end of the windpipe. He puts another white shell where the lungs join, and a red stone on the diaphragm. He puts turquoise on the liver, in the middle of the backbone, on the bladder, and on the anus. He makes small slits to insert each stone. Then standing and walking clockwise around the bear, he places turquoise on each of the paws, on the shoulders, and in both ears. Finally, the old man turns the bear onto its belly and pulls the hide back over it. He sprinkles pollen in a neat line up its back, from the end of the tail to the nose, and then carefully lays his club between the ears.

He is finished. Leaving the bear, his club, and all his shells and stones behind, he is about to return to his village. Before he goes, he kneels close to the bear's head and tells it, "You will come back to life now."[1]

THE WAY THIS NAVAJO killed the bear in the mountains of Arizona is not very different from the bear hunt of a northern Athapaskan or a northern Algonquian. Although the Navajo inhabit the Southwest, they are related to woodland Indians of western Canada and Alaska. They speak Athapaskan, the language of the western subarctic. A thousand years ago they lived in a boreal forest and made their living much the way northern Athapaskans do today, by gathering roots and berries, catching salmon, hunting moose, caribou, beaver, and bear. When they migrated south along the Rockies, they ended ultimately in the latitudes of Arizona, in a land with a wholly new terrain and climate. To survive, they modified traditions many thousands of years old. By observing surrounding tribes they learned to hunt new animals, gather new plants, and prosper in a land spare of water and trees. Their hunts and ceremonials took on attributes of the more sedentary southwestern agricultural tribes such as the Pueblos, but the foundation of their culture remained Athapaskan. Navajo bear hunts reflected this union. Their beliefs and many of their attitudes toward bears resembled those of southwestern agricultural tribes. However, the way they prepared for a bear hunt, how they killed bears, and their treatment of the carcasses paralleled the traditions of subarctic hunters. Both the Navajo and subarctic tribes, for example, hunted bears at their dens. Both preferred to use clubs or spears over bows and arrows or rifles, which were safer. Both spoke to the bears before and after they killed them. The Navajo decorated carcasses with sacred stones and pollen. Tribes of the western subarctic smeared bear hides with red dye and sprinkled them with swan's-

Petroglyph depicting a man spearing a bear. Utah.   *Illustration by Janet McGahan.*

down. Both groups held solemn feasts of bear meat, although the Navajo only ate bear meat when they were on the verge of starvation. After these feasts, the Navajo, like northern tribes, disposed of bear bones in a ritualistic manner. Sometimes the Navajo placed the skull of a bear they had killed in a piñon tree so that it faced the den; Algonquian and some northern Athapaskan tribes placed bear skulls in trees or on special poles. For the Navajo and subarctic tribes alike, it was taboo to utter the specific word for bear before or during a hunt. Instead, they used kinship terms such as grandmother, cousin, or elder brother. Or they used metaphorical expressions or a descriptive phrase. Navajo names included "Reared in the Mountains," "Fine Young Chief," or "That Which Lives in the Den."

Nonetheless, the Navajo bear hunt did differ in some important ways from that of the northern tribes. Northern Athapaskans and Algonquians were avid and sophisticated bear hunters who loved bear meat. The Navajo rarely hunted bears and only killed them when circumstances left them no other choice. When a bear took to stealing sheep or raiding camps, the people would wait until winter, track the bear to its den, and kill it there. When a Navajo singer needed bear paws or other bear medicine for a ceremony, he, or someone else in his village who knew the sacred name of Bear, its

"It May Change into Anything"

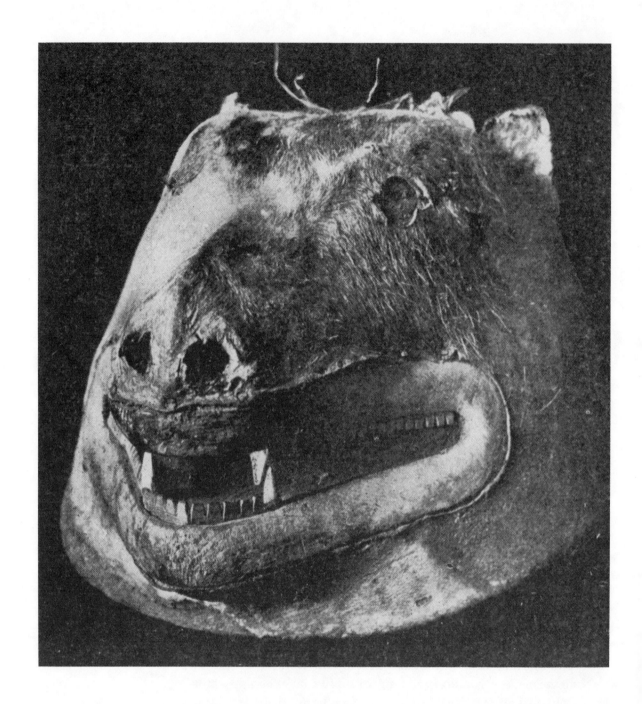

song, and special prayer, hunted the mountains for an occupied den. When he found one, he called the bear out and killed it, took the paws and whatever other medicine he needed, and left the carcass behind, its head facing the den entrance. Starvation was the only other reason Navajos killed bears and the only time they ate bear meat.

The Navajo believed that killing a bear or eating bear meat, except under special circumstances, could make you crazy, give you a fever, make your limbs swell and ache, and make you become fat and listless. In their words, "If you go up in the mountain where the bear is bedded down . . . [and] . . . you bedded down there, it will get you that way . . . make your head go wrong." Or, "Sometimes if you cross a bear's path and pick up some ants the bear rolled over, or slept on, you are liable to have mental troubles."[2]

The Navajos' reluctance to hunt bears, their distaste for the animal's flesh, and their seemingly pathological fear of both black and grizzly bears, seem to have been adopted from neighboring cultures in the southwest. Pueblos, for example, rarely killed bears. To do so, they believed, might invite retribution from the bear's spirit. If a man inadvertently killed a bear, one of the medicine societies performed an elaborate healing ritual for him.[3] Implicit in the bear traditions of many Pueblo communities was the fear that a bear, like a malevolent shaman, could make you sick.

The Pueblos also disliked killing bears because they thought of them as transformed people, and eating one came close to cannibalism. Elsie Clews Parsons, who had a bearskin rug in her home when she was working among the Pueblos, wrote that a woman, who sometimes came to visit her, never stepped on the rug without apologizing to the bear, "who was once someone like us."[4]

The Pima, too, who live just to the south of the Navajo, zealously avoided bears. They believed bears caused a peculiar kind of bloating disease. They said that if you killed a bear without saying the right things, you would get a fever, an aching head, and swollen limbs. Simply stepping on a bear track could make your legs swell up so badly you could not walk. The remedy for this malady was to sit alone for a day, fast, and sing the bear songs.[5]

Why did these tribes fear sickness from bears while other tribes killed bears for food? Perhaps southwest Indian beliefs and traditions have something to do with the fear of physical attack, although when Navajos or Pimas talk about bears they rarely touch on physical threats such as mauling. They speak instead, often in veiled ways, about the spirit of the animal and about its power. A bear, they say, knows and does things that other animals cannot. It hears men talking, even when they are miles away. Sometimes it travels across the land very fast, as fast as a whirlwind. It appears and disappears, moves in and out of mountains like a ghost. The bear, they believe, is like a great shaman; powerful, unpredictable, and dangerous.

The owner of this Tlingit grizzly bear hat acquired it and the exclusive right to use it after he killed a grizzly bear with his ax. The bear had killed many people. There is a gash on the top of the hat, which represents the lethal wound. *Photo courtesy of the Smithsonian Institution, National Anthropological Archives.*

Even the northern Athapaskan tribes that actively hunted bears for food feared them for these reasons. Examining their beliefs, it is easy for one to understand how the Navajo, an Athapaskan-speaking tribe that originated in the north, came to adopt some of the beliefs of southwestern tribes. Northern Athapaskan women feared bears. The men, who loved to hunt bears, were careful in the way they talked about them. They rarely used the word bear. They said it infuriated the bear so that it attacked or fled. Instead they called it "Grandfather" or some other name that bestowed honor.

Mimbres bowl with painting of a man and a bear (from the tenth to twelfth century). *Illustration by Janet McGahan.*

GIVING VOICE TO BEAR

Some northern Athapaskan-speaking tribes made up riddles as an indirect way of talking about bears. Richard Nelson, in his book on Koyukon world view, *Make Prayers to the Raven*, describes an example of the tradition:

> The late Chief Henry, when just a boy, was traveling on foot through the forest with a group of people. Somewhere along the way he heard a strange thing, an old man off in the timber, shouting to the others, "I found a place where a white man froze to death back here last fall!" Everyone understood what he meant—that he had killed a hibernating black bear in its den—and that he used cryptic language so he would not offend its spirit.[6]

A Koyukon man might say, "Wait, I see something: I am looking everywhere for a lost arrow." The people knew he was seeking a bear den because they knew that a person had to search for a lost arrow in the same way that he looked for a bear den.[7]

For the Kutchin, another Athapaskan tribe of Alaska, there was only one kind of riddle—the bear-telling riddle—and it could be posed many ways. A man could, for example, act it out by moving around like a bear. This was called *gwizhii ideegwidlii* (literally, "wisdom that is performed"). Or he could tell it, which was called *gwizhii ideeridlii* ("wisdom that is told").[8] In the words of Abel Tritt, a Kutchin man, Kutchin riddles worked this way:

> *Gwizhii ideegwidlii* is used when a man finds a bear den with a bear in it. Look it over real good and then go home. Go over to the person who lives next to you and purposely sit very close to him. When he offers you food, you ask him, "Where's the fat and grease that goes with it?"...When you say this to a smart man, he finds out right away. When you say these things but his mind is not on the subject, you ask him in another way, and sometimes you walk around roughly and clumsily in his house....Sometimes you enter your friend's house and walk past him, brushing against him real hard on purpose....If a man is smart, he'll find out right away.[9]

To say he found a bear, a Kutchin man might ask, "What's that brown stuff on your cheeks?" Or he might walk around pigeon toed like a bear and ask, "How come you walk around like this?" He could scratch his back on a tree and then, turning around, exclaim, "Hey, it looks like there's some hair left on there!" Or he might return from a hunt and announce, "Gee I saw a lot of berries out there!"[10]

There were other tribes in North America besides those in the southwest that did not hunt bears. Of the Great Plains tribes, only the

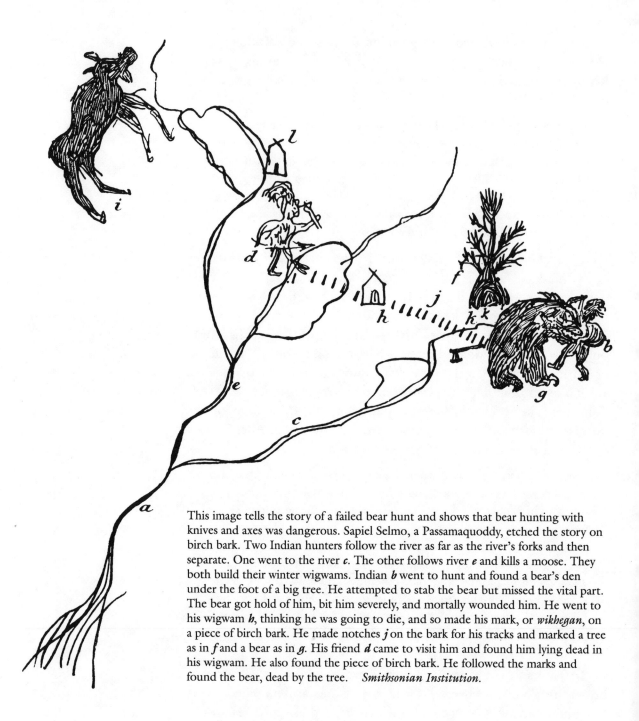

This image tells the story of a failed bear hunt and shows that bear hunting with knives and axes was dangerous. Sapiel Selmo, a Passamaquoddy, etched the story on birch bark. Two Indian hunters follow the river as far as the river's forks and then separate. One went to the river *c*. The other follows river *e* and kills a moose. They both build their winter wigwams. Indian *b* went to hunt and found a bear's den under the foot of a big tree. He attempted to stab the bear but missed the vital part. The bear got hold of him, bit him severely, and mortally wounded him. He went to his wigwam *h*, thinking he was going to die, and so made his mark, or *wikhegan*, on a piece of birch bark. He made notches *j* on the bark for his tracks and marked a tree as in *f* and a bear as in *g*. His friend *d* came to visit him and found him lying dead in his wigwam. He also found the piece of birch bark. He followed the marks and found the bear, dead by the tree. *Smithsonian Institution*.

Plains Cree, Plains Ojibwa, and Assiniboin hunted bears for food. The Blackfeet had a strong taboo against killing, eating, or using the hide of the animal, although their shamans could use hides for ceremonial purposes and warriors could possess claws. James W. Schultz, a white man who lived with the Blackfeet in the late 1800s, wrote that they would rather starve to death than eat the flesh of a bear. When Blackfeet went out hunting in bear country, they talked to the bears saying, "We are not looking for you. Keep out of our way."[11]

Other plains tribes such as the Cheyenne and Arapaho also refused to eat bear meat, although the Cheyenne occasionally killed black bears. They considered bears to be ancestors, so eating bear meat was like eating the flesh of a relative. Fearing a rash that would turn their skin black, Cheyenne and Blackfeet women would not handle bear hides until they passed menopause. The Lakota said, "If a menstruating woman tans a bearskin, then she will become a bear. She will turn hairy and black all over. Therefore women are very much afraid of bearskins."[12]

Like most of the plains tribes, some California and southwest tribes avoided bear hunting. The Yavapai of western Arizona viewed bears as humans without fire and refused to kill them. As a consequence, the bears that lived around them fed and sunned themselves quite near their camps.[13]

In the northwest, the Tlingit had a similar attitude toward grizzly bears, although they often killed black bears. They still tell a story about a woman who married a grizzly bear and gave birth to two cubs during her winter in the den. Even today the Tlingit do not eat grizzly bears because of this belief. They say, "That is why you never eat grizzly bear meat. Now people eat black bear meat, but they still don't eat grizzly meat, because grizzlies are half human."[14]

Tribes that hunted bears in the west, where there were both black and grizzly bears, thought of the grizzly as a distinctly more powerful and dangerous animal. The Kootenai, for instance, considered the grizzly bear to be the most powerful of the spirit guardians. They believed that the black bear was so spiritually weak, however, that it was unable to act as a spirit helper. The Blackfeet word for black bear was *kyaio*, which may be translated as bear, while their word for grizzly bear, *nitakyaio*, means real bear.[15] Many of the tribes that hunted black bears for food avoided grizzly bears altogether. Those that did hunt grizzlies treated them in a more circumspect manner. Richard Nelson writes of the Koyukon:

> Nearly everything that is done to respect and placate the black bear
> is also done for the brown [grizzly] bear; but the acts and emotions

are intensified, the danger and fear are greater, the consequences of error more grievous. I noticed the people's voices often became lower and softer when they talked of this animal. This, as much as the words they spoke, revealed the meaning of the bear in their lives. For nothing else that visibly or invisibly occupies the wildland did I hear this change of voice.[16]

Some of the tribes that hunted bears considered bear hunting the equivalent of going to war. Like the Tlingit, they thought bears were enough like humans that they should be treated as such. Young Cheyenne men counted coup on bears they killed as they would on a slain enemy.[17] When Assiniboin warriors recited their war deeds, they included all the bears they had killed.[18] The Fox, a Great Lakes tribe, scalped a bear after killing it, as they would a human enemy, and then cremated the body.[19]

Some Pueblo communities, on the rare occasions when someone killed a bear, treated the carcass as a slain enemy. At Jemez, warriors returning from a battle would stop a mile or so from camp and shout their return. A man who killed a bear did the same, and all the men ran out to meet him as if he were returning from a war. The hunter gave each of them a piece of bear meat to wrap around the barrels of their guns, and they all rode into camp shouting and singing. As they entered camp, women charged out to meet them and to beat the dead bear with sticks and fire pokers. They called the successful bear hunter a war chief, and they danced a war dance to celebrate. Five days later they set up an altar and held a ceremonial feast, its purpose to convert the bear from enemy to friend. At the close of the ceremony, in an act symbolizing the adoption of the bear's spirit into the tribe, a holy man washed the bear's head and placed it, together with miniature red-painted weapons, in a shrine. They treated the scalps of human foes in the same way.[20]

The bear's nature, especially the grizzly bear's, inspired awe and respect. Some Indians considered the grizzly bear a warrior's warrior. They said that in battle it was powerful, aggressive, and fearless. Conjuring these qualities for themselves, warriors from these tribes wore grizzly bear claws and painted bears on their shields. On the plains, bear dreamers, the men who had the bear as their guardian spirit, fought by imitating bears.

On the coast of what is now British Columbia, the Kwakiutl hunter who killed a grizzly acquired its powers. He became fierce and violent and unpredictable, desirable traits among the Kwakiutl. When a Kwakiutl man hunting for grizzly bears finally came upon one, he addressed it saying, "Be ready friend, that we may try our strength. You dreaded one. I am of the same kind, for I am dreaded also. . . . Listen to me, Supernatural One, now I will take by war your power of not respecting anything, of not being afraid, and your wildness, great, good, Supernatural One."[21]

The primary reason for killing bears, though, was for food, especially in forested areas where there were no buffalo and tribes utilized every available game species. In the wooded east, Indians hunted bears as food animals from Hudson Bay to the Gulf of Mexico. In the densely forested western and central subarctic, tribes also hunted bears and ate bear meat. And tribes up and down the northwest coast, on the Columbia Plateau, and in parts of California killed black and grizzly bears for food. Only on the Great Plains, where buffalo replaced woodland game, and in the deserts of the southwest, were bears not generally hunted for food.

In the areas where bears were an important source of meat, many of the tribes believed that bears had control over the supply of other game. For example, hunters of several plateau and northwest coast tribes sang a song after they killed a bear:

> You cause the other animals to do as you have done.
>> Even you, you have laid down for me;
>> Now, you cause the bucks to lie down.
>> You have given up to me;
>> Now, you cause the good looking women to give up to me.[22]

Except for the reference to women, the song is similar to the prayers the Cree said over the bodies of the bears they killed. It suggests that these tribes also connected the bear with their success in hunting any game. Perhaps the bear represented for them, as it did for the Cree, the renewal of those animals that were hunted for food.

Indians also killed bears to obtain only claws or perhaps hides. This was especially true of shamans or warriors, who hoped to gain some of the bear's power by killing it and wearing some part of it. Often these men did not eat the meat. Some tribes, such as the Navajo and the Apache, would kill bears to get paws or gall for tribal ceremonies.

Sometimes Indians killed bears to protect human life and property. The occasional bears that attacked people or broke into lodges or food caches were usually considered to be bad bears and were hunted down and killed. Often only spiritually powerful individuals, those who possessed the bear as a guardian spirit or knew the bear-hunt songs, attempted to go after them.

The means of killing bears were diverse. In the north, Indians preferred to take a bear at its den with a club or a spear. To see if a den was occupied, they poked a long pole with a split end into it.

> If you feel [a bear] you twist the pole and get some hair . . . and you take that hair home. You don't want to kill the bear right then. If it's old time, and [the hunter] wants to kill it for his brother-in-law, he takes the hair and puts it in his [brother-in-law's] hand. And he doesn't say anything. He keeps quiet because it is a secret from the rest of the camp, and the bear would know, too, what you think. I think you put the hair in the fire too. U.Q. knows it from my father. He knows the song too."[23]

Northern tribes also attacked bears in the open with spears and trapped them with snares or deadfalls. The snare, probably the most common method of trapping bears, was made by placing a rawhide loop about twenty inches in diameter in a narrow spot on a trail where bears were known to travel. The hunter anchored the other end to a large downed log or to a young living tree that would bend and not break. Spared a dead pull, the rawhide could hold a bear. Sometimes a hunter set up his loop on the trail, then ran the snare line through the crotch of a large tree and fastened it to a heavy log

One type of deadfall used to kill bear in the subarctic. The fall log is positioned over the bed log and is guided by the stakes (1 – 4). The bait stick is positioned under (or over) the samson post. The top of the pen is covered with brush to disguise the trap and to prevent the bear from entering except through the front. The bear enters at *E*, tugs at the bait, and upsets the samson post. The fall log drops on its back or neck. *Smithsonian Institution.*

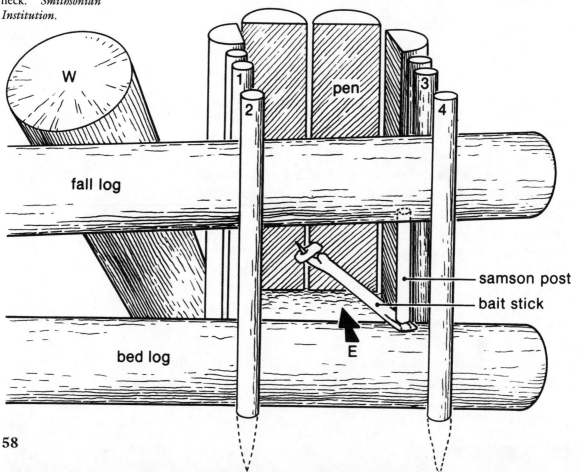

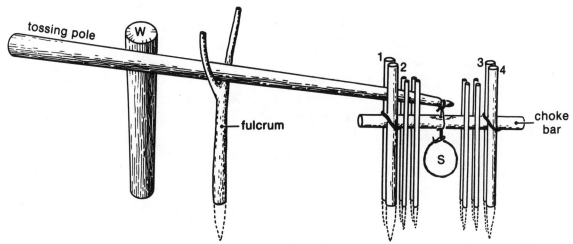

tossing pole

fulcrum

choke bar

A snare trap used for bear. A single perforated choke bar is lashed tightly between the uprights (1 – 4). The snare line passes through the hole in the choke bar and is tied to the tossing pole, which is held down by a catch loop. Brush is piled under the noose and on both sides of the framework. The bear's head enters the noose, the catch loop is released, and the weight of the log to the left of the fulcrum causes the tossing pole to pull up and choke the animal against the choke bar. *Smithsonian Institution.*

propped three to five feet above the ground. A bear, in its struggle to free itself, invariably caused the heavy log to fall and was hoisted into the air and choked to death. Snares had to be strong. In the Yukon and Alaska they were made of twisted vine. The Inland Tlingit believed that if a bear broke the snare line someone in the hunter's family would die.[24]

The deadfall trap was made by bracing five or six heavy logs between two or more trees about five feet above the bear's trail. The hunter connected the brace to a pin-type trigger in the trail, which he had covered with grass and brush. When the bear stepped on the trigger, the logs dropped and pinned the bear or crushed it to death.[25]

In the Yukon, the Inland Tlingit often hunted bears with dogs. To make a puppy a good bear dog, they scratched its nose with a claw from the "right hand thumb of a bear" until it bled. They put a few drops of the blood into a hole in the head of a dead gray jay while saying, "I wish that dog to be good at bear hunting."[26]

Several plateau tribes also hunted bears with dogs. The dogs, trained to recognize the scents of both black and grizzly bears, trailed a bear until it climbed a tree or turned to fight, then held it at bay until a man could approach and kill it with a bow and arrow. These tribes believed that dogs, like people, had spirit guardians who helped them hunt, and they fed bear-hunting dogs bits of a grizzly claw mixed with pemmican to encourage a visit from the grizzly spirit. Sometimes they would wrap a dog tightly in a fresh bear hide and keep it bound until it quit struggling.[27]

The Maidu, a California tribe, hunted grizzly bears in groups of five or six. Upon spotting a bear, the men crept as close as they could without alerting it, and each man chose a hiding place behind a tree or rock. With a signal from the leader, one man showed himself to the bear and shot at it once or twice. If all worked well, the grizzly would chase this man, who ran as fast as he could to where another hunter was hiding. The second hunter jumped out and diverted the bear's attention by shooting one or two arrows at it, and then he ran. The bear chased him. This hunter led the bear to a third man who did the same. Eventually, the bear tired. The hunters circled and finished it.[28]

Among the Lower Carrier Indians, a bear hunter would put fish oil on the bottoms of his moccasins and then walk until he knew a bear followed, attracted to the fish smell he trailed behind him. The hunter led the bear to exactly where he wanted it and then killed it. Though effective, this was a dangerous method. Grizzly bears, lured by the strong fishy smell, sometimes chased the hunters down and ate them.[29]

Most tribes considered the rich and oily bear meat to be a delicacy. Bear feasts were always considered special meals, celebrations really, for both spiritual and dietary reasons. All fleshy parts of the animal were eaten, the meat being either boiled or roasted. Some tribes, such as the Koyukon, made an assortment of meat and organ dishes. Other tribes, such as the Inland Salish of the Columbia Plateau, simply pit-roasted the entire bear.

Subarctic Indians considered fat to be one of the most important parts of any animal. Bears carry a thick blanket of body fat and were, therefore, highly valued as food animals, especially in the winter months. Northern Indians rendered the fat and served it as a separate dish prized by all. One Ojibwa man described it: "I remember the taste of my mother's milk. It tasted rich and good like bear fat."[30]

These tribes always saved some bear fat and burned it in their lodges to provide light during the long dark winters. The Cree used it ceremonially. They smeared it on parts of their lodges and in their hair on special occasions. Many tribes considered bear fat mixed with medicinal herbs to be a potent emollient.

Hides were used for a variety of purposes, from parka ruffs and mittens to blankets, although some northern tribes such as the Koyukon refused to use a grizzly hide right away because of its spiritual potency. After killing a grizzly they stretched and dried the hide and then put it away for several years. Most often, these "mellowed" hides were used as doors on traditional winter houses. The Koyukon never placed a hide where someone, especially a woman, might step over it.[31]

Shamans and warriors who possessed the bear as a guardian spirit wore skins as well as claws and teeth. They kept certain parts of the animal, especially claws, in their medicine bundles. In the eastern woodlands and the subarctic, hunters kept tongue sinews, pieces of hide, knee bones, and scapulas to use as charms or for divination. The bones not used for charms or ceremonies were kept away from dogs and eventually bundled and placed in a tree, returned to the bear's den, or simply burned. Hides, too, if not used for clothing or rituals, were sometimes returned to the den or burned.

Tribes generally disposed of the remains of the bears they had killed with the same attitude of caution and respect that they possessed during the hunt. Most believed that a bear's spirit stayed with its bones and hide long after it died. Bones and hides had power. They could divine the future, bring luck, or, if ill-treated, invite retribution. Most tribes disposed of bones in prescribed ways from which there was little deviation.

For whatever reason Indians hunted bears—whether to obtain food, to acquire power, or to protect one's camp or family—the hunt was always steeped in reverent, sometimes fearful ceremony. The people endeavored always to please the animal's spirit, to preserve a harmony between humans and animals, a harmony as fragile as autumn ice.

5

"A Bear Will Devour Your Flesh"

THEY EMERGE SUDDENLY from the trees, walking on snowshoes, a boy of perhaps fourteen years and a man who appears too old to be the boy's father. They are Beaver Indians of the western subarctic, and it is a mild day in February. The sun is bright on the heavy snow, and a warm wind gusts at their backs.

They have come far—half a day's walk from their winter camp. The boy has led most of the way, the old man guiding from behind. They have passed seven caribou, a moose, and three beaver, but they are not hunting today.

Now the old man moves ahead. His pace quickens, and they cross a frozen lake. On the other side they re-enter the trees, which quickly become dense, almost impassable, and they crawl for a while until they emerge into a small clearing against a wooded hill. Raising his hand, the old man signals the boy to move quietly. They creep to the base of the rise and stop. "Now," the old man whispers, "you will hear The Old One sucking his paws."

On hands and knees they crawl to a yellowed, fist-sized opening in the snow. Gently, the old man takes the boy's arm and eases him closer to the hole. Both hold their breath and listen, and they hear, faintly, muffled sucking sounds from the bear. They smile.

On the way home, after a long period of silence, the old man tells the boy, "When you are ready to fast like The Old One in the den, it will be your time." A short distance farther they spot the same seven caribou. The old man says it is a good sign. They sit for a while, watching the animals wander out of sight.

MANY HUNTING TRIBES thought of bears as the shamans of the animal world. According to Yavapai myth, at the dawn of time the first great shaman was Bear. In a tale told by tribes of the western subarctic, the bear is portrayed as an animal shaman, who uses his powers to

Bearskin-clad shaman found in an earth-work enclosure of the Hopewell Culture (400 B.C. to A.D. 400) at what is now Newark, Ohio. *Photo courtesy of the Ohio Historical Society.*

prophesy the future—and his own death. Another tale, told in the eastern woodlands, tells of a spirit war between a bear and a shaman, the kind of fight that normally involved two shamans.

Coexisting with these mythic narratives was an universal belief among northern hunters that bears possessed powers analogous to those possessed by shamans. Indians believed that bears, like shamans, could tell the future. Many said that bears changed their form to become persons, other animals, or even inanimate objects. The Tlingit said, "People must always speak carefully of bear people since bears [no matter how far away] have the power to hear human speech. Even though a person murmurs a few careless words, the bear will take revenge."[1]

And in turn, those shamans who had the bear as a spirit helper wrapped themselves in the skins of bears, wore necklaces of bear claws, painted bear signs on their faces and bodies, and smoked pipes carved in the shapes of bears. In their medicine bundles they kept bear claws and teeth and other parts of the animal. They used bear claws and gall and bear grease in their ceremonies. They ate the plants bears ate and used them as their medicines. They danced as they thought bears danced, and they sang power songs to the animal. Here is a grizzly bear song of the Tlingit, in which the shaman expresses his sense of oneness with the bear:

A shaman's charm. The carving depicts a bear devouring initiates. Tlingit. *Photo courtesy of the Department of Library Services, American Museum of Natural History.*

> *Whu! Bear!*
> *Whu Whu!*
> *So you say*
> *Whu Whu Whu!*
> *You come.*
> *You're a fine young man*
> *You Grizzly Bear*
> *You crawl out of your fur.*
> *You come*
> *I say Whu Whu Whu!*
> *I throw grease in the fire.*
> *For you*
> *Grizzly Bear*
> *We're one!*[2]

Many Indians believed that shamans could transform themselves into bears. In the early part of this century, the Chukchansi of southern California told of a female shaman who, on being killed and buried, emerged from the ground in the shape of a bear.[3] The Ojibwa of the Great Lakes region and the Pomo of California told

GIVING VOICE TO BEAR

"A Bear Will Devour Your Flesh"

Skeletonized bears believed to be shamanic in origin. Igloolik area, Southern Ellesmere (left) and Belcher Island (right). *Photos courtesy of the National Museums of Canada, Ottawa.*

stories of bearwalks and bear doctors—shamans who traveled the countryside disguised as bears.

That Indians associated bears with shamanism stems in part from the similar and overlapping roles the bear and the shaman played in native American hunting cultures. Both bear and shaman were conceived of as spiritually powerful entities, both potentially dangerous. The shaman, like the bear, served as a messenger to the Owner of the Animals in the quest for game, and during divination rites the people consulted both bear and shaman about future hunts, especially during times of scarcity. The shaman healed the sick; likewise the bear was considered to have potent healing powers.

There were also similarities in the way they lived. Bears are solitary creatures. The shaman, too, was a loner who sought his wisdom and spiritual knowledge in isolation, in the wilderness. On the subject of solitude an Eskimo shaman named Igjugarjuk told the Danish explorer Knud Rasmussen how a shaman must live. "True wisdom," he said, "is only to be found far away from people, out in the great solitude, and is not found in play but only through suffering. Solitude and suffering open a person's mind to things unseen, therefore a shaman must seek wisdom there."[4]

Shamanic initiation rites were bear-like. To acquire power, the future shaman, like a bear entering hibernation, withdrew from his village and suffered a long bout of fasting. Igjugarjuk recounted his initiatory experience to Rasmussen in the early part of this century.

> When I was to be a shaman, I chose suffering through the two things that are most dangerous to us humans, suffering through hunger and suffering through cold. First I hungered five days and was then allowed to drink a mouthful of warm water. . . . Thereafter I went hungry another fifteen days, and again was given a mouthful of warm water. After that I hungered for ten days, and then could begin to eat though it only had to be the sort of food on which there is never any taboo. . . . I was to keep this diet for five months, and then the next five months might eat everything; but after that I was again forced to eat the meat diet that is prescribed for all those who must do penance in order to become clean . . .
>
> My instructor was my wife's father, Perqanaq. Perqanaq built a small snow hut at the place where I was to be, this snow hut being no bigger than that I could just get under cover and sit down. I was given no sleeping skin to protect me against the cold; only a little piece of caribou skin to sit upon. There I was shut in. The snow hut in which I sat was built far from the trails of men and when Perqanaq had found the spot where he thought it ought to be built, he stopped the little sledge at a distance and there I had to remain

GIVING VOICE TO BEAR

seated until the snow hut was ready. Not even I, who was after all the one to have to stay there, might set my footprints in the vicinity of the hut and old Perqanaq had to carry me from the sledge over to the hut so that I could crawl in . . .

My novitiate took place in the middle of the coldest winter and I, who never got anything to warm me and must not move, was very cold, and it was so tiring having to sit without daring to lie down, that sometimes it was as if I died a little. Only towards the end of the thirty days did a helping spirit come to me, a lovely and beautiful helping spirit . . .

When a new moon was lighted and had the same size as the one that had shone for us when we left the village, Perqanaq came again with his little sledge and stopped a long way from the snow hut. But by this time I was not very much alive any more and had not the strength to rise. In fact I could not stand on my feet. Perqanaq pulled me out of the hut and carried me down to the sledge and dragged me home in the same manner as he had dragged me to Kingarjuit. I was now completely emaciated that the veins on my hands and body and feet had quite disappeared. For a long time I might only eat very little in order to again get my intestines extended, and later came the diet that was to help cleanse my body.

Later, when I had quite become myself again, I understood that I had become the shaman of my village, and it did happen that my neighbors or people from a long distance away called me to heal a sick person or to "inspect a course" if they were going to travel. When this happened, the people of my village were called together and I told them what I had been asked to do. Then I left the tent or snow house and went out into solitude, away from the dwellings of man. But those who remained behind had to sing continuously, just to keep themselves happy and lively.

These days of "seeking for knowledge" are very tiring, for one must walk all the time, no matter what the weather is like and only rest in short snatches. I am usually quite done up, tired, not only in body but also in head, when I have found what I sought.[5]

Although there were variations between tribes, the way of becoming a shaman was surprisingly consistent throughout North America, even among tribes with very different cultural backgrounds. Shamanic initiations, like other initiations, turned on the mystical experience of a symbolic death and resurrection, but the intensity of the shamanic initiation set it apart from all others. Like Igjugarjuk, other shamans experienced long and difficult ordeals that often took them to the limits of human endurance.

Having first prepared for initiation with an elder shaman, the aspirant went into the wilderness to a piece of ground considered powerful or sacred. Sacred geography—landforms or grounds where spirits were believed to live or frequent—was part of every tribe's territory.

A Klamath tale tells about a sacred lake, one of the places where Klamath shamans sought their power. A man went there one day and saw a bear standing upright in the water. "This is what I am looking for," he said. The bear disappeared into the lake, and the man dove in after it but did not come back up. Later, his relatives found him lying unconscious on the shore. A stream of dark blood flowed from his mouth and pooled around his head. They carried him home and took care of him. After several days he recovered and became a shaman. They called the spot at the lake where he had received his power *Wita'mumpsi*, which means "Black Bear's Place." After that, people went there to get power.[6]

Shamans used buttes, mountaintops, and caves for their initiations, especially in the west and in the arctic.[7] Aspiring Pomo shamans sometimes excavated their own caves to sit in.[8]

The climax of the ordeal came when the candidate received a vision of a spirit. Spirits took the forms of animals, such as buffalo, eagle, and bear, or of mythical beings such as the thunderbird. Generally, Indians considered the bear to be one of the most powerful spirits, and so shamans often sought it as a spirit helper. Among some Eskimo groups, the spirit that came to a future shaman always manifested itself as a bear. The shamans of some tribes, however, considered the grizzly bear spirit too powerful to control. Tlingit shamans, for example, did not want the grizzly bear as a spirit helper.[9]

In the vision, the aspirant offered his flesh for the spirit to eat. The spirit tore the candidate's body apart, drank his blood, and ate the meat from his bones. The future shaman's soul rose to where he could look down on what remained of his body. He saw his bones, stripped of all flesh, scattered on the ground. He watched them reassemble and saw new flesh grow. His body became whole. He reentered it and came back to life.

Knud Rasmussen, writing of the Eskimo, explains:

> Though no shaman can explain to himself how and why, he can, by the power his brain derives from the supernatural, as it were by thought alone, divest his body of its flesh and blood, so that nothing remains but his bones. And he must then name all the parts of his body, mention every single bone by name. . . . By thus seeing himself naked, altogether freed from the perishable and transient flesh and blood, he consecrates himself, in the sacred tongue of shamans, to his great task, through that part of his body which will longest withstand the action of sun, wind, and weather, after he is dead.[12]

The historian of religion Mircea Eliade has written that "bone represents the very source of life, both human and animal. To reduce oneself to the skeleton condition is equivalent to re-entering the womb of this primordial life, that is, to a complete renewal, a mystical rebirth."[11]

Usually the spirit became the shaman's guardian or helping spirit and stayed with him for the rest of his life. Sometimes, however, a shaman's helping spirit came to him later and was different from the one he had encountered during his initiation. Many shamans had more than one spirit guardian. Spirit helpers came to them in visions throughout their life. A helping spirit guided, counseled, and protected a shaman from less friendly spirits or human enemies. They came to the shaman anytime he needed assistance in this world or in the world beyond.

Bear effigy pipe. Pawnee. *Illustration by Janet McGahan.*

The bear rites of northern hunting tribes correspond with the ritual tradition of the shaman. In the eat-all bear feast, the hunter and his family dismembered the slain bear's carcass and cooked and ate the flesh in an all night feast, as the spirit of the bear looked on. They consumed the animal entirely, leaving only the bones, which they boiled clean of meat. The people believed that if they carried out the ritual properly and if they kept the bones away from dogs and were careful not to break or chip them, then the bear would be born again.

An Eskimo describes the shamanic equvalent: "The bear of the lake or the inland glacier will come out, he will devour all your flesh and make you a skeleton, and you will die. But you will recover your flesh, you will awaken, and your clothes will come rushing to you."[10]

Hunting tribes, in general, believed that the soul of a slain animal or deceased human survived death and for a time resided in the skeleton, principally in the skull. They stressed that injury to the bones caused insult to the soul, even after it had departed. Thus their reverent dealings with bones: painting bear skulls with red ocher and lashing them to poles or trees with offerings of tobacco, reassembling the other bones at the den or bundling them to hang with the skull. At all times they kept dogs, which they considered unclean, away from the bones of the bears they had killed.

In an Apache tale, Fox manages to kill Bear. Fox not only cut all the meat from the legs of Bear but he also broke Bear's bones with his knife, so Bear would not come back to life.

During his initiatory death, the shaman would leave his body and move about, however briefly, in the spirit realm. Having once experienced the separation and reuniting of soul and body, the shaman could then leave his body and travel in that other realm whenever he wished. He summoned his helping spirit and entered a trance. His soul separated from his body and entered the spirit realm. When the shaman's soul accomplished its goal in the other world, it reentered his body and the shaman awoke. Thus, shamans traversed the threshold of life and death at will, by crossing into a world where the living did not ordinarily venture. In this sense, every trance was a death experience and the shaman's practice was, in essence, one of periodic death and resurrection.

There were different levels of trance. During the shaking tent performances of the Cree, the shaman remained conscious and communicated with both spirits and the people watching the performance. During a deep trance, however, the shaman became completely unconscious. His body grew rigid, as if he were in a cataleptic state. On long and difficult journeys, such as to the land of the dead, a shaman might remain unconscious for many hours. These mystical soul flights were the source of the shaman's power. As a soul journeying in the spirit realm, the shaman communicated directly with spirits that were ordinarily inaccessible and recruited their help. He asked them things only they knew, and saw things otherwise invisible.

An important role of the shaman was to assist in the hunt, especially when times were hard. When hunters were unsuccessful and famine threatened, the shaman, in a trance, visited an Owner of the Animals to ask for release of food animals. Often the Owner of the Animals responded that someone had broken a taboo. Perhaps a child had wasted meat or a menstruating woman had handled a bear hide. Whatever the transgression, the shaman asked for forgiveness and pleaded for the release of the animals. Then he returned from his mystical journey, and, if the Owner absolved the people of their sins, the game returned to the hunting grounds.

The shaman's soul journey to the Owner of the Animals is comparable to the journey of the dead bear's soul in the bear hunting rites of northern tribes, in which the dead bear's soul was sent to the Owner of the Bears with a plea for more bears or for more food animals in general. Both traditions—the journeys of the shaman and the slain bear to the Owner of the Animals—lay at the foundation of

Petroglyph of a man receiving power from a bear. Dakota County, Nebraska. *Illustration by Janet McGahan.*

Native American hunting cultures, because they provided a way for the people to communicate with the spirit beings that controlled the supply of food animals. It is interesting, however, that in the bear hunt the role of the shaman was often restricted to the pre-hunting divination rites. Perhaps the shaman stayed out of later parts of the ritual to acknowledge the bear's primacy.

Petroglyph of bear tracks and human figures. Wyoming. *Illustration by Janet McGahan.*

Another parallel between the role of the shaman and that of the bear has to do with curing (see chapter 6). One of the most important roles the bear played in native North America was that of a curing animal. Curing was also a primary function of shamans. And often, the two, shaman as healer and bear as healer, came together. Nearly all the plains tribes considered shamans with bear power to be the greatest healers of all. The list includes the Lakota, Yanktonai, Assiniboin, Pawnee, Blackfeet, Cheyenne, Ponca, Mandan, Arapaho, and Iowa. The eastern woodland and prairie tribes that employed shamans' bear power to cure sickness included the Potawatomi, Winnebago, Huron, Fox, Cree, and Ojibwa. In the southwest, the Pueblo word for shamans who cured the sick was the same as the word for bear.

In all of these tribes shamans imitated bears when they performed their curing rites, and they all had stories of shamans who were capable of crossing the line and actually becoming bears. The Zuñi told of one man who painted his body red; wrapped yucca around his wrist, chest, and the crown of his head; and then tied a red eagle feather in his hair. Finally, "He put a bearskin on his back and he became a bear."[13]

Stories about bear shamans with great healing powers who transformed themselves into bears were common on the Great Plains. A Lakota story told about a man who one day gathered his people together to demonstrate his power.

The man was well known among the Sioux as a holy man, capable of bringing the dead back to life. After saving a young hunter who had been knocked off his horse and gored in the stomach by a wounded buffalo, he announced a public display of his powers. Because of his reputation, word spread quickly, and people came from surrounding villages to watch. He asked them to set up a circle of lodges in a large clearing by the river. While the people worked, the holy man erected a special lodge in the center of the circle. He asked that a cedar tree and several plum trees be stuck in the ground outside its entrance.

Later, the people gathered and seated themselves around the circle of lodges. Soon the shaman emerged from the center lodge carrying a grizzly bear skin. He walked around the inside of the circle four times. Then, pausing by the cedar tree, he pulled the skin over his shoulders so the bear's head covered the top part of his head and the rest hung loosely over his back. He then tied it across his chest and waist. He tied the loose hanging legs around his own arms and legs. The drums started and he began singing the grizzly bear songs. As he sang, he again walked around the circle four times, this time his body bent forward so his hands almost touched the ground. His arms and legs moved like a bear's legs and his head hung down like a bear's head. His singing stopped and he began to cry like a bear. He came back to the cedar tree and sat down. He sat a long time with his head down and made bear sounds. Then, suddenly, he was a grizzly bear.

He lifted his head and looked around. When he saw the people he started chasing them. Although they scattered in all directions, he caught one man and tore him to pieces. He devoured the body and left only the bones. In the distance the people watched in terror and began to wail for the dead man. The bear went into his lodge and the dead man's relatives ran into the circle to gather his bones. But the bear came out again and chased them away. Once more the bear walked around the circle. His head hung down and he growled. He passed the dead man's bones four times. On the fourth time the bones regained their flesh and the man came back to life.

The bear went over to the plum tree and shook it. Though the tree had no plums, many plums fell on the ground. The bear hit the earth with his paw and turnips appeared. Then he sat down under the cedar tree and put his head down. When he lifted it again the people could see the holy man's face beneath the bear's head. He had changed back into a man.

The people said that sometimes a small grizzly bear came out of the man's mouth and walked around the circle. When this happened, the shaman fell to the ground as if dead. Then the bear went back into his mouth and he recovered.[14]

Like the Lakota, many tribes believed that shamans could change themselves into bears, although not all believed bear shamans were benevolent. Tribes of central California, such as the Pomo, told of shamans who donned bearskins to become bears so they could steal and murder with impunity. The Pomo called them *gauk burakal*, which means literally "human bear."[15]

The Algonquian-speaking tribes of the eastern woodlands also believed that malevolent shamans assumed the form of bears. The Ojibwa called them bearwalks, and they had a great fear of this kind

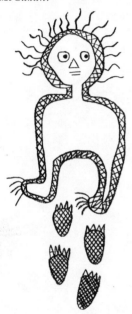

A bearwalk. After a drawing in Dewdney, *Sacred Scrolls of the Southern Ojibway*. Illustration by Janet McGahan.

GIVING VOICE TO BEAR

of sorcery. The belief was that old people who practiced bad medicine foraged about in the woods like bears for special plants. They mixed roots and herbs together and ate them to become bear-walks.[16] When a bearwalk intended to kill someone, it visited that person's wigwam for several nights and each time left some of his medicine behind. The victim might never see the bearwalk, or if he did he might think it was a real bear. But the medicine it left made him sleepy and sick and in a few days he died. There was no anti-dote, unless someone could kill the bearwalk.[17]

In a fashion similar to the berserkers of northern Europe, shamans of some tribes may have worn bearskins into battle or to disguise themselves so they could move undetected through another tribe's territory. This may have been the case with Pomo bear shamans or the *gauk burakal*, who wore elaborate bearskin suits constructed of three layers. First, the bear shaman wrapped strands of shells or beads around his stomach, chest, arms, and legs, and then covered these with a layer of woodpecker skins. These two layers served as an armor, over which he pulled a bearskin, sewing it together so it would fit tightly over his body. The bear's head was sewn over an openwork basket of white oak, with openings for eyes, nose, and mouth.[18]

The association of shamans with bears occurred everywhere in North America where there were shamans. Part of that association probably arose out of the correspondences between the role of the shaman and that of the bear, especially among northern hunting tribes. But shamans themselves identified with bears because many of them possessed the bear as a spirit helper, and because their initiation resembled a hibernation. Perhaps, as the Yavapai believe, Bear was the first great shaman.

Necklace worn by a Lakota bear doctor when treating the sick. The owner's name was Bear-With-White-Paw. *Photo courtesy of the Smithsonian Institution, National Anthropological Archives.*

Digging for Medicine

I N THE WEST there is a lodge as high up as the clouds. Inside the lodge I was deeply attentive. Men who were painted red sat in the lodge and they showed me a man with a gaping wound whose mouth was red with blood. Speaking, they put medicines in my hands: "Boy, human man . . . with these sacred medicines you will make those who lie suffering among your people [able] to stand."

. . . They are called bears—those, they are the ones. So humbly I tell their words. Alas! Without these I am nothing.[1]

THIS WAS THE VISION of a Lakota bear medicine man. He would recite it in the *wakan* (sacred) language of his people each time he doctored a patient. Using a bear claw, he would then clean the wound and treat it with plant medicines that had been told to him in a vision by the bear spirits. After the treatment, he would remain with his patient until he was certain of a recovery.

The Lakota considered the bear to be a curing animal. They associated their medicinal herbs with bears, and they believed that their most powerful doctors acquired powers to cure from the bear spirit. They were not an exception. Most of the tribes in North America associated bears with curing. Canadian Eskimo shamans revered bears as the strongest of the spirit protectors and called upon them when they diagnosed an illness and when they performed their curing rituals. In the southeast, a bear dance highlighted a Cherokee winter ceremony performed to protect against diseases brought by Europeans. Miami Indians suspended bearskins smeared with green dye in their wigwams to prevent sickness. The Cheyenne and other Great Plains tribes believed that bears could heal themselves and other bears with herbs. When the Plains Cree butchered a bear, a sick or injured person would cut out a piece of the bear's flesh corresponding to the place on his body that was hurt. If he had a pain in his shoulder he would remove a part of the bear's shoulder saying, "I have a pain in my shoulder and now I cut it out."[2]

The American Indian's perception of the bear as healer proceeds from a knowledge of bear behavior. Although bears are omnivorous and eat some meat, the vast bulk of their diet is vegetation. Yet bears are different from other animals that feed on plants. Ungulates, such as deer and elk, eat grasses, forbs, and a few woody plants. Bears, on the other hand, eat grasses and forbs as well as many of the vegetable foods that people eat—roots, seeds, grains, fruits, berries, nuts, stems, and mushrooms. Consequently, Indians probably saw bears not as hunters or grass eaters, but as the plant gatherers of the animal world.

Indians gathered plants for medicines as well as for food. Every tribal group relied heavily on herbal remedies to treat their sick and injured, and every tribe used plants as sacred objects in healing rites. Not only did bears eat nearly all the plants that Indians used for food, they also ate most of the plants used as medicines or in cere-monies. Some of these plant medicines were principal bear foods. It was a natural step from observing this behavior to associating bears with healing, especially herbal healing. As animal gatherer of herbs and roots, the bear served as guardian of the first medicines and communicator of the knowledge of healing.

A Cheyenne suffering from a cold would drink a tea steeped from yarrow leaves. The Cheyenne often observed bears, both grizzly and black, eating yarrow. Hence, among the Cheyenne and many other Great Plains tribes, yarrow, a common medicinal herb, became iden-tified with bears. Similarly, when a Crow pulverized the leaves of kin-nikinnick and applied the powder to his canker sores, he very likely knew that bears consumed the leaves, berries, stems, and roots of

Bear curer. Effigy vessel from Colima, Mexico.
Photo courtesy of Peter Furst.

GIVING VOICE TO BEAR

this plant. One of the common native names for kinnikinnick, which was considered sacred by many tribes because of its use in ceremonial rites, is bearberry.

A root used by the Cheyenne to treat diarrhea and to relieve pain in the bowels was called "bear's food." The Crow relied on a plant known as "bear root," chewing it to soothe their sore throats, applying it as a poultice to reduce swellings, and burning it as ceremonial incense. The Prairie Potowatomi called the roots of a plant they used in doctoring wounds "bear potatoes." Their Bear Clan members always kept a few of them wrapped in their medicine bundles along with grizzly claws and bone daggers (which they used in surgery). The Ojibwa of southern Ontario referred to one of their most potent medicines as "bear medicine." They used it to treat headaches, earaches, coughs, and heart troubles and chewed it to purify their bodies. They cut it in small pieces and strung the wedges on a cord in such a way that they resembled bear claws on a necklace.

Plant medicines were often named for the bear partly because the bear first discovers them in the myths and tales of many tribes, and it is the bear who offers the knowledge of them to the people. A Hupa tale illustrates how Bear discovered a medicine for pregnant women:

> While walking in the middle of the world Bear got this way [i.e. pregnant]. Young grew in her body. All day and all night she fed. After a while she got so big she could not walk. Then she began to consider why she was in that condition.
>
> "I wonder if they will be the way I am in the Indian world?"
>
> She heard a voice talking behind her. It said, "Put me in your mouth. You are in this condition for the sake of Indians."
>
> When she looked around she saw a single plant of redwood sorrel standing there. She put it in her mouth. The next day she found she was able to walk. She thought, "It will be this way in the Indian world with this medicine. This will be my medicine. At best not many will know about me. I will leave it in the Indian world. They will talk to me with it."[3]

A common remedy such as redwood sorrel or yarrow or kinnikinnick might be used by everyone within a tribe. Often, however, the bulk of the knowledge concerning herbal healing, especially the treatment of more complicated or life-threatening ailments, was kept secret by individual medicine men and women or medicine societies. In most medicine societies, one had to be properly initiated before being taught the secrets, many of which concerned the plants themselves. The body of knowledge comprised information on hundreds of species, and medicine healers were respected not just for their ability to cure but also for their plant knowledge. They were thought of as master gatherers and, accordingly, likened to bears. Of the Zuñi Pueblo, whose word for doctor is the same as that for bear, anthropologist Ruth Bunzel wrote, "The medicine societies are, in fact, medical guilds...which guard their secrets jealously. The combined esoteric knowledge and ritual held by these groups is enormous, and...genuinely esoteric...no knowledge is more closely guarded than this."[4]

Secrecy was so important to some of the medicine societies of the Algonquian-speaking tribes that they gave medicine plants secret names. Among the Ojibwa, some bands never named many herbs; initiates learned them by looking at dug samples. It was common practice for Ojibwa healers to grind or mutilate a plant beyond recognition as soon as it was gathered, then scent it with another aromatic herb, so as to obscure its identity.[5] Members of the Ojibwa medicine society, the Midewiwin, were said to "follow the bear path," in part because of their special plant knowledge. Another group of Ojibwa practitioners, individuals who used their herbal medicines and poisons for malevolent purposes, were known as bearwalks.[6]

The relationship between the bear and herbal healers is well illustrated by healing societies of the Great Plains, such as the Lakota Bear Dreamers Society. The Lakota recognized the bear to be "the only animal dreamed of that offered herbs for the healing of man," an association that was built into the Lakota cosmology. Their emergence myth tells that in the beginning the Lakota lived beneath the present world. They were happy living under the ground; their lives were easy, their hearts content. Then, one day, Iktomi, the trickster, seduced them into coming out to live on the earth's surface. From the moment they emerged, they suffered terribly. The sun burned their eyes and skin, the air was bitter cold, and the wind never stopped blowing. They were always hungry. The spirits were angry at them for leaving the middle earth, so the people had nothing but bad luck. Bear, however, took pity on them and gave them medicines so they could protect and care for themselves.[7]

The Lakota said that any man who dreamed of the bear would be an expert in the use of plant medicines. They considered bear medicine men the most powerful of healers (as opposed to elk, bird, or buffalo medicine men): besides healing ordinary diseases bear medicine men also treated the wounded.[8] (Apparently other healers did not.) Black Elk, the great Lakota holy man and medicine man, said that he received his power to cure from the bear spirit.[9]

Lakota bear doctors used therapeutic medicines, mostly herbal, to treat the sick. In a fraternity of sorts, they taught each other plant lore, songs, and invocations. The songs were part of the medicine: if a person did not know a medicine-plant's song, the medicine would not work. The words to one such song were:

Small bags of medicine and a spoon used by the bear doctor Eagle Shield to treat the sick. *Photo courtesy of the Smithsonian Institution, National Anthropological Archives.*

> *A root of herb you will eat,*
> *at that place it stands.*
> *A Bear said this to me.*[10]

And another song used with wild licorice:

> *My paw is sacred,*
> *the herbs are everywhere.*
> *My paw is sacred,*
> *all things are sacred.*[11]

In her association with the Sioux, the ethnologist Francis Densmore was impressed by an incident involving a Lakota bear doctor named Eagle Shield. In the early 1900s, a man living on the Standing Rock Reservation attempted suicide by shooting himself in the side, just below his left arm. He was aiming for his heart but the bullet missed and tore through his body, shattering one edge of his

GIVING VOICE TO BEAR

right shoulder blade. The wound completely paralyzed his arm. He was taken to a hospital where he was treated by two white physicians. Both said he would never regain use of the arm and recommended amputation. The man refused and returned to his home, where Eagle Shield took care of him by treating him with yarrow and songs and ritual. The man regained full use of his arm. (As compensation, Eagle Shield received one hundred dollars, a new white tent, a revolver, and a steer.)[12]

The entire Bear Dreamers Society, which might include a dozen or more men, sometimes performed public healings. Thomas Tyon, a Lakota mixed-blood, described such a ritual. In his words:

A man dreams of the bear and so he is very *wakan*. Also he belongs to the Bear Society. The man who dreams of the bear is leader of the whole society. . . .

When a man is wounded, a big tipi is set up in the middle of camp and the wounded man moves into the tipi. Inside the tipi the entire floor is completely covered with sage. And all those who consider themselves Bears, these and only these, move into the tipi with the wounded men. And when the Bears doctor, they all have round drums. They sing many very good songs. And so the bear leader moves about. All those who have been wounded stand and move about. Those who have different types of medicine move about. They are all thought to be very *wakan*. There is a very white medicine and it smells very good. All men find it very pleasing. When they smell it, then the wounds do not fester. They are cured. So it is that for four nights the ones who were wounded will participate in ceremonies.

Then all those who had been wounded will come out. So an old man goes about proclaiming this aloud. Perhaps some of the women are menstruating, so none of them come near. The old man goes along. Around the camp on the inside of the camp circle, the crier goes along. So then the people stir about and men crowd all around the Bear tipi. Then, as the Bears sing, all of the people stand looking intently at the entrance to the Bear tipi. Suddenly the Bear leader begins to move quickly towards the tipi entrance. Growling ferociously, he comes out of the tipi. His body is painted entirely red and his hands white; he carries a knife. All of the onlookers flee. Then one of the wounded comes out after him, carrying a short staff painted entirely red. Slowly he comes out. The staff is forked at the end. And then the Bear singers come out, singing as loudly as they can. Therefore, the Bear leader and the one who was wounded bend down and move about furiously. . . .

Well now the wounded begin to walk and they stand facing the south. Then they turn and stand facing the west. Again they turn and stand facing the north. Again they turn and stand facing the east. They all stand with their arms raised in prayer. Throughout,

Eagle Shield, a Lakota bear doctor. *Photo courtesy of the Smithsonian Institution, National Anthropological Archives.*

they sing songs. Therefore, the bear leader moves about. And now when they have completed the four directions they go back to the tipi from which they came. Again they go inside. The doctors place the wounded at the *catku* [place of honor in the rear of the lodge]. At last they apply the healing root. Throughout they command that no woman come near. . . .

Sometimes the leader of the bear dreamers sleeps in his tipi during the day. And then suddenly they wake him up; they frighten him and he becomes wild, it is said. Finally his canine teeth grow very long and become visible, it is said. Then, lying down, he paws at the earth and a wild turnip slips out from it, it is said. And again, he comes outside and he goes around a wild plum tree, growling like a bear. He grasps the plum tree in his hand and shakes it. And then some plums stick to it, it is said. . . .

Well, there is another thing. Bear dreamers imitate the bear, it is said. The bear skin completely covers his head and on the right side of the back, an eagle tail feather is fastened, it is said. Then from the center of the camp he goes around the inside of the camp circle, it is said. He has a knife in one hand and even though someone shoots him with a gun, he does not die, it is said. He himself often says he is going hunting. He thrusts his knife into something and he heals the wound, it is said.[13]

Like the Lakota and other Great Plains tribes, many of the Pueblo peoples made a strong association between the bear and healing. The Pueblo word for bear is the same as that for doctor. In many Pueblo

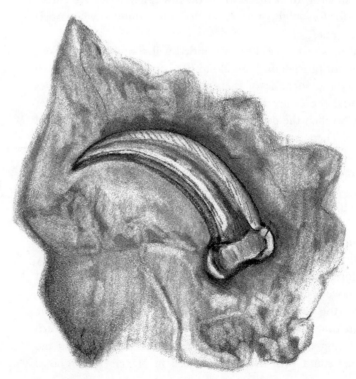

Bear claw used by Eagle Shield in treating the sick. When the claw was photographed it had been in his possession for forty-eight years. From a photo in Densmore, *Teton Sioux Music*. *Illustration by Janet McGahan*.

communities, when a doctor practiced he wore a bear claw necklace and bear paws pulled over his hands like mittens. These people perceived the bear to be the most powerful of their beast gods. The bear was one of the priests of long life and the giver of medicine, both plants and the power of healing.

The Taos Pueblo told a tale about Bear Old Man digging for his medicines:

Bear Old Man was living in the burnt timber. People were living at the Mouth of the Red Willows. Bear was coming down to dig medicine at the place called *klaa'ata*. He got his cane and came down. He sang:

> *hina nina i a*
> *hina nina i a*
> *hina nina i a*
> *ya he i ha*
> *a he ina a*

He was now halfway from his home to the village. He paused there and said to himself, "People are seeing me. I must dance harder." Then he began to sing again,

> *hina nina i a*
> *hina nina i a*
> *hina nina i a*
> *ya he i ha*
> *a he ina a*

Then he got to *klaa'ata*. He spit with his medicine in four directions. Then with his cane he dug [sunwise] and he sang. Then he dug, and he chewed and dabbed on his body and legs. Then he put the medicine on his back. Then he started back home. The people said, "Lazy Bear Old Man came again to dig his medicine."

Then he went back singing again. He went half way and he stopped and he said, "People are looking at me. I must dance harder." He sang.

He got to his home and said, "People call me Bear Old Man lives in Steep Woods. The village people ask good luck of me for themselves and here I remain at my home at Steep Woods."[14]

One of the strongest medicines used by Pueblo healers was a plant they called "bear medicine" or "bear root." They gave it to their patients, and, because it induced a trance-like state when ingested, doctors themselves ate it before diagnosing an illness so as to see the cause of sickness.[15]

Priests of the Giant Society in a kiva in New Mexico's Sia pueblo. They are evoking the power of the bear to heal a sick child. They wear bear-claw necklaces and hold eagle wing plumes and gourd rattles. Behind them are the skins of bears' forelegs. After a photo by M.C. Stevenson taken about 1888. *Photo courtesy of the Smithsonian Institution, National Anthropological Archives.*

Besides its association with medicinal herbs, the bear was also a spirit helper for many shamans. Unlike medicine men and women, shamans did not depend upon the therapeutic effects of plants to treat the sick. They relied instead on their spirit helpers. Sometimes shamans included plants in their rites, but as part of the ceremony, not as a therapy. For example, a Yokut shaman named Supana would lie down beside his patient and begin talking to the bear spirit. As he spoke he would scratch the person's back with a soap root brush which had been given to him by the bear spirit in a vision. The soap root had no medicinal value. It was the means by which Supana summoned the spirit of the bear to cure the ailing person.[16]

Most Native American groups considered the bear to be among the most powerful of spirit helpers, and shamanic healers and some of the bear societies drew on the bear's spirit power to effect cures. George Catlin saw it when he watched a Blackfeet shaman try to help a fatally wounded warrior in 1830. The man had been shot twice in the stomach at close range in a battle with a neighboring tribe and was nearly dead. A large crowd gathered around him in a circle. The crowd became still, a pathway opened, and a shaman

GIVING VOICE TO BEAR

Blackfeet shaman painted by George Catlin.   *Smithsonian Institution.*

Digging For Medicine

entered the circle. He wore a yellow bearskin draped over his head and body. The bear's head covered his head like a mask, the paws hung loosely from his wrists and ankles. The pelts of dozens of smaller animals and various animal parts hung from the skin. In one hand the shaman carried a gourd rattle, in the other, a spear. With lilting steps he approached the dying man. As he came closer, his gait broke into a wild dance, and he began shaking his rattle. He grunted and growled like a bear and prayed to his spirit guardian. Over and over he charged, leaped over, and pawed at his patient. As he danced, some of the people in the audience shouted, others screamed. The dance continued until the wounded man died, about a half hour later.[17]

The healing power of the bear spirit also played a part in the Winter Solstice Ceremony of the Zuñi Pueblo, in the Bear Dance of the Winnebago, and in healing rituals of the Huron. In the Zuñi ceremony, the oldest and most learned medicine men pulled bear paw mittens over their hands and began to act like bears. Using powers acquired from the bear spirit, they peered into crystals to see any hidden sickness. If they saw an illness in someone, they drew from his or her body the foreign substance that had caused it.[18]

In the Winnebago Bear Dance, dancers circled like bears around a mound of earth called *ma'warup'uru*, which represented a bear's den. The four sides represented den entrances. The center of the mound was said to be the home of the bear. Dance leaders put tobacco and red feathers in the center and at each of the four entrance points. As they moved around the mound the dancers stretched out their arms, growled, and huffed like bears. They took tobacco from the den and ate it. The sick people for whom the dance was performed also took tobacco from the den, chewed it, and asked to live.

The description of a Winnebago Grizzly Bear Dance that follows conveys the sense of personal power that came from imitating a bear. The dance was performed late in the last century at a village on the Rock River in southern Wisconsin for a man named Little Priest and was recorded by Paul Radin. Little Priest had been wounded in many places and was, according to witnesses, unconscious and close to death. His relatives decided to perform the Grizzly Bear Dance for him, as Little Priest's guardian spirit was the grizzly bear. (Grizzly bears had come to him in a vision when he was young.)

> The dance was to be given at the lodge of an Indian named Good Soldier. They carried Little Priest to the lodge in a blanket, so that

GIVING VOICE TO BEAR

they could sing for him and permit him to show the powers he possessed. He was unable to move on account of the wounds and the bruises he had gotten. The man who sang for him at that time was South-Wind. There were all in all ten Indians, entirely naked, except for their breechcloths. Little Priest had told South-Wind that he was a grizzly bear and that he could heal himself [no matter how badly he had been wounded].

As soon as the songs and dancing commenced Little Priest began to move his little fingers. Soon he was able to move his arm as far as his forearm, and gradually he regained the power of moving the entire arm. Finally he sat up and began to keep time on the drum. Then he tried to stand on his feet, but owing to his weakness it was only with the greatest difficulty that he could straighten out his body. Finally he stood erect. Then he started to walk around the lodge very slowly. The second circuit he made more easily, and by the time he had made his fourth circuit he was dancing just as the other dancers were with all his strength restored. Then he walked to the *ma^{n}warup'uru*, took some earth, rubbed it on his wounds and they were healed immediately. There was only one wound that he could not heal, which was situated on a part of his back that he could not reach with his hands.[19]

Among the Huron, when someone was very sick the shaman asked twenty or more women and men to gather at the patient's lodge. When everyone had arrived, three of the oldest women sat near the patient and began singing steadily while they beat short sticks on dry tree bark. To the accompaniment of the singing, the other men and women brought gifts forward and laid them before the sick person.

After all the gifts had been bestowed, the three old women raised their voices together in a long wail. Everyone rose and moved to the edge of the lodge, where they pulled on bearskins so that the bears' heads covered their own. With everyone singing, the old women danced slowly toward the patient. They were followed by the younger women, and finally by the men. As they moved with short steps, in imitation of bears, they growled, ate berries and nuts, and pretended to hide like bears. After a while the old women gently lifted the sick person, so that she might join the dance. At first the patient moved only slowly and rested often, hanging on to the old women. But in time (dances like this often lasted all night) she danced as well as the others.[20]

Many tribes believed that bears could cause sickness as well as cure it. The Kootenai performed a ceremony called the Growling to

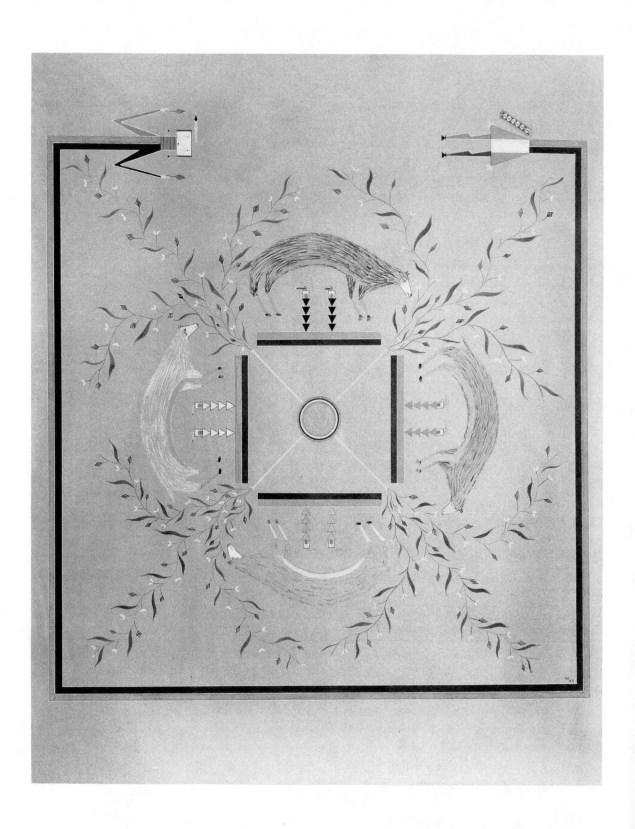

"let no sickness be in my family." They prayed to the bear, "Do not make us sick."[21] The Chickasaw called a disease that caused pains in the abdomen and loose bowels bear sickness, and they treated it with the bark of a particular tree.[22] The Creek believed that the bear caused two diseases. The first was accompanied by an intense fever, an unquenchable thirst, and violent diarrhea. The other caused one to vomit blood. They treated both with herbs. The Pima believed that stepping on a bear track or stepping over bear feces caused swelling limbs, headaches, and fever. The remedy was to sing the sacred bear medicine songs throughout the day. For example:

> *I am the black bear.*
> *Around me you see the light clouds extending.*
> *I am the black bear,*
> *Around me you see the light dew falling.*
> *I drink the reddish liquor which kills the spirit.*[23]

Among southwestern tribes such as the Pueblos, Navajo, and Apache, it was believed that fright could cause sickness. Because bears were particularly fearsome, bear sickness was a serious threat. Indians from these tribes went to great lengths to avoid contact with bears. Only under extreme circumstances, such as starvation, would they kill a bear. Navajo Indians would not gather piñon nuts from a place where a bear had gathered them, nor would they make a baby's cradle from a tree upon which a bear had rubbed. Even seeing a bear in the wild could cause an illness of overwhelming tiredness, swollen arms and legs, vomiting, and diarrhea. One could be cured only through an elaborate and expensive nine-day ceremony or chant called the Mountainway. It was believed that Bear-Old-Man gave the ceremony to the Navajo. The Apache had parallel beliefs and a similar ritual.[24]

Healing for American Indians was essentially a process of renewal. In the Winnebago Grizzly Bear Dance described earlier, Little Priest, who was near death, was given new life, as was the ailing Huron woman lifted by village elders who were dressed in bearskin robes. The Lakota man Thomas Tyon said that bear medicine men were the most highly regarded of medicine men because they could bring the gravely ill back to life. He said that people were consistently astonished by the power of the bear medicine men.[25]

Indians brought the bear into these and other healing ceremonies in part because the bear presided over the plants of medicine and therefore tendered powers of curing. But the bear was also the most powerful icon of spring's triumph over the long winter. It therefore symbolized the rebirth of health, the reawakening of spirit, and the moving from near death to life.

People of the Myth. The second painting from the Navajo Male Mountainway Ceremony. The center is water with the yellow moss around it. The four animals are: the white bear, the blue bear, the yellow bear, and the black bear. The triangular figures under the bears are clouds, the little clouds are the little bear men. The plants are the Sarvis-berry which the bears feed on, and the border is a rainbow. Painting by Mr. Colville about 1910. The singer was Sam Chief. *Photograph by Sonny Lee. Courtesy of the Wheelwright Museum of the American Indian.*

The tepee of Ayanyan, a chief of the Assiniboin. A scarlet pennant fluttered from the head of each of the black grizzly bears painted on the sides of the tepee. After an 1833 painting by Carl Bodmer. *Illustration by Janet McGahan.*

7

"Ah Bear, We are the Same Person!"

Mahchsi-Karehde (Flying Eagle), a Mandan warrior, wearing a Great-Plains-style bear-claw necklace. After an 1833 painting by Karl Bodmer. *Illustration by Janet McGahan.*

MY NAME IS SDIPP-SHIN-MAH (Fallen from the sky). I am Flathead. I am going to tell you now about the time when the grizzly spirit gave me its power.

One day when I was a girl just about six or seven winters, my mother told me we were going berrying in the mountains. We rode double on her horse and went high into the mountains. It was getting late in the evening. I saw a patch of bushes. I told my mother, "Look, there are some berries and plenty of them."

She said, "Child have patience, a little farther up is the place where we will get our berries."

So we went on and on until when the sun was just about going down she stopped our horse and said, "Here is the place where we are going to pick."

She put me off the horse and got off also. She started picking and put some berries on the ground for me and said, "Sit here and eat on these berries while I go down here to see if there are more below."

She spread out my robe, and I sat on it and began eating. She got on the horse and reminded me to stay where I was, and she said she would be back soon. She disappeared in the bushes. I was not afraid. I ate berries and talked to myself about the trees. Then I saw night was coming and my mother was not yet back. I became frightened and called for her. I called for my mother but saw no sign of her. I called and called while crying, not knowing what to do. I just cried and cried and called for my mother all night. But there was no use. She had left me and went back home leaving me alone in the high mountains.

When I could not cry any longer, I got up and took my robe and walked not knowing where I was going. It was still night and very dark. I went on until I got tired and sleepy and lay down and went to sleep. When I woke up the sun was way up already, and it was nice and warm. At first I thought I was sleeping with my mother at home. Then I remembered I was high in the mountains, and my mother was not there. I started to cry again. When I stopped crying I began to walk and eat the berries growing there. I kept on until I got to a deep gulch fully covered with trees. While I sat there I thought of my home and my mother. I began to cry again. Then I barely heard a sound that I thought was human voices. I listened closely but heard nothing and thought it must be the cry of a bird or something. Then I heard a sound again, and as I listened I heard it again and again and knew it was the sound of humans laughing and talking loudly way down in the bottom of the gulch. I could not see them as it was covered all over with trees and bushes, but I could tell they were coming toward me.

Just where I was sitting was on a ridge and below on the hillside was an open bald place. The sound came from that way and I was watching closely and was surprised with joy to see a woman with two little ones coming. I thought it was someone from my tribe. They were running and chasing each other. Laughing and shouting, they came pretty close. I saw the woman was a very handsome woman, well clothed all in buckskin and clean. One of the children was a boy and one was a girl. They were also well dressed, all in buckskin.

This woman said to me, "Poor girl, this is not the place for you especially to be alone. I am sure you are thirsty by this time. Come, we will bring you down to the stream to drink." Then she told her children, "Do not bother your little sister, she is thirsty and tired."

While we were going down, the children were playing and laughing and tried to get me to play with them but the mother always stopped them saying, "Your little sister is tired so leave her alone."

When we got to the stream we all had a good drink. I was last to finish my drink and when I stood and looked, instead of seeing my little sister and brother and mother there was sitting there a grizzly bear and two cubs. I was afraid. The bear spoke, "Do not be afraid, little child. I am your mother bear and here is your little brother and sister. We will not hurt you."

Then she told me this: "Listen closely. I am going to give you medicine power by which you will be a great help to your people in the future. This time will come after you pass middle age. But do not try to do more than I am allowing you or granting you because, if you do, it will be nothing more than false and you will be responsible for sufferings and even death. One of my gifts is that you are going to be helpful to women especially those that are having hard times and suffering giving the birth of a child." She said this. Then the grizzly bear mother and her cubs took me back to my people.[1]

SDIPP-SHIN-MAH WAS NOT A SHAMAN, but, like a shaman, she possessed an animal spirit helper who gave her powers that she used throughout her life. The concept of the guardian spirit is related to that of shamanism. Anthropologist Robert Lowie once described the idea of the guardian spirit as "democratized shamanism." The chief

A bear-painted tepee cover of the Kiowa Apache Chief White Man. Chief White Man's maternal grandfather, Lone Chief, had a vision of a bear hugging a tepee. The bear told Lone Chief, "make this tepee and I shall always hold you up." *Photo courtesy of the Smithsonian Institution, National Anthropological Archives.*

difference was that anyone could acquire a guardian spirit, whereas only a few were called to the practice of shamanism. A shaman and his helping spirit experienced a more potent relationship than that between a person and his or her guardian. Shamans possessed more power and entered trances. In most cases those who simply possessed a guardian spirit did not. There are enough similarities between the two traditions, however, that many scholars believe that one evolved out of the other.[2]

People obtained guardian spirits principally through their dreams and visions. Sometimes visions came spontaneously, but most were solicited on vision quests. These quests often took place during a child's initiation into adulthood (although a guardian could appear in a dream or vision at anytime in a man or woman's life). Most vision quests fit within a pattern: At or just prior to puberty, a youth, having purified himself by sweating and taking emetics, would go to a secluded spot—a mountain top, a cave, or a special place chosen by an elder—and fast. After several days, if all went well, a spirit would appear in human or animal form and grant the child some special power, which the child would have for the rest of his or her life. In return, the spirit asked the child to honor it by observing some rule such as not killing or eating animals of its kind. (Although sometimes the animal spirit not only allowed the hunter to kill its kind,

A shield cover from one of the Upper Missouri River tribes, invoking the protective power of the bear. *Photo courtesy of the Smithsonian Institution, National Anthropological Archives.*

GIVING VOICE TO BEAR

but gave him special luck in the hunt. This was especially true among the Plateau tribes.)

In the vision, the spirit often gave the child instructions for making a medicine bundle. For the rest of his or her life, the child would treat the bundle as a manifestation of the spirit itself. The spirit also taught the child a medicine song, which the child could use to call the spirit. A free translation of one such song from the Omaha is:

> *Here at this place*
> *I came, I stood.*
> *Grizzly Bear I was;*
> *As Grizzly Bear I appeared.*[3]

Before disappearing, the spirit would leave something—a claw, some fur, a horn—some piece of its body to be kept and protected during the child's life, and perhaps to be placed, with other items, in the medicine bundle.

Generally, Indians held that humans were spiritually less powerful than animals. Humans, in fact, were the only creatures born essentially powerless. To live well in the world, that is, to hunt or gather well enough to feed one's family, to avoid being killed in battle, to contribute to the tribe, one had to gain power. This power usually originated from an animal or a mythological being.

Many received power from bear spirits. In the east, where there were no grizzlies, the black bear spirit was respected as a powerful vision, and many men and women pursued it as a guardian. But grizzlies, wherever they occurred, were always considered to be different from black bears.

Women who acquired the grizzly as a guardian were unusual. The Nez Perce, perhaps because of their belief in a terrifying mythological being called Grizzly-bear Woman, considered the grizzly to be a proper guardian spirit for a man but not for a woman. The grizzly was too wild and dangerous; its spirit was too hard to control. The Nez Perce associated the malevolent side of the bear with women and believed that, if a woman had the grizzly for a guardian, the spirit might possess her instead of her possessing it. She might bring ruin on her family or village.[4]

Other groups held similar beliefs. Women and girls from Athapaskan tribes avoided contact with grizzly bears, even dead ones. Like the Nez Perce, northern Athapaskans feared that contact might cause women to change into grizzlies.[5] Early white explorers of the MacKenzie Delta reported that among the Eskimo, "The possession of a brown bear skin is much desired by those who have growing boys, as children sleeping on such a skin will become quick to anger and of an unforgiving disposition. Growing girls should never be allowed to sleep on one of these skins, for women should be of a mild and forgiving temper."[6]

The Kwakiutl were less concerned. They desired the grizzly bear's power as a food gatherer for their daughters. They said, "If the right fore-paw of a bear is placed on the palm of the right hand of an infant girl, she will be successful in picking berries and digging clams."[7]

For some men, also, the grizzly was not a good guardian to have. Tlingit men tried to avoid the animal because they believed that it was too unpredictable. A Shoshoni medicine man once warned, "The bear is an animal that gets mad, therefore no good *puha* (guardian spirit) for a family man; he will get mad over nothing. One man with bear *puha* was Pinjiz (Cross-legged), a good, strong medicine man. When he got mad he growled like a bear, and the hair on his head stood up like the hair of a bear."[8]

Nevertheless, for the men of many tribes, particularly on the Great Plains, the grizzly bear was a powerful, if not benevolent, spirit guardian to have. Many men hoped to dream of the animal—only a few did. An account follows of how a Hidatsa man named Crow Bull obtained power from the bear. The story is told by his great grandson, Bears' Arm.

> Crow Bull went out fasting on the hills called Rainy Buttes for seven days and nights at a time. Each time he fasted he had a good dream, but none of them satisfied him. He thought that if he fasted more he would see something with his own eyes without having to dream about it. On the seventh day of the seventh time out, during the middle of the forenoon, he cut off the first finger next to the thumb. He cut all the flesh off with a piece of sharp flint and the blood spurted out.
>
> He cried from the top of the butte. Soon he heard someone in back of him singing, "He is the one I can depend on."
>
> He looked up as a small cloud passed over the butte. There was a large bear standing on the butte, also, trying to look over the rim to see who was doing the singing. All this time Crow Bull could hear the singing at his back. The singer said, "When he [the grizzly bear] does that, he always overcomes what he has in mind."
>
> Then the cloud over the butte passed on. The voice said, "You have always wanted to see these things with your own eyes and not in a dream; now you have seen them."[9]

There were ways other than vision to obtain a guardian spirit. Among a few tribes, the Pueblos and Pawnee for example, the belief was that each person was born with a guardian. On the northwest

coast of Canada, individuals inherited a helping spirit from a deceased relative. Indians of the northern Great Plains could purchase helping spirits from others who had obtained them in a vision. Among these tribes, a man might trade his spirit guardian for horses or other valued material possessions. The actual transfer of the spirit took place in an intense, private ceremony in which the medicine bundle representing the spirit went to the purchaser. After the transfer, all the power and protection bestowed by the guardian spirit went to the new owner; the former owner could claim nothing. Some men willingly relinquished their spirits because they had grown old, and the powers were no longer of use to them. Others tired of the rigorous obligations involved with maintaining a medicine bundle. And some, who possessed an unpredictable and potentially dangerous spirit such as the bear, let it go out of fear. Bears are easily angered, and an angry spirit can mean disaster for a man or his village.

Bear knife of the Blackfeet. *Illustration by Janet McGahan.*

A bundle famous for its power among the Blackfeet and an allied tribe, the Gros Ventre, was the bear-knife bundle. It held a single long knife with a handle made from the jaw bone of a bear. Its power came from the bear and protected its owner in battle. The Blackfeet, famous for their great warriors, knew bears as "fighting animals." The bear was a guardian for their best fighters.

The transfer ceremony for the bear-knife bundle was so brutal that few tried to purchase it. One who did was a Piegan named Black-bear. He described the ceremony, which took place near Browning, Montana, sometime around 1870. First, to prepare for the transfer, Black-bear said that he had to build seven sweat lodges for the man who owned the bear-knife bundle, one lodge for each of seven days. In each lodge he made a pile of seven rocks, which would be used to make parsnip root smudges. (Parsnip roots are one of the bears' favorite foods. Plant parts, such as parsnip roots, smoldered on rocks, produce a thick, purifying smoke called a smudge.) On the day that a lodge was to be used, Black-bear tied the bear-knife bundle to its top.

Before each sweat, the owner waited in his tepee. He wore a red painted buffalo robe, hair side out. Earlier in the day he had painted his face red and, with his fingers, made black streaks across his eyes and again at the sides of his mouth to represent bear's teeth. When the sweat was ready, someone from camp came and kicked the side of his tepee, and he made a sound like a bear. The person kicked the lodge again and again, and each time he made bear sounds. On the fourth kick, the owner left his lodge and ran to the sweat. He entered it crawling backward.

Inside, he smoked a pipe given to him by Black-bear and prayed. He picked up parsnip root and sang, "The earth is my medicine," and he placed some of the root on each of the seven stones. Then he threw water on the stones fourteen times.

After the seventh sweat, the owner of the bundle returned to his tepee, where he piled rose bushes or hawthorne branches in a row at the back. He made a smudge of parsnip root and put some red and black paint into birch bark cups, placing the cups to the left of the thorns. Other men entered carrying seven drums and sat on the far side. The owner of the bundle and Black-bear were naked and sat down on either side of the thorns, the owner on the left, Black-bear on the right. When all was ready, the other men in the tepee began to drum. Soon someone started to sing. Others joined in. The noise grew louder as some of the men began to shout and shake the tepee poles. The owner became agitated and started to move about like a bear. Then, in the midst of the tumult, he flung himself on Black-bear, threw him on the thorns, and began to paint him. He used the red on Black Bear's face and body and the black to make the familiar scratches around his eyes and mouth. The thorns cut Black Bear's flesh and made him bleed. The drumming and singing and shouting went on.

After painting Black-bear, the owner made another parsnip root smudge. He picked up the bear-knife bundle and passed it four times through the smoke. Then he opened the bundle and, holding the knife in his right hand, stabbed at the air. Again, without warning, he charged at Black-bear, threw him on the thorns, and began to beat him with the flat of the knife, first on the chest then on the back. The two crawled on hands and knees to the north side of the lodge. There, the owner held and beat Black-bear again. They moved to the west side, and he beat him a third time, then to the south for the final beating. The transfer was complete.

Black-bear left the lodge of the owner and painted his horse. He used red on the maine and forelock, the backbone, and the tail, and made red hand prints in key places along the sides. That evening, and on the three that followed, Black-bear rehearsed the songs that belonged to the bundle and that had been taught to him by the former owner. They were all war songs. On the fifth day he went into

GIVING VOICE TO BEAR

Tepee with bear images at a Sun Dance encampment of the Blood Indians in southern Alberta. *Photograph by Philip Arrowtop.*

the hills with the bundle and fasted for seven nights. He hoped to dream of a bear.

Afterwards, Black-bear painted his robe red and wore it with the hair out. Before a raid or fight he painted his face the bear way, and in a battle the only weapon he carried was the knife. In summers he kept the knife unwrapped and tied to a lodge pole in his tepee near his seat, as the bear had instructed the original owner. When the bears entered their dens, he took the knife down and wrapped it. All winter he kept the bundle tied to a tripod near his lodge and made parsnip root smudges three times a day.[10]

Although it was not part of Black-bear's ceremony, most bear-knife bundle transfers ended with the owner throwing the knife as hard as he could at the buyer, who was required to catch it without injury. Feather Head, a Sarcee, had such a bundle, which he had made after dreaming of bear. In his dream the bear handed him a similar bundle and said, "My son, just as I never turn aside when I pursue some object, so when you give this bundle to anyone don't let him turn away. Throw the knife straight at the man's chest. If he catches it in both hands, good; but if it cuts his hands or his chest he will die soon afterwards."[11]

On the Great Plains and areas adjacent, men and women with the bear as a guardian spirit formed exclusive societies. Many of the Siouan tribes and some Algonquian groups—the list includes the Assiniboin, Dakota, Lakota, Mandan, Iowa, Omaha, Ponca,

Painted tepee cover. The bear images suggest the owner had a speial relationship with bears.
Illustration by Janet McGahan.

Winnebago, Plains Cree, and Arapaho—had what ethnologists have designated as bear cults.

The Assiniboin bear society was typical. Only men who had dreamed of bear could join. In battle or in ceremonies they painted their faces red and made black circles around their eyes and mouths and scratch marks on their cheeks. They wore bear claw necklaces and yellow-painted buckskin shirts perforated with dozens of small holes. They shaved the front part of the top of their heads and rolled and tied their hair into two small clumps to look like bear's ears. In battle, a man from the society carried a shield with a bear painted on it, and his primary weapon was a knife with a handle made from the jaw bone of a bear. Some of these men painted bears on their tepees.[12] Bad-horn, a Hidatsa bear society member, always oriented his lodge like a bear den. "My gods are grizzly bears," he said. "The mouths of bears' dens always face north; therefore I want my lodge to open towards the north."[13]

Periodically, to celebrate certain occasions, society members held feasts. For the Assiniboin the meal was berry soup. They served no meat, and they never ate bear meat. Their guardian forbade it. Painted and dressed as bears, the men at the feast sang bear songs and danced as bears. They thought of themselves as bears. The people of their tribe called them bears.

In battle, Assiniboin bear dreamers rushed the enemy with bear-knife and shield and painted face. They made noises like a bear, "Huh, huh, huh!" They believed the power of the bear would protect them.

GIVING VOICE TO BEAR

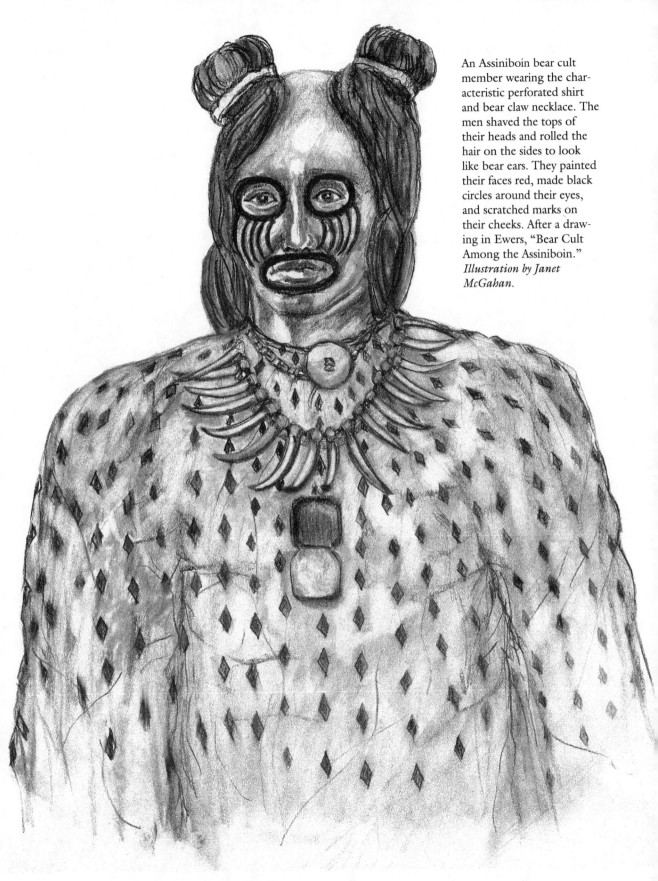

An Assiniboin bear cult member wearing the characteristic perforated shirt and bear claw necklace. The men shaved the tops of their heads and rolled the hair on the sides to look like bear ears. They painted their faces red, made black circles around their eyes, and scratched marks on their cheeks. After a drawing in Ewers, "Bear Cult Among the Assiniboin." *Illustration by Janet McGahan.*

"Ah Bear, We are the Same Person!"

Lakota war shield painted
with four bear tracks.
*Photo courtesy of the
Smithsonian Institution,
National Anthropological
Archives.*

The bear dreamers of other tribes also excelled as warriors. The Blackfeet said that those with bear power were seldom killed. They claimed that the appearance of the bear-knife "frightened everyone into submission, after the manner of bears."[14] Although they were not members of a bear society, the two leaders of the Crow Big Dog Society wore belts made from a bearskin with the legs and claws attached. Like Assiniboin bear society members, they bunched their hair to resemble bear's ears before a battle. But unlike the Assiniboin, they painted their bodies with mud. They vowed that, during a battle, they would walk straight into the enemy's camp and never retreat. It was their charge to rescue any other Crow who had been wounded or trapped in the fight, regardless of the danger.[15]

In contrast, the Lakota considered bear power to be unlucky for warriors. "The bear," they said, "is slow and clumsy, and apt to be wounded; and although savage when cornered [the bear] is not as likely as some animals to escape harm."[16]

Bear dreamers of the plains tribes were usually powerful healers as well as great warriors, and many were known more for their abilities as curers than as warriors. The bear societies were often the most powerful of the curing societies. The Lakota tradition described in chapter 6 is characteristic.

Most bear doctors were herbal doctors, who used plants, many of which were bear foods, for their medicines. But some were also sucking doctors, who used their mouths or a straw to suck disease out of their patients. An example from the Omaha is described by a man whose father was a grizzly bear doctor.

My father had the Grizzly Bear power. He got that from a sacred man called Black Grizzly Bear. He didn't pay for it; he didn't get it from the supernaturals. He went to Black Grizzly Bear's tipi. He fasted outside that tipi crying to *Waka da* for power for four days and four nights. Then Black Grizzly Bear who had got it from the supernaturals gave it to my father. He took my father far over the hills to where the supernatural grizzly bears live below ground. There Black Grizzly Bear caused my father to see the grizzly bear vision.

My father's powers were doubted by the other grizzly bear doctors. They were all assembled over a patient with bad stomach trouble. They picked on my father to treat the patient. He sucked out rattlesnake poison and passed it round in a basin for them to inspect. Then he swallowed the rattlesnake poison. They were all dumfounded. Then others sucked from the patient's stomach. Only one other got more rattlesnake poison. The others got only blood. My father and the other who got rattlesnake poison were the best of the Grizzly Bear Society Doctors.

Once my father was ill and he went off alone. I was sent to look

Zuni shield. *Smithsonian Institution.*

for him. I found him down by the river making noises like a bear and cutting his side with a knife to bleed himself.[17]

Men only comprised most bear societies of the plains tribes, although among the Kiowa, one of two female societies was the *Sate-tsow-hee*, or Bear Woman Society. This religious group was secretive, so little is known about it. It was a small society, with only ten or eleven members. When a Bear woman became old, she chose her daughter or sister to succeed her. When these Bear women danced, they imitated the motions of bears with their hands. No one was allowed to watch their ceremonies. According to one Kiowa, everyone feared Bear women.[18]

In some cultures, the grizzly spirit came to women through their husbands, who possessed the bear as a guardian. This was true of a Hidatsa woman who had participated in the transfer ceremony when her husband purchased a grizzly bear bundle. In the midst of the transfer, a ceremonial leader announced, "We are going to sing the Female Bear song. Any of you women who know the Female Bear dance should get up and dance." Several of the women rose and danced. Like bears, they shuffled past the man purchasing the bundle. He gave each of them four ball-shaped cakes of corn. Then the men placed a full, freshly skinned bearskin on a buffalo robe and asked the woman whose husband was buying the bundle to sit on the robe. The woman came over to it and took off her dress. She picked up the bearskin and pressed the hair of it to her naked breasts, holding it there for a few moments before letting it fall back to the ground. The Hidatsa said that this action made her "granddaughter to the bears." After this, if her husband died, only another man with a bear bundle could marry her because "other men would be afraid of her."[19]

Men feared her because any person identified with a potent animal spirit such as that of the bear possessed some numinous quality. In so far as the spirit was mysterious and sacred, a part of a person who was possessed by the spirit was also mysterious and sacred. When someone had a strong relationship with his or her guardian spirit, the spirit's presence was palpable to everyone, but the person who possessed the spirit felt it most keenly. If it was an animal such as the grizzly bear, it made people uneasy.

Bear dreamers acquired the character of the animal and decorated their clothes and weapons with its fur and claws. They danced like a bear, not because they wanted to be like bears, but because they thought of themselves as bears. A Crow named Otter-chief became ecstatic and acted like a bear any time he ate chokecherries. Another

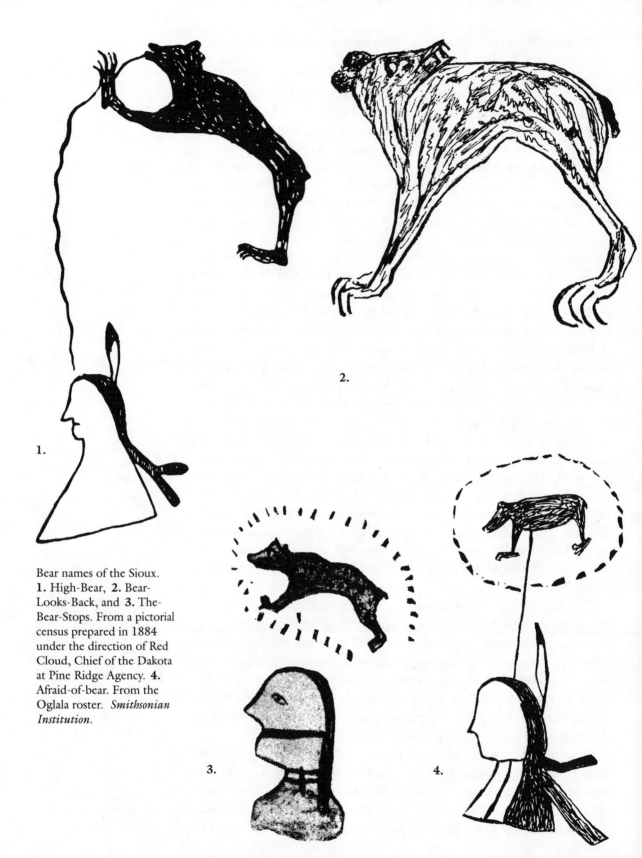

Bear names of the Sioux.
1. High-Bear, **2.** Bear-Looks-Back, and **3.** The-Bear-Stops. From a pictorial census prepared in 1884 under the direction of Red Cloud, Chief of the Dakota at Pine Ridge Agency. **4.** Afraid-of-bear. From the Oglala roster. *Smithsonian Institution.*

106

Crow man, Plenty-bear, frequently terrified onlookers by opening his mouth and showing bear's teeth.

Some felt so tied to their guardian spirits that they believed their bodies to be inhabited by a miniature version of the animal. The Lakota and other plains tribes tell of bear dreamers who, on those occasions when they lost consciousness, would have small grizzlies crawling out of their mouths.

An Ojibwa woman named Maggie Wilson had a lump in her neck where, she said, her guardian, the bear, resided. One time a sucking doctor drew it out of her. She looked at it before he put it back and said it looked like a tiny black worm. Another Ojibwa, Chief George, said that two bears lived curled up in his back, one on each side of his lower spine. One time, when he became ill, his back began to spasm, and the doctor told him "the bears were suffering." He cured him by prescribing certain herbs and a sweat.[20]

The concept of the guardian spirit is often confused with that of totemism, but totemism refers to the mystical relationship between a *kinship group* and an animal. Kinship groups were exogamous and are termed clans or gentes depending on whether the lineage was matrilinear or patrilinear in its reckoning. The group identified with an animal species, their totem, because they considered themselves mysteriously connected to it. Often, they claimed they were directly descended from the original mythic being of the species. The chief difference, then, between the guardian spirit and the totem is that a guardian spirit belonged to an individual, the totem animal belonged to a tribal division or group.

Bear tattoo of one who claims descent from bear. Haida. *Smithsonian Institution.*

There were many bear clans and bear gentes in North America. Members of the Bear Clan of the Yuchi Indians of the southeastern United States claimed descent from the bear, and because of that members could not kill bears (but they ate the meat and used the hide from bears killed by members of other clans). They prayed to the bear and danced for it at a New Year ceremony. At his or her puberty ceremony, each Bear Clan member obtained protection from the bear. They called on it for help when in trouble.[21]

A Fox Indian described the relationship with his totem: "There is no difference between a bear and one who goes by the name of a bear; both are the same, they are like brothers and sisters. . . .Bears are present at all gatherings of the Bear-people; they are not always visible yet they are there, and their presence is always felt. Bears, and people of the bear name, are still brothers and sisters."[22]

The Sauk Indians, a tribe linked historically with the Fox, had thirteen gentes, one of which was the Bear, or *Mu'kwa.* Bear Gens members claimed descent from a bear that came from under the

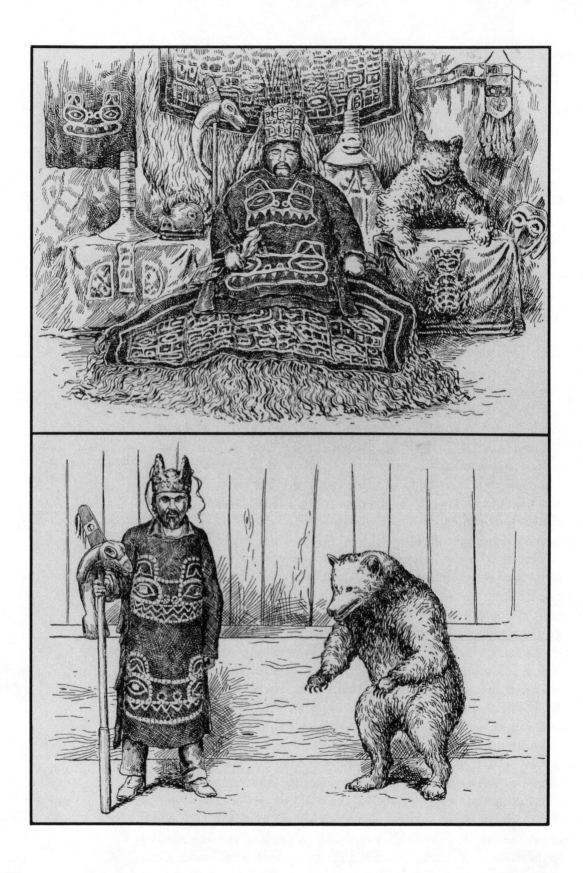

GIVING VOICE TO BEAR

ground. Members wore necklaces of yellow grizzly bear claws and otter fur. One of the names they gave to their children was a gens name, chosen to recall their bear ancestor, such as: Long-claws, Big-feet, Bob-tail, Bear-cracking-plums, Bear-excrement, Fat, Bear-old-woman, Imprint-of-buttocks-on-sand, Sits-tight-in-hollow-tree, Erect-standing-man, Twinkling-eyes, or Grandmother-earth.[23]

Among the Sauk, Bear Gens responsibilities included holding the annual maple sugar feast, during which they prayed for permission to tap the maple trees. The Winnebago Bear Clan gave two bear feasts a year: one in January, the bear month, and one in the spring. They served berries and sugar at the feast, but no meat, and they ate in the dark (like bears in a den), using only their left hands. The Bear Clan of one band quit giving the feast because once, when it was time to give the feast in the first bear month, the daughters of the host were menstruating and were fasting. Just before the meal, their mother stole some of the sacred food for the girls, who boiled and ate it. The following spring they were tanning hides with their mother when a bear attacked and killed them. The Winnebago claimed that it was not an ordinary bear. Its body was covered with blue clay, and it came out of a spring to kill the girls because they had eaten the sacred food when they were unclean.[24]

Carrier Indian beliefs seemed to merge the concept of the totem with that of the guardian spirit. In this Athapaskan-speaking tribe of western Canada, an initiation ritual brought a boy or girl together with his or her totem. The idea was that, by living like the animal, one could *become* the animal for a time, both in mind and body. A boy undergoing initiation stripped naked, pulled a bearskin over his body, and disappeared into the forest. For the next four days and nights he lived as a bear lives. He used his fingers to dig roots, which he ate in bear fashion. Traveling on all fours, he moved with a bear's gait and swung his head from side to side. The people of his village thought of him as a bear. Every evening at dusk a group from the village came out to search for him. They yelled, "*Yi! Kelulem!*" (roughly, "Come on, Bear!") The "bear" always answered them, but with growls and huffs. The hunters raced toward the sound, yelling again, "*Yi! Kelulem!*"—only to find him gone. They heard him growling from another place. In this hunt the "bear" was seldom found. After his ordeal ended, he returned to the village of his own will. When the people saw him coming, shouts went up and they charged out to capture him as if he were a wild bear invading the camp. The entire village led him to a ceremonial lodge where he partook in various rites. The ceremony reached its climax when the initiate danced as a bear. After the dance came a potlatch, a gift-giving celebratory feast characteristic of northwest coast Indians.[25]

Tracing descent from the bear. In the top illustration, the body of the Tlingit head chief, Shakes, lies in state. He is dressed in a ceremonial attire decorated with his totem animal the bear. A bear mask is to his right and a stuffed bear to his left. The lower illustration is a Tlingit enactment of a legend that traced Chief Shakes descent from the bear. *Smithsonian Institution.*

"Ah Bear, We are the Same Person!"

Finally, there was one other important way for Indians to derive power from bears, and that was by killing and eating part of the animal, usually the heart. Eating bear meat to gain its power lacked the depth and reciprocity of both the guardian spirit tradition and totemism; it did not result in a lifetime relationship with the animal. Plenty Coups, a chief of the Crow, ate grizzly bear meat as a youth to become a strong warrior. Kwakiutl nobility did the same. But, by this act a man did not ask for the animal's power—he took it by force.

After killing a grizzly bear, a Kwakiutl man addressed it, saying, "You have been overcome by me, friend. Now we have pressed together our killing hands, for now I have inherited your power of catching easily salmon and of doing all your work. Also, that your wild hands come to me, that I may be like you, and that there may be nothing that is not massacred. I mean this, great, good Supernatural One, all this I have inherited because you were greatly feared, friend."

The man skinned the animal and cut out its heart. When he returned home, he cut the heart into four pieces and boiled them. If he had a son, he called him over to where he was sitting and, when the meat finished boiling, he told him, "Now, child, you will eat part of this wildness of the grizzly bear." He gave him the first piece of meat and said, "Now take care, child, of this true Supernatural One, of these ways of this owner of this heart. Now eat this, what makes the grizzly bear get everything easily, so that you also may get easily all kinds of property." His son would eat the meat. He gave him another piece and told him, "Now eat this, the receptacle of the wildness of the grizzly bear, that you also may be wild." The child ate it. He gave him a third piece. "Now eat this, the grizzly bear's receptacle of having no respect that you also may have no respect of anything." He took the last piece of the heart and said, "Now you will eat this, the grizzly bear's power of killing things before he is struck, that you may also kill things before you are struck, for indeed, I wish you to be a warrior, son, as I am a warrior." When his son had eaten the last of the heart, the man told him, "Now my child you have in your stomach four things that come from the heart of the grizzly bear. Now you will for four days purify yourself in the pond and rub your body with hemlock branches in the morning and in the evening when our whole tribe goes to sleep. Now wish for a good dream about the grizzly bear when you always think about what you have done when you ate the four pieces of the heart of the grizzly bear; the wild animal, for I wish you to be of the same kind, child."[26]

Whether it was eating bear meat, believing they were descended from bears, or seeking the bear as a spirit guardian, Indians wanted to join with the animal, "to be of its kind," to have its power, and thereby to share in the grandness of its being.

8

Giving Voice to Bear

IT IS WINTER, and outside the night sky is dark and full of stars. This night is windless and, like all such nights, deeply silent. A heavy blanket of new snow covers the ground and bends the limbs of trees. The air smells new. Clustered within a stand of tall spruce trees are a group of birch bark lodges. Within each a fire burns, the firelight shining through the bark coverings and throwing a low orange-yellow glow on the surrounding trees and snow. The only sound that can be heard comes faintly from inside one of the dwellings, a single aged voice chanting the stories of The People.

Inside, among the scents of hide, smoke, and food, the men and boys sit or lie propped on elbows and piles of furs. Their bodies form a crescent on one side of the fire. The women, girls, and infants sit on the other side. A tiny grey-haired woman is telling the stories. Shrunken with age, she sits slightly hunched in the rear of the lodge, opposite the doorway. Her husband sits next to her, on the men's side. The smallest children are sleeping and lie curled beneath furs close to the fire.

Everyone is quiet, listening. If an infant starts to cry, it is nursed. If the children talk, they are hushed. "Listen to your Grandmother," their parents say. But there is frequent laughter; the storyteller is often funny and so are the stories. Occasionally she picks up her drum, beats it gently, and sings.

Her voice is constant, her cadence easy. Her words conjure vivid images. She speaks of a time when animals looked, talked, and behaved as humans, a time when even plants and rocks could speak, a time of strange and mysterious happenings. The tales are dreamlike, yet to the men, women, and children seated inside the lodge they are stories about things that actually happened in the "long time ago."

Others have told the same stories, but not in the same manner. Yet she recounts the events just as she heard them when she was a young girl, some sixty years ago. She goes on late into the night. By the time she finishes, the fire has burned low, and all of the children are asleep. The adults rise quietly, thank their grandmother, gather up babies, and step outside into the cold night. They feel, for a few moments, the icy air on their faces, and then disappear inside their lodges to rekindle fires before going to sleep.

Pictograph of bear and wolf. Medicine Rocks, Saskatchewan. After a drawing in Grant, *Rock Art of the American Indian*. Illustration by Janet McGahan.

THESE PEOPLE ARE OJIBWA INDIANS of the eastern woodlands, and this winter scene was repeated in tepees and wigwams throughout North America until about one hundred years ago.

Indians loved to tell stories. News about far away places or relatives, the events of a day spent hunting or in camp, an unusual observation of an animal's behavior, knowledge about a specific plant, advice—all were likely to be relayed in the form of a story. A story provided depth, precision, and richness, and most important, a context. Among the Cree, if a man had been gone for an extended period of time, he was expected, immediately upon returning, to tell his story, even if he was hungry and exhausted. The people at home wanted to know what had happened and exactly how it happened. "What did you see? What did you do? Tell us!"[1]

When it came to the winter recitation of myths and tales, the best storytellers were generally the elders. Older people simply knew more stories than anyone else. Because they had listened to and practiced stories all their lives, they were skilled at narration. They had led long and active lives hunting, gathering, and fishing and so knew more about the landscape and the plants and animals than anyone else. The elders knew best what kind of personality to give each animal or plant that took on human attributes in the myths and tales, and how each might sound when it spoke.

Sometimes Takelma story-tellers of southwestern Oregon represented grizzly bears by emphasizing each syllable spoken. According to linguist Dell Hymes, this gave their speech a quality of "lumbering ungainliness and clumsiness."[2] Takelma narrators carefully prefixed selected words or sentences spoken by bears with an L- sound or an s- sound. Hymes believes the s- prefix (which made a kind of lisping sound) ingratiated an audience.

Brown Bear, who, unlike Grizzly Bear, is usually harmless in the tales, hears girls at a puberty dance singing about him and making fun of his anus. He goes to the dance and announces his arrival with a "Hau, hau, hau, hau." In Takelma this phrase is ordinarily the characteristic threat of an angry bear. But Brown Bear's "Hau" is prefixed by an s- sound and because of it, his threat loses all its power and amuses instead. Brown Bear does not avenge his tormentors.

According to Hymes, the expressive L- prefix, used only by grizzly bears in certain situations, indicated coarseness and stupidity and was intended to elicit disdain. In one tale, Grizzly-bear Woman is tricked into eating the roasted livers of her own murdered children. When she discovers the deception, she cries, "L-so it is L-my children? So it was their livers that I ate?" And in another story, the L-prefix was used humorously to indicate a crude denseness on the part of Old Man Grizzly Bear and his wife. The two are so old that they have lost all their teeth and have to be fed the soft parts of slaughtered humans by the younger grizzly-bear men. But the two old bears seem to be unaware of their toothless condition, or they know it but pretend out of vanity that they still have their teeth. Repeatedly they tell each other to sharpen their "L-teeth."[3]

Obviously, most, if not all, of these details are lost when a story is translated, but there are other, perhaps more serious problems with translating Indian tales. For example, modern Indo-European languages are aesthetically quite distant from native American languages. The great linguist Edward Sapir hinted at this when he wrote, "Single Algonkian words are like tiny imagist poems." A single word in Algonquian can encompass a whole cluster of concepts or perceptions. Sapir's statement implies that Algonquian words possess a completeness and evocativeness missing from individual words in analytic languages such as English. Hence, translated stories lack the perceptual intensity and potency of the original, and a simple passage describing an angry bear charging down a trail looses its full impact when it is translated.[4]

Indians who were literate in English were aware of these problems. Archie Phinney was a Nez Perce Indian educated at Columbia University and trained by Franz Boas. He went home to the Lapwai Reservation in Idaho to transcribe the myths and tales of his people. In a letter to Boas, Phinney lamented, "A sad thing in recording these animal stories is the loss of spirit—the fascination furnished by the peculiar Indian vocal tradition for humor. Indians are better storytellers than whites. When I read my story mechanically I find only the cold corpse."

The stories are artifacts. Although in many places in North America native peoples still gather in winter to hear stories told in their own language, the stories themselves (as several of the tales that follow) may be thousands of years old. They are openings into the world of the Indian as it was before Europeans arrived on the continent. The bear myths and tales in this chapter reveal, at least on one level, how Indians thought about bears. But these tales are not full of biological information. They reveal what the bear was like in the Indian mind, and it is a different bear from the one most of us know today.

There are hundreds of American Indian bear tales. Those that follow were selected because each possessed a plot element or theme that was widespread in North America. The first two tell about people who married bears, perhaps the most popular kind of bear stories. The third was chosen from a group designated here as grizzly-bear-woman tales and is about a monster she-bear. The fourth tells of a culture hero who slays a murderous bear to make the world safe for humans. The fifth portrays the bear as a powerful but benevolent spirit animal, a helper of humans. In the last two, the bear encounters a trickster.

*   *   *   *

The story that follows is adapted from a version of a bear wife tale told by the Indians of the southern Yukon. An elder Tagish woman named Maria Johns told the story to Dr. Catharine McClellan. Maria's daughter, Dora Austin Wedge, translated it from the Tagish dialect of Athapaskan. McClellan wrote that Maria Johns, in her eighties, was a gifted raconteur. "She pantomimed frequently, changed her voice to indicate that different characters were speaking, and imitated the sounds of the dogs and bears." She volunteered this story immediately when McClellan asked her if there were any ritual observances for bears. The tale accounts for the way the Tagish treat slain bears.[5]

The Girl Who Married the Bear

Once there was a girl who picked berries in the summer. She went with her family, and they picked berries and dried them. When she went with her women folk, they would see bear droppings on the trail. Girls have to be careful about bear droppings. They shouldn't walk over it. Men can walk over it, but young girls have to walk around it. But this girl always jumped over it and kicked it. She would disobey her mother. All the time she would see some bear droppings and kick it and step over it. She kept seeing it all around her. She did this from childhood.

When she was quite big they went out picking berries. She picked with her mother and aunts and sisters. She saw some bear droppings. She said all kinds of words to it and kicked it and jumped over it.

When they were all coming home, they carried their baskets of berries. The girl saw some nice berries and stopped to get them. The others went ahead. When she had picked the berries and was starting to get up, her berries all spilled out of her basket. She leaned down and was picking them off the ground.

Soon she saw a young man. He was very good looking. She had never seen him before. He had red paint on his face. He stopped and talked to her. He said, "Those berries you are picking are no good. They are all full of dirt. Let's go up a little ways and fill your baskets up. There are some good berries growing up there. I'll walk home with you. You needn't be afraid."

After they had gotten the basket half full of berries the man said, "There is another bunch of berries up there a little ways. We'll pick them too."

When they had picked them all, he said, "It's time to eat. You must be hungry."

He made a fire. They cooked gopher, quite a lot of it, and they ate some. Then the man said, "It's too late to go home now. We'll go home tomorrow. It's summer, and there's no need to fix a big camp."

So they stayed there. When they went to bed, he said, "Don't lift your head in the morning and look at me, even if you wake up before I do."

So they went to bed. Next morning they woke up. The man said to her, "We might as well go. We'll just eat that cold gopher. We needn't make a fire. Then we'll go pick some berries. Let's get a basket full."

All the time the girl kept talking about her mother and father. All the time she wanted to go home, and she kept talking about it.

He said, "Don't be afraid, I'm going home with you." Then he slapped her right on top of her head, and he put a circle around the girl's head the way the sun goes. He did this so she would forget. Then she forgot. She didn't talk about her home any more.

They left again. He said, "You're all right. I'll go home with you."

Then after this she forgot all about going home. She just went around with him picking berries. Every time they camped, it seemed like a month to her, but it was really only a day. They started in May. They kept traveling and going.

Finally she recognized a place. It looked like a place that she and her family used to dry meat. Then he stopped there at the timberline and slapped her. And he made a circle sunwise, and then another on the ground where she was sitting. He said, "Wait here. I am going hunting gophers. We have no meat. Wait 'till I come back." Then he came back with the gophers. They kept traveling. Late in the evening they made camp and cooked.

Next morning they got up again. At last she knew. They were traveling again, and it was getting late. And she came to her senses and knew it. It was cold. He said, "It's time to make a camp. We must make a home." He started making a home. He was digging a den. She knew he was a bear then.

He got quite a way digging the den, then he said, "Go get some balsam boughs and brush." She went and got some. She broke the branches from as high as she could and brought the bundle.

He said, "That brush is no good. You left a mark, and the people will see it and know we were here. We can't use that. We can't stay here."

So they left. They went up to the head of a valley. She knew her brothers used to go there to hunt and to eat bear. In the spring they took the dogs there, and they hunted bears in April. They would send the dogs into the bear den and then the bear would come out. That's where her brothers used to go. She knew it.

He said, "We'll make camp." He dug a den and sent her out again.

"Get some brush that is just lying on the ground—not from up high. No one will see where you get it, and it will be covered with snow."

She got it from the ground and brought it to him, but she bent the branches up high too. So she let them hang down so her brothers would know. And she rubbed sand all over herself—all over her body and limbs.

And then she rubbed the trees all around, so that the dogs would find where she had left her scent. Then she went to the den with her bundle of brush. She brought it.

Just when the man was digging, he looked like a bear. This was the only time. The rest of the time he seemed like a human being. The girl didn't know how else to stay alive, so she stayed with him as long as he was good to her.

"This is better," he said, when she brought back the brush. Then he brushed up and fixed the place. After he fixed the den, they left. The grizzly bear is the last bear to go into his den. They go around in the snow.

They went hunting gophers for winter. She never saw him do it. She always sat around when he was hunting gophers. He dug them up like a grizzly bear, and he didn't want her to see it. He never showed her where he kept the gophers.

Nearly every day they hunted gophers and picked berries. It was quite late in the year. He was just like a human to her.

It was October. It was really late in the fall. He said, "Well, I guess we'll go home now. We have enough food and berries. We'll go down."

So they went home. Really they went into the den. They stayed there and slept. They woke up once a month and got up to eat. They kept doing it and going back to bed. Every month, it seemed like another morning, just like another day. They never really went outside. It just seemed like it.

Soon the girl found that she was carrying a baby. She had two little babies—one was a girl, and one was a boy. She had them in February in the den. This is when bears have their cubs. She had hers then.

The bear used to sing in the night. When she woke up she would hear him. The bear became like a shaman when he started living with the woman. It just came upon him like a shaman.

He sang his song twice. She heard it the first time. The second time the bear made a sound, "Wuf! Wuf!" And she woke up.

"You're my wife, and I am going to leave soon. It looks like your brothers are going to come up here soon, before the snow is gone. I want you to know that I am going to do something bad. I am going to fight back!"

"Don't do it!" she said. "They are my brothers. If you really love me you will love them too. Don't kill them. Let them kill you! If you really love me don't fight! You have treated me good, why did you live with me if you are going to kill them?"

"Well, all right," he said, "I won't fight, but I want you to know what will happen!"

His canines looked like swords to her.

"These are what I fight with," he said. They looked like knives to her. She kept pleading.

"Don't do anything. I'll still have my children if they kill you!" She knew he was a bear then. She really knew.

They went to sleep. She woke again. He was singing again.

"It's true," he said. "They are coming close. If they do kill me, I want them to give you my skull—my head, and my tail. Tell them to give them to you. Wherever they kill me, build a big fire, and burn my head and tail and sing this song while the head is burning. Sing it until they are all burnt up!"

So they ate and went to bed, and another month went by. They didn't sleep the whole month. He kept waking up.

"It's coming close," he said. "I can't sleep well. It's getting to be bare ground. Look out and see if the snow is melted from in front of the den."

She looked, and there was mud and sand. She grabbed some and made it into a ball and rubbed it all over herself. It was full of her scent. She rolled it down the hill. Then the dogs could smell it. She came in and said, "There is bare ground all over in some places."

He asked her why she had made the marks. "Why? Why? Why? They'll find us easy!"

They went to bed again, just for a little while.

Next morning he said, "Well, its close! It's close! Wake up!"

Just when they were getting up, they heard a noise. "The dogs are barking. Well," he said, "I'll leave. Where are my knives? I want them!"

He took them down. She saw him putting in his teeth. He was a big bear. She pleaded with him.

"Please don't fight. If you wanted me, why did you go this far? Just think of the children. Who will look after my children if you kill them? My brothers will help me. If my brothers hunt you, let them be!"

When he went, he said, "You are not going to see me again!"

He went out and growled. He slapped something back into the den. It was a pet dog, a little bear dog.

When he threw the dog in, she grabbed it and shoved it back in the brush under the nest. She put the dog there to hide it. She sat on it and kept it there so it couldn't get out. She wanted to keep it for a reason.

For a long time there was no noise. She went out of the den. She heard her brothers below. They had already killed the bear. She felt bad, and she sat down. She found an arrow. She picked it up, and then others. Finally she fitted the little dog with a string around his back. She tied the arrows into a bundle. She put them all on the little dog, and he ran to his masters.

The boys were down there dressing the bear. They knew the dog. They noticed the bundle and took it off.

It's funny," they said. "No one in a bear den would tie this on!" They talked about it. They decided to send the youngest brother up to the den. A younger brother can talk to his sister, but an older brother can't.

The older brothers said to the youngest brother, "We lost our sister a year ago in May. Something could have happened. A bear might have taken her away. You are the youngest brother. Don't be afraid. There is nothing up there but her. You go and see if she is there. Find out!"

He went. She was sitting there crying. The boy came up. She cried when she saw him. She said, "You boys killed your brother-in-law! I went with him last May. You killed him, but tell the others to save me the skull and tail. Leave it there for me. When you get home, tell Mother to sew a

Tlingit bear hunter's decorative face painting.
Smithsonian Institution.

GIVING VOICE TO BEAR

dress for me so I can go home. Sew a dress for the girl and pants and a shirt for the boy. And moccasins. And tell her to come and see me."

He left and got down there and told his brothers, "This is my sister up there. She wants the head and tail."

They did this, and they went home. They told their mother. She got busy and sewed. She had a dress and moccasins and clothes for the children. The next day she went up there. They dressed the little kids. Then they went down to where the bear was killed. The boys had left a big fire. She burned the head and tail. Then she sang until all was ashes.

Then they went home, but she didn't go right home. She said, "Get the boys to build a house. I can't come right in to the main camp. It will be quite a while. The boys can build a camp right away."

She stayed there a long while. Towards fall she came and stayed with her mother. All winter. The kids grew.

Next spring her brothers wanted her to act like a bear. They wanted to play with her. They had killed a female bear that had cubs, one male and one female. They wanted their sister to put on the hide and to act like a bear. They fixed little arrows. They pestered her to play with them, and they wanted her two little children to play too. She didn't want it.

She told her mother, "I can't do it! Once I do it, I will turn into a bear. I'm half there already! Hair is already showing on my arms and legs! It is quite long."

If she had stayed there with her bear husband another summer she would have turned into a bear. "If I put on a bearhide, I'll turn into one!," she said.

They kept telling her to play. Then her brothers sneaked up. They threw the hides over her and the little ones. Then she walked off on four legs, and she shook herself just like a bear. It just happened. She was a grizzly bear. She couldn't do a thing. She had to fight against the arrows. She killed them all off, even her mother. But she didn't kill her youngest brother, not him. She couldn't help it. Tears were running down her face.

Then she went on her own. She had her two little cubs with her.

That's why the bear is partly human. That is why you never eat grizzly bear meat. Now people eat black bear meat, but they still don't eat grizzly meat, because grizzlies are half human.[6]

The Girl Who Married the Bear is an old tale. Versions of it were told over large parts of northern North America, and similar stories have been recorded from Siberia.[7] In North America it seemed to center in what is now western Canada and Alaska. Of all the tales told by the northern Athapaskans and their neighbors, this was one of the favorites. McClellan, who has worked for years among the Tagish, Tutchone, and Tlingit, writes that it remains today the tale of first choice among both men and women, young and old.[8] And it is

Ivory carving depicting a woman and a bear (Dorset Culture). Marriage-to-bear tales and tales of women that had intercourse with bears were common among the Eskimo, and many other North American tribes. From Naujan, Repulse Bay, N.W.T. *Photo courtesy of the McCord Museum of Canadian History, Montreal.*

no wonder; through a series of agonizing dilemmas, the story addresses two of the most fundamental and decisive issues of life: marriage and death.

In exogamous cultures, the roles of both boys and girls were changed with marriage, but girls' lives were transformed dramatically. Overnight, a girl moved from daughter to wife, and often to expecting mother. In that rupture, her mother, father, brother, and sister suddenly became more distant, and in their place came a stranger, a spouse who was foreign in his person and ways. For the young woman, the man was an unknown, an outsider, and potentially dangerous.

Tales provided a circumspect way of dealing with this disruptive passage. For these northern Indians, the bear with its almost human body, alien ways, and threatening presence, was an appropriate symbol of the husband, and marriage to a bear was an ideal metaphor for marrying out.

The metaphor seemed to work on a broader, community level as well. In his book *The Way of the Masks*, Claude Levi-Strauss suggested that exogamous cultures are constantly mediating between marriage that is too close and marriage that is too distant. There is danger at both poles. Marriage to a bear, or marriage to any animal or supernatural being (such tales are plentiful) represented a marriage that was too far out (what Levi Strauss calls extreme exogamy) and therefore unworkable. The consequences of such a mistake, as in this tale, could be tragic.[9]

McClellan points out that there are other reasons for the story's popularity. The real drama begins when the girl betrays her husband and is faced with the terrible dilemma of choosing her loyalties: she must decide between her bear husband or her own kin. She makes her choice. She begs her husband not to kill her brothers. "Allow yourself to be killed instead!" she pleads. "Think of our children!" He, in what is both appropriate and honorable behavior for a brother-in-law among northern Athapaskans, gives himself to the men, but only after telling his wife how to treat his carcass (and so the carcasses of all slain bears).

She returns home with thick coarse hair growing on her body. She has lived too long with her husband. When her brothers torment her she becomes a bear, and she murders her own family and then disappears into the forest with her children.

Most tribes in the region considered bears to be almost human, so it is not surprising that many thought that male bears were attracted to women. Tribes of the western subarctic saw bears as powerful animal shamans. Male bears, like human male shamans, were assumed to be strongly interested in girls and women. A shaman sometimes used his powers to get women, and a bear, like the one in this story, might do the same.

Consider how women and girls from Alaska and Yukon tribes viewed and addressed the bears they encountered in the wild. Believing that the bear understood human speech, Tagish women meeting a bear while out gathering might say something like, "Be sorry for me brother, I'm just around for berries like you." The Tagish say their women always address the bear as brother because "you are shy to your sister."[10] By calling the bear "brother" (marriage that is too close), they hoped to avoid a marriage that is too distant.

The Koyukon say that a woman threatened by a bear "should expose her genitals to it and say, 'My husband, it's me'. This will shame the animal, quiet it down, and it will leave."[11]

The tales reflected the fears of women, but they also raised the possibility that the bear might take them away not to eat but to marry. "All Indians fear bears," McClellan writes, "but women seem to have an almost pathological reaction to grizzlies, as much because of their spiritual as their natural aspects."[12] To this day some Koyukon believe that if a woman is not careful, she will end up marrying a bear.

When a Tutchone girl was out berrying she never used the word for bear at all. "I saw Great Grandfather's feet," she would say when she saw the tracks of a grizzly. She might take some soil from the tracks, toss it behind her, and walk quietly away without looking back. She threw the soil to avoid contact with the animal. She did not say the word bear and she stepped around its dung to keep from

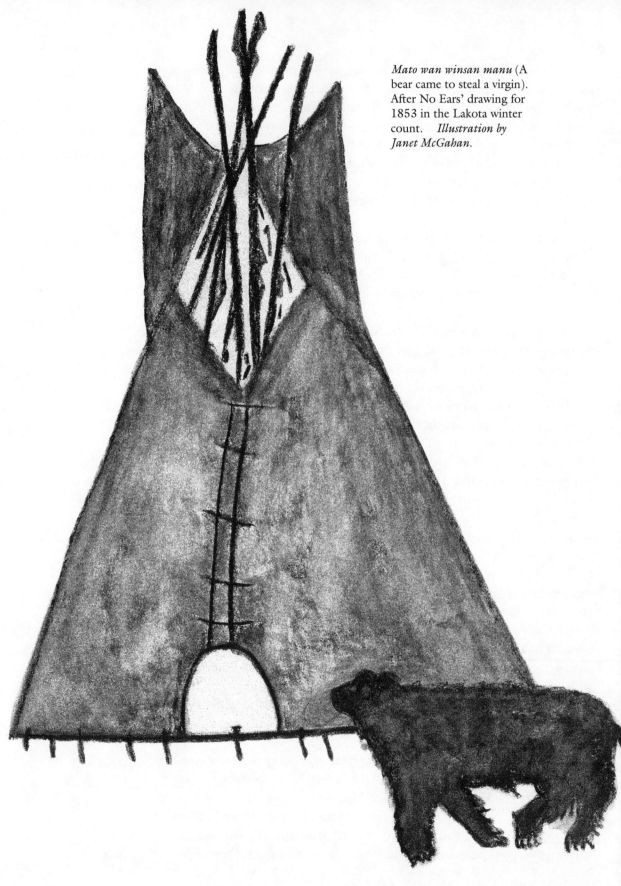

Mato wan winsan manu (A bear came to steal a virgin). After No Ears' drawing for 1853 in the Lakota winter count. *Illustration by Janet McGahan.*

insulting it. Teslin women said that it is good to talk to the bear and also necessary to give it something, a berry basket perhaps.[13]

The idea that bears, especially grizzly bears, seek women is not restricted to the western subarctic. The Navajo and Apache have similar tales. A Lakota winter count records for 1853: *Mato wan winsan manu*, "A bear came to steal a virgin."[14] The bear was caught entering a lodge at night and was killed. The people said that it was trying to steal a wife, just as some bad men did. In the old days, a man could make a woman marry him if he just touched her genitals, even while she slept.

There are other tales about women who flirt with bears. One such Algonquian story tells of an old woman who smears red paint on her face to attract a bear lover.

Within the last two decades some researchers have suggested that menstruating women may attract bears, although there is not strong scientific evidence to support the idea.[15] Still, largely because the question is unresolved, the United States Forest Service and the National Park Service both recommend that women not camp or hike in grizzly bear habitat when they are menstruating. It is tempting to attribute native beliefs about women and bears to an actual physiological attraction of bears to menstrual odors (recall the Lakota belief, "If a menstruating woman tans a bearskin, then she will become a bear and the woman is black all over and her face is hairy all over, it is said. Therefore women are very much afraid of bearskins."[16])

Athapaskan women are still very much afraid of bears. In 1978, Richard Nelson, a northern ethnologist, described in his journal what happened when he and two of his Koyukon teachers chanced upon a grizzly.

> Catherine saw the animal before any of us, and even though it was far off she mumbled softly that "a dark thing" was on the far riverbank. When we did not understand, she finally said, "a big animal is over there," without pointing and while looking in the opposite direction. Our boat drifted toward the animal. It showed little fear, and as we approached Catherine remained silent, her eyes averted and her back partly toward it, her entire countenance almost morose. Everything about her expressed the danger of a woman coming so close to a creature of such spiritual power. I do not believe I ever saw her more serious than during those minutes before the great bear finally turned and ambled into the bush.[17]

*   *   *   *   *

Sometimes in the tales it is a boy who marries a female bear and the bear comes to live with him. Ethnologist Edward Gifford recorded one such story in 1932, a Western Yavapai variant of a Southern Athapaskan epic. Gifford heard it from an aged Yavapai man named Jim Stacey. Stacey's son served as translator.[18]

The Bear Woman with the Snapping Vagina

[An] old woman and her grandson were living together. The grandson went out hunting deer continually. He killed deer all the time. Every time he went out he got one. The old woman said to the boy: "When you go out in the mountains and kill a doe, be sure not to cut it on the left side at first, but on the right side."

He did as his grandmother told him, but he thought about what she had said and his curiosity was aroused. He said to himself he would cut the next one on the left side and see what happened.

He killed a doe and cut her on the left side. He did all the left side cutting first. He was still cutting off the skin by the hind legs, when he heard something making a noise in the bushes. He looked into the bushes and saw a naked woman approaching. She came to him as he was cutting the deer meat. She was standing there watching him.

She said, "I want to tell you that I want to have intercourse with you at once."

The boy did not answer her. Again she repeated her statement, again, and again. The boy kept working on the venison. He was thinking about what his grandmother had said about not cutting on the left side first. He piled up the venison, tied it with a buckskin cord. She came close to the boy and touched him on the arm and said: "I want to have intercourse."

The boy answered her, "You say that to me all the time, 'I want to have intercourse'. Can't you say something else? Your talk is no good. It is not good for a woman to be asking a man for intercourse. Talk to me good or tell me a story and after a month or so we may live together. But to live right away together, no!"

He packed up his meat and went home. The woman followed him. She kept on saying the same thing, "I want to have intercourse!"

The boy kept going and did not answer her. Finally they arrived at his home.

The grandmother was staying in the house. He told her what had happened. "You told me not to cut on the left side. I cut on the right side. Then I wanted to see what would happen if I cut on the left side, so I did. That woman came to me right away. She wanted me to marry her. I ran home and she followed me almost to the house."

The grandmother said, "That happened because you cut first on the left side. Now you have found out."

After a little while, the woman came to the grandmother's house. The old woman and her grandson were sitting inside the house. The woman entered and sat beside the fire. She said to the boy, "You be my husband." She said it again and again.

The boy said, "Go over there and cut wood and fix up a hut with a bed in it and have a fire going. We will not live together without a house."

The woman went into the mountains for house wood. The boy's grandmother said, "That woman has teeth in her vagina. Men get killed when they have intercourse with her. She has killed many men. You lie with her, but don't have intercourse with her. Wait and I'll make something for you first."

She made a penis of clay for her grandson. The woman built a house near-by. In the evening the boy went in. He did nothing with her the first night, or the second night. The first two nights she begged him, but he refused. The third night he used the clay penis. Her vagina had teeth like a bear's teeth. The teeth broke the clay to pieces. On the fourth night, he used a rock penis and put the salty effervescence from lemon berries on its distal end. The teeth wore out on the rock. The boy struck the teeth with the rock penis and broke them off. He pulled out the teeth and threw them away.

A few days after the woman did not feel well. She went out to dig mescal. When she came back she said to her husband, "I saw a wild animal with a pretty hide. I want you to go over there and get it for me, so I may wear the skin. It looks warm."

He did not go over there. He went to his grandmother's for advice. She said, "You go over there. If this woman has relatives over there, she has stayed with them over there and now tells you to go to them. Bears are her relatives."

The woman went out every day for four days. Every evening she came home and said the same thing to the boy. The fourth evening the boy said, "All right, I'll go." He went to the mountain she pointed out.

At the place he went to he saw something as he approached. Four bears came out. He climbed a little hill and went down behind it. He saw a dead tree stump standing there.

He took his buckskin shirt and leggings off and put them over a bush to give it the appearance of a man. Over the top he put an imitation scalp, so the whole thing looked like a man. He hid in some bushes where he could watch. He heard the bears coming. He watched them approach to attack the dummy man. He drew his bow and killed the four bears, shooting only four times. Now he heard his wife approaching. She shouted, "Save me his clothes." She came along shouting that way. He asked her what she meant by saying that. He said, "I thought you wanted meat to eat. There it is. Eat it."

She wailed over her brothers. She felt for their teeth but could not find them. Then she went back home with her husband.[19]

*   *   *   *   *

Giving Voice to Bear

Like the girl who danced over bear dung, the young hero in this Yavapai tale violated a taboo that disrupted his relationship with the animals. As a consequence, he too marries a bear. Whereas the girl married a virtuous character (her husband sacrificed himself for her and his children), the boy's new wife is a devouring monster. Both tales address the question of marriage. But this narrative, from the male's perspective, seems to be more concerned with male anxieties about marriage and the undercurrent of hostility that exists between affines than with the problem of immoderate exogamy.

C. Patrick Morris, a scholar of American Indian culture with a particular interest in the uses of metaphor in mythic narrative, has identified a series of story elements that, in the beginning are wild and undomesticated, but at the story's end are brought under control and tamed. "Affines," Morris writes of the story, "are never talked about openly or directly but rather are the subject of implicit metaphors constructed from elements taken from nature. Hero's camp is the consanguineal world of order and safety. In contrast, affines are seen as outsiders whose uncontrolled appetites are likened to bears and the world of nature."[20]

In the Yavapai story, the young man domesticates the bear woman. She is forced to make a hut, a bed, and a fire. Her husband, the hero of the story, knocks out her vaginal teeth and kills her brothers. In the end, the bear woman is cut off permanently from her own people and her wild home.

That the bear is a symbol of nature is evident as well from the larger narrative of which this story is only part. The boy is in fact the Yavapai culture hero Monster Slayer, who goes about restoring the natural order by destroying monsters in order to make the world safe for people. The bear is one manifestation of uncontrolled nature and the danger it represents.

There is also an element of the devouring female in this story. (In a Navajo variant of this same tale, the bear wife is called *bijosh yeda'a'*, "the overwhelming vagina.") As the Western Yavapai story opens, the bear appears as an overwhelmingly aggressive naked woman with an unbridled sexual appetite. Later, through the grandmother we learn: "She is a bear, and she has teeth in her vagina! She goes from place to place catching boys, and then crushes their penises with her vagina. She has killed many men that way."

The bear in this tale, as animal metaphor, unites two aspects of the world, both of which are dangerous to the male and must be controlled. The first is untamed nature, which threatens his culture. The second is the negative, devouring side of the feminine, which threatens his culture as well as his masculinity. By the tale's end both are domesticated by the male culture hero.

When the northern bear-wife tale and the southwestern bear-husband tale are juxtaposed, the two seem opposite. In The Girl who Married the Bear, the girl, who becomes the bear, devours her family, including her tormenting brothers who murdered her husband. In the end she returns to the forest. It is, in this tale, the bear, the power of nature, and the feminine that prevail.

In the Yavapai tale the male culture hero wins over the bear, nature, and the feminine. The bear-woman is domesticated, her brothers are slain, and the vagina is made safe.

*   *   *   *   *

In the American Indian oral tradition, the bear often represented untamed nature, which the next two tales illustrate. In the first, a Nez Perce story, the bear is a devouring female who threatens to transform all human females she meets into other grizzly-bear women. In the second, a large male bear endangers Indian survival.

A sixty-year-old Nez Perce woman named Wayilatpu told the story that follows to her son, Archie Phinney, who translated it into English. Grizzly-bear Woman is a familiar character in the mythology of the Nez Perce and other tribes of the area.[21]

Wali'ms and the Grizzly-bear Women

Once upon a time the people were dwelling there. There came to them a baby which everybody loved and fondled. It was a girl and always various persons carried it about and nursed it because it was so lovable. Far away the bears, five sisters, dwelt and they heard about the baby girl. They plotted to steal the baby from the people.

"We are going to kidnap her," they agreed, and they set out for the encampment of the people. They arrived in the evening.

"Who shall ask for the baby?" they asked one another.

"Let me," the eldest said right away. "I will present myself thus," and she went into an exuberance of baby talk, talk that was soft and loving.

"Huh," replied the youngest. "You must think yourself very coy to try that kind of talk; it will sound so incongruous that they will suspect you at once. I myself am going for the baby and I will present myself thus, 'We, too, have come to pay our respects to your baby girl, and to fondle her awhile'."

She spoke in a curt, straightforward way. The sisters were impressed and allowed her to go. So it was that the youngest went to the parents of the baby girl and asked for the privilege of fondling the infant.

The mother replied to her request kindly, "Just now they have brought her in, and I must feed her first."

The bear waited. Presently the mother gave the baby to the bear, who carried it now to her sisters who were waiting at the outskirts of the camp. From there they ran away with the baby to the mountains.

The people soon missed their favorite daughter and in the morning everybody was gravely concerned about her mysterious disappearance.

"The five bear sisters were here; it must be that they have taken her. Let us search for them," they decided.

The baby girl had a brother, Red-headed Woodpecker. He watched the hopeless search of the people and he said to them, "My sister was very dear to me, and now I, myself, am going alone in search of her."

He traveled long and far, searched everywhere and stayed away so long that the people began to think that he, too, was lost forever. But it was only that he continued the search for his sister.

One day he shot a prairie chicken and as he carried this along he looked and he saw in the distance a girl digging roots. He went toward her, and while he was yet some distance away she recognized him and shouted, "Brother, brother, I am kept by the bears and badly treated. They always distrust me."

The boy in his joy replied, "Here, take this prairie chicken."

"No," said the girl, "they will suspect me."

"Then take your digging stick and spear it, then you can tell the bears that you are bringing home your own kill; later this evening I will arrive too. What do they do to you?"

"In the evening when I reach home the five sisters will dash out to meet me and wipe their buttocks on my head, first the eldest, then the next and next, all of them. Then I must peel all the roots I've dug during the day, grind and mix them into a mush. The bears then eat this, giving no portion at all to me. Oh, very badly I am cared for."

She left her brother and went home. The bears ran out to meet her saying, "Why are you late?" and at once they began wiping their buttocks on the girl's head. Her brother had put some sharp grass in her hair, and this gashed their buttocks painfully. They scolded her for this, and she told them it was only their own dried dung scratching them.

They noticed the bird and asked, "Wali'ms, (that was the girl's name) where did you get the pheasant?"

"Oh, I speared it today while digging roots."

"All right," replied the bears, "then prove it by spearing it again." She responded to this by taking up her digging stick, facing to the side, and quite casually spearing the prairie chicken.

"Yes, you must have speared it all right. You will mix it with the mush," said the bears.

For a long time she busied herself at cooking, waiting for her brother to come. She dished out the mush for the bears, and they began to take off their clothes (it was their custom to eat nude). They began to eat their mush, making much noise in doing so.

The girl still waited for her brother, when shortly she heard footsteps on the outside, and the door slowly opened. A handsome youth entered, and the bears hastily snatched up their clothes and covered themselves. Woodpecker seated himself and joined them at supper.

A bear then addressed Wali'ms, "Take for yourself some mush," by way of impressing their guest that she was being well cared for. They finished their meal and they all went to bed. Woodpecker slept with one of the bear sisters. He now began a siege of keeping them awake by tossing around and talking incessantly until finally they became very, very tired and sleepy, but he persisted, trying all the harder to keep them awake.

Presently one of the bears remonstrated, "Friend, tomorrow we will resume our fellowship again and go to bed again, but now let us sleep."

The bears had become extremely sleepy by this time and very quickly they fell into a deep, sound, sleep. Woodpecker even rolled them around without waking them. He then tied each one by her hair to a tent pole. He turned to Wali'ms, "Where are you? Let us go now! Get together any of your belongings you wish to take."

They went outside and prepared to set out, and just before leaving he set fire to the lodge, from the door all the way around.

"Do not take anything or even touch anything of theirs," he advised her. "Come let us go."

"Wait," replied the girl. "Let me watch them." By this time the bears were burning and their eyes were exploding and popping like gunshots.

"Hurry, come along," repeated Woodpecker.

"Wait, I wish to watch the fire," replied Wali'ms.

Suddenly the girl heard a voice saying, "Wali'ms, take teeth." And quickly she reached into the fire and received the bear's teeth without her brother noticing.

Wali'ms and her brother Woodpecker then started, traveling long and far. While they were going along he suddenly heard the angry snorting of a bear behind him, "Xaw, xaw!"

"What do you mean by that, Wali'ms?" he asked her.

"Oh, I am just imitating the bears; they used to do that," she answered.

"No," he said. "Very likely you have taken something of theirs."

"No," she denied, "it is just that I am imitating them."

They would go on for a distance and again he would suddenly hear, "Xaw, xaw!" and he would become frightened.

He asked of Wali'ms, "Do not say that."

But as they went along she would repeat the snarl of a bear from time to time, each time resembling more the bear's angry voice.

Now the brother became greatly suspicious, and suddenly he looked around and saw behind him, not his sister but a bristling, angry bear. He thought to himself, "She has become transformed into a bear; it is something she has taken of theirs."

He quickly said to her, "Wali'ms, what are you doing?"

It was to no avail, for the bear bristling angrily now gave chase. She chased him, storming madly along, but Woodpecker soon outdistanced her by far. As he fled along he saw ahead of him five women digging roots. He ran toward them and, as he approached, shouted, "My cousins, hide me! A bear is chasing me."

They replied, "Why do you call us cousins. Express our kinship differently; that one is not right."

He now addressed them by other forms of kinship, "My sisters-in-law, hide me!"

"No," they replied, "Closer yet make our friendship."

Finally he said to them, "My wives, hide me."

Now they seized him very quickly and hid him in a pile of roots they had been digging. They went on digging roots unconcerned-like.

They saw the bear coming. As she dashed up to them she said, "Has the one I am chasing to kill and eat gone past here?"

They paid no attention to her and she repeated, "Do you hear me? Has the one I am chasing to kill and eat gone past here?"

Now the women replied, "Your talk is bothersome; Your are not causing the human race to come all by yourself, already we have done it."

Thereupon the bear left them, giving up hope [of finding Woodpecker].

In this tale Grizzly-bear Woman is represented by the five grizzly-bear sisters. Reading just this one tale, one might judge her to be dangerous but not absurdly so. It is only after hearing or reading several of the stories about her that one begins to appreciate how cruel and murderously insane she is, and how bizarre her behavior is. As outsiders, we are at a disadvantage, since storytellers assumed a certain background knowledge and did not feel obligated to explain everything in each tale.

Dell Skeels, a folklorist, has studied the oral literature of the Nez Perce and has described the character of Grizzly-bear Woman by identifying personality traits she possesses in the fifteen or so myths in which she appears. (According to Skeels, she is the only female character who appears in a principal role in more than one of the stories.) The traits, which follow, apply equally well to the grizzly-bear woman found in Clackamas Indian tales and the tales of other neighboring tribes.[22]

First, Grizzly-bear Woman is extremely violent, and her violence is unrestrained and sadistic. Melville Jacobs, who studied her character in Clackamas literature, calls her a murderous psychotic.[23] In virtually every story in which she appears she either kills or attempts to kill almost everyone she meets, including her own relatives. In one of the Clackamas stories she not only kills her co-wife, but skins her and wears the skin.

Second, she is indecent. She eats in the nude (as did the grizzly sisters, who quickly dressed when Woodpecker entered), which, in the Nez Perce view, is crude and vile behavior. Even more disgusting, the grizzly-bear sisters wipe their buttocks on Wali'ms' hair. In a Clackamas tale Grizzly-bear Woman does the same to her husband's younger brother. In another Clackamas example of her indecency, she paints her face with her own menstrual blood. In another, Cottontail Boy insults her by telling her that her vulva is as large as "the land that extends up the valley." To catch him, she makes her giant vulva into a trap by smearing it with pitch from a fir tree.

The third trait that Skeels has identified is Grizzly-bear Woman's passion for kidnapping children, boys or girls. She steals girls to use as slaves and treats them miserably. She kidnaps boys for sex and goes into jealous fits of rage when other women show an interest in them. Sometimes she merely eats her victims. This aspect of her character must have made Grizzly-bear Woman especially terrifying for children listening to the stories.

Perhaps the most disturbing aspect of her character is that she has the power to change the human women she comes in contact with into grizzly-bear women, even after she is dead. Thus, she is never entirely destroyed. When Wali'ms watched the grizzly sisters burn, she heard a voice, "Take the teeth." She took them and became a grizzly-bear woman herself.

The last characteristic that Skeels noted is Grizzly-bear Woman's association with blood. Before she kills, blood gushes from her mouth. "It is not my blood," she announces, "but the blood of the men I am going to kill!" When she dances and sings, blood pours from her mouth. After she kills she smells of blood. In other narratives she is menstruating or confined to the menstrual hut. In the Clackamas story where she paints her face with her own menstrual blood, she goes about asking the trees to compliment her on her looks.

When you consider all the stories in which Grizzly-bear Woman appears, the image is horrifying. The Clackamas said that although she was a bear she looked "just like a person. That was the way her flesh was, like ours, but her breasts were very long."[24]

In these tales and in the snapping vagina tale from the Yavapai and similar tales from other tribes, the bear represents the dangerous side of the feminine: the terrible devouring creature with her overly aggressive nature and unbridled sexual appetite. Like the Yavapai bear woman, Grizzly-bear Woman is inimical to society. Skeels argued that she represented "the lure and temptation of the basic drives of the animal world untempered by any taming influence; for the sake of communal life she had to be put down and denied."[25]

*   *   *   *

In a tale from the Naskapi of northern Quebec, the bear is a monster called *Katcheetohuskw*, "Stiff-legged Bear." The Naskapi describe it as an animal "of very large size, being man eating, and having head and ears like a bear." This bear, however, is male.[26]

Stiff-legged Bear

A long time ago an old man, his wife, and daughter lived together. One day, the old man and his wife, who was now pregnant, left camp to cut birch for ladles. A large monster bear called Katcheetohuskw heard the two chopping wood. He charged out of the trees and attacked them. There was no time to run. He tore the bodies to pieces and began to eat them. When he came to the unborn child carried by the woman he tossed it aside. It was unclean.

The daughter of the old man and woman waited at her family's lodge a long time. When it was clear to her something bad must have happened, she followed her parents' tracks to where they had been killed. She found their clothing and saw bones scattered about. All around were the tracks of a giant bear. She wailed at the site. Then, she heard a baby cry. She found it in the grass. It was a boy. She cleaned him with moss and put him in a wooden cup to keep him warm as she walked home. She named him Djakabish.

In the days that followed, Djakabish grew quickly. He began walking quite early. Within months he played in the forest and killed rabbits with stones. The girl decided to make him a bow. She made one of wood but the first time he stretched it, it broke. She made him one of deer ribs, but he broke it too.

He told his sister, "I will make a bow that will not break."

"No," his sister said, "you are too young and too small."

But he went out anyway, and cut a dry juniper, and from it he made four arrows. He cut a spruce and made a bow from it. Then he told his sister he was going hunting for squirrels, but really he planned to hunt for Katcheetohuskw, the monster bear that killed his parents.

Djakabish had not gone far when he found large bear tracks deep in the snow. He sang his hunting song. Katcheetohuskw heard him and told Black Bear, "go and kill the one who is singing."

Black Bear went out and approached Djakabish.

"Are you the one who killed my father?" Djakabish asked him.

"No. That was another," Black Bear replied.

"Then go and tell the one who did I am hunting him," Djakabish said, and he started to sing again.

Black Bear returned to the monster bear and told him the human boy was hunting him. Katcheetohuskw then sent White Bear to kill Djakabish.

White Bear went out. Djakabish saw him coming. He asked, "Are you the one who killed my father?"

White Bear said, "No, I did not."

"Then go and tell the one who did I am hunting him," and he started to sing again.

White bear returned and told Katcheetohuskw the boy was coming after him. Katcheetohuskw then sent Brown Bear. Soon Brown Bear returned with the same message. Katcheetohuskw asked him, "How big is this human boy?"

"He is not big at all. He is very small," replied Brown Bear.

"Alright," Katcheetohuskw said, "I will go and kill him myself!" and he went after the boy. Soon he saw Djakabish, and indeed, he was quite small. He was inside one of Katcheetohuskw's tracks trying to climb out. His bow and arrows were far below him. Katcheetohuskw hit him with his nose and Djakabish fell to where his bow and arrows lay. The blow made Djakabish grow much larger. He stood up and faced the monster bear.

"Who killed my father?" Djakabish asked.

"I did!" Katcheetohuskw thundered.

"How hard was my father to kill?" Djakabish asked. He had grown very big now.

"About as hard as dry juniper!" the monster replied.

Djakabish shot one of his arrows into a juniper. The tree shattered. "That was not hard enough," he said.

"No, he was hard as a rock," the monster said.

Djakabish shot an arrow at a nearby rock and it exploded into small pieces. Frightened, Katcheetohuskw started to run. Djakabish shot him in both hips with his two remaining arrows.

"You have killed me!" Katcheetohuskw yelled. "Cut my body into small pieces, eat my head, but keep my ears for your bed." Then he died.

Djakabish did what the monster bear said. He cut the carcass into pieces, and threw some of them into the air. These became birds and flew away. Some he dropped on the ground. These became animals and ran away.[27]

The slaying of a monster bear who has been killing people, killing all the food animals, or hoarding nuts or roots was a common motif in native America. Many of these stories are classified as culture-hero tales, since the slayer is generally responsible for making the world safe for people. The bear he destroys (usually it is a bear, although sometimes it is a mythological monster) is huge and possesses supernatural powers.

The Stiff-legged Bear tale was common to the entire eastern subarctic. But the distribution of closely related tales, tales considered part of the same legend complex, is much larger.[28] The sequence of events in the Djakabish version are: (1) monster bear kills hero's parents; (2) hero, who was still in mother's womb, is thrown away by bear; (3) hero is saved by relative and born from wooden cup; (4)

hero is precocious; (5) hero is given or makes bow and arrow; (6) hero meets and slays monster bear. The famous Bloodclot Boy story told by the Blackfeet, Gros Ventre, Arapaho, Dakota, Ponca, Iowa, Pawnee, and Kiowa is a simpler variant of the same story: monster bear kills hero's parents, hero grows miraculously in cup, develops precociously, and slays monster bear.

Bloodclot Boy is in turn related to another tale, the Twins tale, which was told by the Ojibwa, Cree, Menomini, Micmac, Sauk and Fox, Seneca, Arapaho, Caddo, and Wichita. The major episodes of this tale are: (1) monster slays pregnant woman; (2) from part of her remains a boy is born who is raised in the normal way (Lodge-boy); (3) from another part, a part that has been thrown away, a twin is born who is raised by animals (Throw-away); (4) Throw-away is caught by the family; (5) together the twins kill the monster. The simple pattern remains: monster slays woman, a part is thrown away, and vengeance is served.

Folklorist George Lankford has suggested that the group of stories evolved from a single and ancient hunting myth. He believes that the Djakabish version (because of the antiquity of Djakabish himself) is one of the oldest, and probably closest to the original.[29]

There are many other tales about heroes who destroy monsters in the form of bears, which do not fall into the Djakabish/Bloodclot/Twins legend complex. One such story comes from the Pueblos; and the Hopi version is representative. A bad bear is living on a mountain where cactus fruits and piñon nuts grow in abundance. The people are hungry and on the verge of starvation, but everyone who visits the mountain to gather food is killed. The villagers give a bow to an ugly boy, Pookong, who resembles a Kachina, and he leaves his village to hunt the bear. He finds it and kills it using his newly acquired weapon. The mountain is made safe. The people are saved.[30]

Another tale, "Night-rainbow and Grizzly Bear," told by the Coos Indians of western Oregon, is similar in many respects to the Djakabish tale of the Naskapi: The Night-rainbow people were living together in a village with their grandmother, Night-rainbow-old-woman. Her daughter and son-in-law are out hunting and find a field of camas. They pick some. Grizzly Bear suddenly appears, demanding, "Why did you pick it? The camas belongs to me!"

Grizzly Bear is so angry that he kills the couple and goes to the village and kills half the people. Rainbow-Old-Woman and her grandson (son of the couple who discovered the camas) survive. The boy grows up precociously. His grandmother makes him a bow. He goes out and finds and picks some camas. Grizzly Bear appears. The two fight, and the boy finally shoots the bear with an arrow and kills it. He returns home and tells his grandmother. The next day, when he goes out again, his grandmother dances the murder dance at home. Again the boy gathers camas. Another grizzly comes, this time a female. "Come!" she yells. "We two will fight. You are my enemy." They fight, and again the boy kills the bear with his bow. With all the evil grizzly bears now dead, the boy and his grandmother travel to the house of Grizzly Bear, where they find their murdered relatives, including the boy's parents. They bring them back to life and return home.[31]

Murderous giant bears and food-hoarding grizzlies are beings that must be destroyed. They threaten people and human culture. They represent a natural world without controls, the dangerous side of nature. The person who destroys these monsters is the culture hero, the savior, the one who makes the world safe for people. In pre-Columbian America, the bear sometimes maimed and killed people. It was the only animal that posed a consistent threat to humans, and it was therefore the proper monster for a hero to destroy. A myth of the Alsea Indians of the Oregon coast begins, "The world was very bad long ago. Everywhere it was so, and this was the cause of it: A bad person was devouring them long ago. Grizzly Bear was devouring them long ago."[32]

That tribes from all over North America so often chose bears for the role of ogre is evidence that Indians feared bears, and that the bear, especially the grizzly bear, was a threat.

*　　*　　*　　*　　*

In contrast, the bear in the next tale is benevolent. The story comes from the Mistassini Cree and was told to Adrian Tanner by Charlie Etap.[33]

The Boy Who was Kept by a Bear

A bear found a boy and kept him like a son for several years. Every summer the bear would hunt for all kinds of food—beaver, porcupines, other animals—and in the fall the bear and the child would collect blueberries. Then they gathered their food and took it to where they would spend the winter.

One fall the bear told the child he could sense the boy's father starting to sing. The bear tried to sing his own song to oppose the father, but the power of the man's singing was too strong for the bear, and it made him forget his song and stop singing.

Later, during the winter, the child's father started to sing again, and again he succeeded in defeating the bear's song. The next day the bear told the child that he could sense the father preparing himself and setting out to find them.

The father began walking straight towards the place where the bear and the child were staying. The bear tried to lead him astray. First, he threw a porcupine out of his den. At the same moment the man noticed the marks where a porcupine had been gnawing at a tree off to the side of his path. But the man just kept on walking straight, intending to kill the porcupine on his way home.

The bear called out, "I cannot defeat him! Straight! Straight! He comes walking to me!"

Next the bear threw out a beaver. At that moment the man was passing a lake, and he noticed it contained a beaver lodge. But he kept on walking ahead, meaning to investigate the beavers on his way home. The bear uttered the same cry, "I cannot defeat him! Straight! Straight! He comes walking to me!"

Finally, the bear threw out a partridge. At the same instant a bird flew out from under the snow near the father, and landed on the other side of his path. But the man kept on walking straight, meaning to kill the partridge later. The bear again makes his cry, "I cannot defeat him! Straight! Straight! He comes walking to me!"

Realizing the man's power was stronger than his, the bear used magic. He lay on his back with all four legs in the air whereupon an object came crashing out of the sky, causing a huge storm. But still the father kept coming towards the bear, and for the last time the bear called out, "I cannot defeat him! Straight! Straight! He comes walking to me!"

Knowing that he was about to be killed, the bear gave the son one of his forelegs, telling him to keep it wrapped up and hanging in his tent above the place where he always sat. He told the child that if he wanted to hunt bears he was to climb to a place where he could get a good view of the surroundings and look for the place where the smoke was rising. He was told that only he would be able to see it, and if he looked at that place he would always find a bear.

Then the child's father began to break through the snow covering the bear's den, the bear went outside, and the man killed him. He took his son home, and the boy looked after the bear's foreleg as he had been told to do. Later the boy got married, and was an extremely successful bear hunter. His hunting group lived almost entirely on bear meat. Sometimes he would tell another hunter where to look for a bear, and the man would look where he was told, and would always kill a bear.

The hunting group was visited by another group. The women of this group were very jealous, because the hero could find bears whenever he wanted, and their own husbands were never able to kill any. While the hero was off hunting for bears, of which he had previously found the location, one of the women of the second hunting group decided to look for the source of his power. She went into his tent, took down the package, and started to unwrap it. At the same moment the hero became aware of what was happening, and immediately returned to camp.

Catlinite effigy pipe. Pawnee. *Photo courtesy of the Linden-Museum, Stuttgart.*

For a while he could be heard outside his tent. Then he entered, but stayed sitting on the doorstep. He asked for the culprit; the woman admitted it was her. He told her that the following day she could find a bear by going to a particular place which he described.

He then removed his ammunition pouch, took off all his clothes, and went to sit at his accustomed place. Immediately, the leg fell down, and both he and the leg disappeared underground, leaving no trace behind. It was said that he had become a bear.[34]

This bear is benevolent. The boy in the beginning of the story was not stolen, seduced, or coerced by the bear. He was, we presume, lost. The bear found him and cared for him. They lived together as father and son. Even when the bear knew he was about to be killed by the boy's father, he remained kind and generous. Before he died, he gave the boy the power to find bears, a gift of great value in Cree society.

The only hint of antagonism is the song fight between the boy's natural father and the bear. Fights like this actually occurred in Cree culture. Shamans often dueled with song. In the end, the bear recognized the superior power of the boy's father and allowed himself to be killed.

The boy left the den but found himself between two worlds: that of his true father and that of his bear father. Being a great hunter of bears, he was respected among men. He was able to see the smoke from dens that bears but not humans could see. In the end he became a bear.

Stories of bears that help humans are as common as stories of malevolent bears. Universally, Indians considered the bear to be an animal of great spiritual power. People, especially men, were always seeking power, so there are many tales about men who acquire power from bears. Often these individuals would return to their home or village and use their power for good, and, sometimes, for evil (bear power is so strong that it is often difficult to control). Sometimes the person would accidentally violate a restriction, and the power would then go bad, or he would be killed by the bear.

*   *   *   *   *

The bear often plays a role in another kind of tale, the trickster tale. When Bear meets Trickster, Bear is slow-thinking, slow-moving, gullible, and usually the loser.

Two of these tales follow. In this first story, from the Arapaho, a group of bear women are visited by the most famous trickster of all, Coyote. The tale was popular across the Great Plains.[35]

Coyote and the Bear Women

Coyote went down the river, and walking near the edge of the shore he saw plums, full ripe. Farther down he saw just the top of a tipi, which was standing alone. He picked a few plums and went to the tipi. He went in and was welcomed by four women. Said they, "Well, Coyote, what has brought you here? What are you going to do?"

"Oh, my sisters and my nieces, I have brought you some plums. I found them close to the river, just a short distance from here. I wonder that you never get plums, they grow so near you! They are nice and good to eat," said he. He gave them to the women, and they ate them.

These women were all nursing babies. "Say, sisters, just make these children go to sleep. I shall look after them while you go and pick the plums."

So these women made hammocks inside of the tipi and placed their babies in them to sleep. When the women had gone, he took a big kettle, went to the river, filled it with water and hung it on a tripod over the fire.

The babies were sound asleep. He took a knife and cut their heads off and put the bodies into the kettle, placing the heads back in the hammocks.

The women returned, bringing plums in rawhide bags. "Say, sisters," said he, "while you were gone, I went out a short distance from here and found a den of gray wolves, and I took them out and killed them, and that is what I have boiling in the kettle for you all to eat."

The women thanked him for supplying them with food. "Well, sisters," he continued, "I am sweating from work, cooking a mess of wolves for you. I will have to go out to cool myself. When the wolves are done cooking you may help yourselves."

He went out and sat down by the door and pushed the edge of his robe inside. When these women dipped out the meat, they looked at one another, but finally went to eating.

One said, "Say, sisters, the meat tastes like our children."

"Oh! Don't say a thing like that; it is a very bad idea. The meat tastes strange because it is from gray wolves," said another of them.

Coyote kept pushing the edge of his robe to cause no suspicion among the women, but at the same time he was fixing to get away.

"Surely, sisters, this meat tastes like our children," said one of the women again.

Coyote cut off the edge of his robe to allay all suspicion and ran away secretly. After he had gone some distance from the tipi, he cried out to the women, "I have cooked your children! This time I have fooled you!"

The women went to the hammocks and found nothing but the heads of their children, which were carefully laid there. They then began to cry and scratch themselves for the love of their children.

Grizzly bear-claw necklace. Sauk and Fox. *Photo courtesy of the Buffalo Bill Historical Center, Cody, Wyoming.*

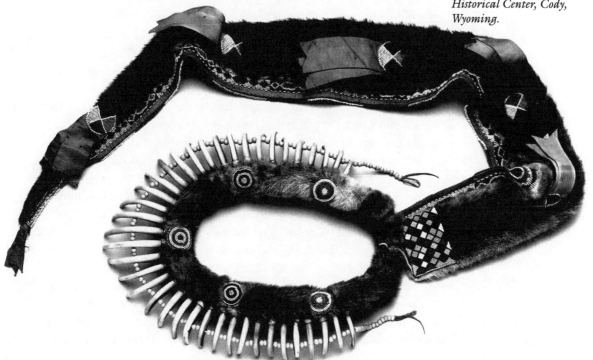

Now these women were female bears; so they started off, chasing Coyote. Coyote was getting away, but the women were about to catch him when he said, "I wish there was a hole in my path, where I am going so I could get to the other side!"

And so it happened, and he went into it and passed out at the other end, and continued to run for safety. The women reached the hole, and went in and came out the same way as Coyote had. Coyote saw them following his trail and cried again, "I wish there was a long hole where I am going."

So he came to another hole, passed into it for refuge and came out as before. The women also passed into the hole, out and after Coyote again. Coyote was now becoming tired, and the women approached nearer and nearer. "Now," said he, "I do wish that there was another hole for me to go into."

So he came to the foot of a hill where there was a hole, through which he passed, but having emerged, he turned and sealed one end, then he ran around the hill and painted himself with white paint to look like a different person. He took a willow stick, put feathers on it, and laid it across one arm. He came again to the entrance of the hole just as the bear-women were entering. "Now what is the trouble?" said he.

"Coyote fooled us," said they. "When we went to picking plums he cut the heads from our children and cooked them for us in a kettle. We are after him. He went into this hole."

Now the women were still crying and were out of breath from crying. "Well," said he, "you let me go into the hole while you stay outside. I will fetch him out all right."

So he went in, but came out again, telling the women that he had seen him inside, but that he looked very strong. Still he said he would go in and engage him this time. So he went in, and the women heard him making a great deal of fuss and howling. Finally he came out, with his face and hands pretty well scratched up, and with his clothing torn. "Say, women," said he, "he is a terrible man, but I am going to try again for your sakes."

But the women said no, that they had better go in themselves. "All right," said Coyote, "I shall watch him at the other end."

So the women went into the hole and looked for Coyote.

When they had gone, Coyote gathered sticks of wood and placed them by the hole and set them on fire. Then he heard one of the women say plainly, "I guess that there is a fire outside." "Oh! The fluttering birds have just passed," said Coyote, "go on and find him!"

He now placed more sticks on the fire, which made it smokey inside of the hole. "I guess that there is a fire outside, because it is smokey in here," said one of the women.

"Oh! The smoking birds have just passed by," said Coyote. He was still placing sticks of wood at the entrance of the hole. The smoke was pouring inside so thick that the women smothered to death. After the women made no effort inside, he went in and found them all dead. He dragged them out and cooked them for himself. Then he said, "What good luck I have, for I relish bear's meat."

*   *   *   *

In the last story of this chapter, Raven takes a turn at tricking Bear. This tale comes from the Tsimshian, but it was told all along the Northwest Coast.[36]

Raven Kills Grizzly Bear

There was no food with which Raven could satisfy his hunger. He began to cry, for he was very hungry; and he went on, not knowing which way to go. Finally he arrived on one side of a large bay, and saw a small house on the other side, and a small canoe on the beach in front of the house. Raven went toward the house and entered. In the house was an old man with his two wives. The house was full of dried fish—halibut and other kinds—and of dried meat of mountain goat, and there was fat and all kinds of dried berries. They spread a mat out, and let Raven sit on it. They gave him some of the good food they had, and while Raven was eating his meal, he said to his new friend, "May I join you tomorrow when you go out to catch halibut?"

Grizzly Bear said that he had no bait, but Raven replied, "We shall have bait from our own bodies." So Grizzly Bear consented and they went to bed.

When Raven knew that they were all asleep, he went out secretly to the creek, caught a salmon and cut off its tail. Early the following morning Raven went down first, launched Grizzly Bear's canoe, and then Grizzly Bear also went down.

They started for the fishing bank. When they reached the fishing ground, Raven pretended to cut off part of his testicles and to tie it on to his hook for bait. Grizzly Bear saw it, but he was afraid to do the same. Grizzly Bear was surprised when he saw what Raven was doing. Then Raven urged him, saying, "Go on! Do the same," but Grizzly was afraid to do so. He threw his knife to Grizzly Bear and Grizzly Bear took the knife, put his scrotum on the thwart, and cut off part of his own body. He fainted. When he woke, he felt that he was dying, he rushed at Raven, trying to kill him. Raven jumped out and clung to the bottom of the canoe. When he heard that Grizzly Bear was dead, he went back into the canoe. Then he went ashore and hurried toward the house.

He said to the two female grizzly bears, "Your husband has fainted, and he will die. If you want to bring him back to life, bring me two stones."

Then the two women went and brought each a small stone. Raven put these stones into the fire, and, when they were red hot, he told the women each to swallow one. The female grizzly bears trusted him. When the stones were red hot, Raven took two wooden tongs, took up the stones, and said to each of the women, "Now, open your mouth and close your eyes!"

They did so, and Raven put the hot stones into their mouths. Then they tumbled about, and Raven struck them until they were dead. Thus Raven

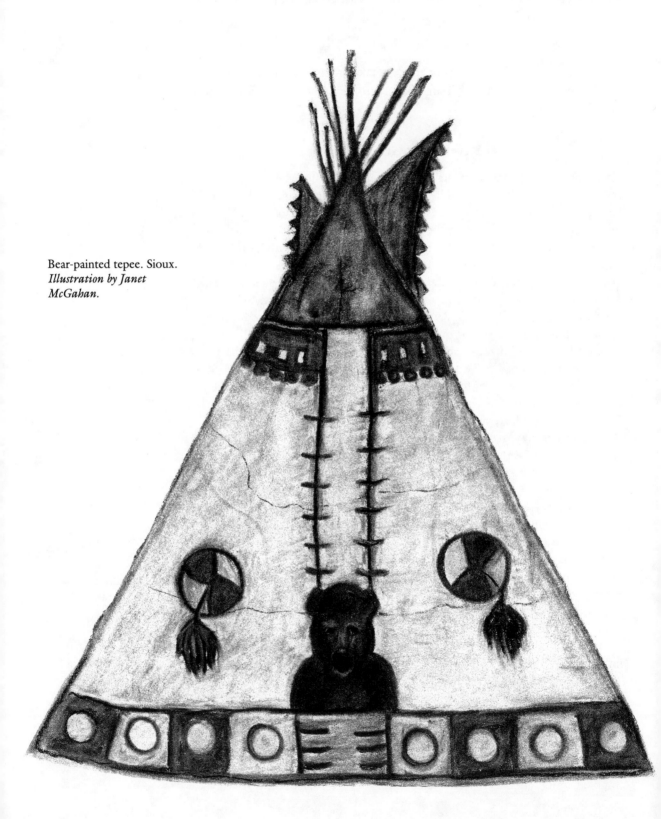

Bear-painted tepee. Sioux.
Illustration by Janet McGahan.

GIVING VOICE TO BEAR

killed three grizzly bears in one day. He went down to the beach at once and took out of the canoe the grizzly bear that he had killed. He cut it up first and then his two wives. Raven stayed there many days. He had a good time, and ate all he wanted every day.

The grizzly bears in these trickster stories are neither evil nor benevolent. They are good citizens minding their own business. But they are trusting, and that makes them easy prey for a prankish trickster. Their gullibility even frustrates their attempts at revenge, making them vulnerable and impotent. Perhaps it was for this depiction of the mighty bear that the Indians told these trickster-bear stories.

By virtue of the tales alone, it is easy to see the fascination that bears evoked in the Indian mind. The bear as seen by the Indian was large enough to encompass a host of characters. There are kind and generous bears in the stories, just as there are malicious and perverse bears. There are noble bears willing to sacrifice their lives for their families, and there are selfish, food-hoarding bears. There are cunning bears and bears that are easily duped, bears that threaten and destroy, and benign bears. Excepting humans, no other character appearing in the tales has that kind of range. Like gods in the Greek myths, bears in the Native American oral tradition possessed all the human fallibilities while retaining their godliness.

Bears invaded the Indian imagination. They demanded stories as they demanded rituals, and they invested those stories with every imaginable character.

The Bear Dance of the Sioux. Painting by George Catlin.   *Collection of the Glenbow Museum, Calgary, Alberta.*

Moving Like A Bear

NE TIME I WAS HUNTING. It was sunrise in the spring and I was looking for buffalo, climbing over hills and looking. I came on a bears' trail. Lots of tracks. I followed them to where the bears stood gathered by a tree, and I watched. They were performing a Sun Dance.

I hid with the wind in my face so they could not smell me. Bears are wicked animals when dancing! If they had seen me, they would have hunted me for miles. They danced in front of a pine tree painted yellow, red, and green. They made four steps forward and four steps backward, all the time they were looking at the pole. They also sang, and their singing was a growling.

They had built a midnight fire there. One of those bears was a *puhagant*, a medicine man. He made the fire. Bears have *puhagant* just like people. When they dance they pray for their children. Bears are smart. They act just like a person.[1]

AN EASTERN SHOSHONI MAN told this story to the Swedish ethnologist Ake Hultkrantz. Men and women from other tribes have also told about watching real bears dancing in the wild. The Pawnee said that when the bears dance they stand on their hind legs and lift their paws toward the sun. In Pawnee belief, that is the way bears receive their power. Pawnee Bear Society members dance with head down and palms up to receive the sun's rays.[2] They receive curing powers from the sun. The bear dances of Indians mimicked the movements of real bears. Indians moved as they saw bears move and as they believed bears moved when they danced.

In central California, in one of the Western Yokuts' most important ceremonies of the year, men and women danced a bear dance immediately after the acorn harvest in the fall. When the time came, those of the bear lineage who had also dreamed of a bear gathered together to decide when the dance would take place, who would participate, and who would prepare food for the visitors. Performed on just one night of the year, the ritual drew people from surrounding villages. As these visitors and the locals came together on the evening of the ceremony, the dancers—four men and one woman—readied themselves. The male dancers tied whole grizzly bearskins over their bodies, put on bear claw necklaces, and hung streamers of flicker feathers from their arms. The woman dancer dressed in her best clothes—a deerskin apron, beads, and a down headband—and carried bunches of crow feathers in her hands.

The five stood in a row and faced the crowd, the woman at the far left. A singer sat to one side and began to shake his rattle and sing, "My store of acorns is on that hill. I am Bear. I will drink from my little acorn mush basket." The male dancers turned to the left, and holding their feet together, they jumped forward three times, their movements slow and stiff. They cupped their hands over their mouths to amplify their voices, and they made the harsh grunting sound of a bear, "Xo! xo! xo!" After the third jump, they returned to their original positions. Then they repeated this pattern twice more. Meanwhile, the woman stood in one place with her hands at her shoulders, fingers spread, palms forward, and her elbows pulled tight against her body. Balanced on the balls of her feet, she bounced, turning the upper part of her body to the left and then to the right, twisting and bouncing as the men jumped.

The dance was short. When it ended, the traditional shouts went up for it to be repeated, but everyone knew that the Bear Dance could only be performed once a year in a single village.[3] People of the bear lineage waited to eat acorns until after it had been performed. This dance was a kind of "first fruits" ritual to ensure the continuing abundance of acorns. Bears ate acorns in abundance, so the Yokuts connected them to the harvest. They said, "Bears often dance with the oak trees so there will always be plenty of acorns."

In the 1920s, ethnologist Anne Gayton interviewed a seventy-year-old Yokuts named Jim Britches, who said that his wife once saw the bears dancing. She, her sister, and a cousin were out gathering seeds and saw a bear near a little white oak tree. They thought that the tree was his singer. As they watched from a safe distance, the bear jumped and grunted three times, then grabbed the tree and mauled it. "Three times he did this and then went off."[4]

Another Yokuts man provided Gayton with a similar account. He was out hunting. It was about sundown when he saw a small bear dancing beside an oak tree. The bear "was standing on his hind legs and holding up his paws; he jumped at the tree three times. Then he

clawed up some earth and threw it at the little tree. The tree was his singer and the little bear was mad because the singer made a mistake."[5]

Arikara bear dancers, dancing without bearskin costumes. *Photo by Edward S. Curtis.*

There were hundreds of bear dances in native North America, performed for many purposes. The Yokuts dance was a harvest rite. Other tribes, such as the Delaware, danced a bear dance to renew the world and the cycle of the seasons. A bear dance was part of a Pueblo winter solstice ceremony. At night, men and women met in a kiva, where they were visited by shamans and war leaders who entered in two lines, wearing bear-leg skins on their forearms and making bear noises and dancing.[6]

Many plains tribes, including the Lakota, performed bear dances to heal the sick and those injured in battle. Other plains tribes, such as the Assiniboin, danced as bears in preparation for war. The Kootenai and Maidu danced to pacify the grizzly bears so none of their people would be attacked. The Plains Cree danced before a bear hunt, donning entire bearskins and bear masks. Some tribes

Arikara bear dancers. After a photo by Edward S. Curtis. *Illustration by Janet McGahan.*

danced bear dances before initiation rituals, and some danced simply to welcome and honor the bears as they emerged from their dens.

Bear dances were ritual dramas with impromptu or fixed rhythmic movements, often sacred reenactments of events that had taken place at the beginning of time. The movement was a way of honoring an aspect of the sacred and of acknowledging something mysterious, such as a bear coming out of the earth in the spring. In the Blackfeet Grizzly Bear Dance, performed as a part of the Medicine Pipe transfer ceremony, a man would pull a robe over himself and dance to imitate a bear coming out of its den. The drummers chanted, "I begin to grow restless in the spring," and the dancer sang, "I take my robe. My robe is sacred. I wander in the summer." Still imitating a bear, the man would pick up a pipe and sing, "Sacred Chief! Everyone, men, women, and children will now behold you." He would then dance with the pipe as the drumming continued and the drummers sang more bear songs. Then he would hold up his hands like a bear holding up its paws. With his feet together he would jump backward and forward. Then he would lumber about, breathing heavily, digging, and lifting rocks as if looking for insects. He blew on his medicine whistle to imitate the Thunderbird and, with his left arm extended, would spread his fingers to represent the wings of the Thunderbird. In Blackfeet belief, Thunderbird comes in the spring, at the same time that the bear emerges.[7]

With their bearskin robes, bear claw necklaces, masks, vocalizations, and mimetic movements, bear dancers must have believed that they became what they portrayed. Those who watched the dancer imitating the bear probably perceived him as a bear. Joseph Epes Brown has written of the merging of symbol and reality in the Native American mind:

> The generally understood meaning of the symbol as a form that stands for or points to something other than the particular form or expression—is incomprehensible to the Indian. To the Indian's cognitive orientation, meanings generally are intuitively sensed and not secondarily interpreted through analysis; there tends to be a unity between form and idea or content. Here the "symbol" is, in a sense, that to which it refers. The tree at the center of the Sun Dance lodge does not just represent the axis of the world, but is that axis and is the center of the world. The eagle is not a symbol of the sun but is the sun in a certain sense; and similarly, the sun is not a symbol of the Creative Principle, but is that Principle as manifested in the sun. When a Navajo singer executes a sand painting of one of the gods, or *Yei*, the painting does not represent the god; the god is really present there and radiates toward all participants at the ceremony its particular grace or power.[8]

This recognition of the symbol as a form or expression of reality is evident in the many eyewitness accounts of bear dancers becoming real bears. These stories were told by Indians from eastern woodlands and midwestern plains tribes, where bear clans and bear societies played an important role. There are similar anecdotes from the northwest coast, the southeast, the southwest, and from the arctic and subarctic.

One sixty-year-old Yokuts man, Joe Pohot, recalled seeing a bear dancer when he was young. He said that the dancer's arms and legs were painted black. A number of people were standing around the dancer and they said, "If you are a bear, let's see your hair!" Pohot said, "At once the black portions turned into hair all over his arms and legs." [9]

Two brothers, Gohil and Tewus, were famous as Yokuts bear dancers at the turn of the century, because they were said to have always turned into bears when they danced. Tewus was "the worst of the two" because he "went around the country scaring people."[10]

The belief in such transformation was reenforced by the often realistic impersonations of bears and the lifelike costumes worn by dancers. When Lakota bear dreamers performed the bear ritual, it was said that they became possessed by the spirit of the bear. They breathed clouds of red clay from their mouths and they stuck grizzly canines under their lips so that the bear's teeth looked like their own. They chased people around and dug up prairie turnips out of the soil or shook wild plum trees to make the ripe fruit fall.

The bear in *pa'nongkasi*, the Maidu Bear Dance, from north central California, provides another example of a realistic impersonation. This dance was performed to protect the people from attack by grizzly bears. On the morning of the dance, the "grizzly bear," a man dressed in a full bearskin, came in from the forest. He shouted to make his arrival known and was answered from the dance house by a ceremonial clown. The bear came in carrying a bundle of sticks, which he gave to the chief. In return, the men in the house gave the bear presents of small skins and beads. When the bear was satisfied, he took off his bearskin, and the women from the village entered. Half a dozen men, wearing feather bands and carrying walking sticks and handfuls of shredded bullrushes, began to dance around the room, first one way then the other. They made four complete circuits and sat down; then the women stood and danced, wearing hats of badger skin decorated with feathers and holding shredded bullrushes against their breasts. When they finished, the men danced again, and then again the women. They alternated this way well into the night, until finally the bear impersonator disappeared behind a screen of mats and emerged wearing the bearskin again.

Seeing the bear, the people all stood and started crying and shouting and clapping their hands, making whatever noise they could. The bear ran one way and then the other around the inside of the dance house. On his third round he attacked a log sitting on the floor of the house. He picked it up and threw it from side to side and batted it with his paws. Four more times the bear disappeared and reappeared from behind the screen. Each time he emerged walking backwards and danced with his back toward the fire burning in the center of the house. He held his paws vertically with the palms in. When he finished the last series of dances, he left the house and returned to the forest, and the ceremony ended.[11]

Not all bear costumes looked as lifelike as the one in this Maidu dance. Some bear dancers wore no costume at all. Others only remotely resembled a bear. The Zuñi bear kachina, *Aincekoko*, was presented in two forms by the kachina dancers, one that looked like a bear, another that did not. In the realistic representation, the dancer's upper body was covered with a bearskin with the head attached. The bear head, with a single red feather ("the bear's feather") attached, covered his head entirely. The paws, decorated with

One of the Zuni bear kachinas. *Photo courtesy of the Smithsonian Institution, National Anthropological Archives.*

Moving Like A Bear

feathers, fit over his hands. He tied yucca around his wrists and wore beads like the Zuñi Society People. Over his lower body he wore a blue kilt covered with buckskin, an embroidered sash, and a woman's belt. On his feet he wore blue moccasins.

The more symbolic kachina had a white mask with red ears and red, blue, and black spots painted on it. The mouth was large and a red tongue hung out. Black hair covered the top of the mask, and a hawk feather came out of each ear. He wore the red bear's feather in his hair, yucca bands over both shoulders, and the beads. His body was painted red, his legs white. He wore a blue loin cloth, and over it a buckskin shirt with an embroidered sash and fox skin, a yucca band on his right wrist, a leather band on his left wrist, and blue moccasins.

The bear kachina came to the Zuñi Mixed Dance. In Zuñi mythology, the bear woke from his winter sleep in the distant east when he heard thunder in the spring. He was lonely after sleeping alone for so long in his cave. He had heard that the people would be dancing, and he wanted to dance with them, so he came down. "Sometimes he comes dressed like a kachina, but sometimes he comes like a real bear in a bearskin dress."[12]

The costume of the Bear Braves of the Blackfeet Bear Society included bearskin sashes decorated with bear claws and eagle tail feathers. Bear Braves made ears from the bearskin and tied them to the sides of their head and used charcoal to draw black lines down from their eyes. Their dance was that of an angry bear. As the dance opened, the Bear Braves sat in holes (representing dens) covered with buffalo robes, their heads bowed. Boys came and pelted them with dry buffalo and horse dung. Offended, the bears dropped their robes and sat up. They threw their bodies about, growled ferociously, and held their hands beside their ears. The youngsters ran away, and the bears covered themselves with their robes. When the boys returned to harass them again, the bears sprang to their feet and began to dance. At one point in the ritual, the bears charged other dancers who carried bags of pemmican. They grabbed the pemmican sacs, sat down, and devoured them.[13]

Another, more lighthearted, Blackfeet bear dance involved both male and female bear impersonators. To the accompaniment of singers, one man and three women rose. They held their hands against the sides of their foreheads with their fingers bent to suggest claws. Each of the women waddled up to a man and grabbed him roughly, as a bear might grab a person, and forced him to dance. Those watching shouted and laughed. Afterwards, the leader cut up a roll of tobacco and gave a piece to everyone. Then he gave them

Nane (grizzly bear dancer). The initiate imitates the bear in his dress and in the way he acts. One of the responsibilities of the grizzly bear dancers was to guard the dance house and punish those who violated the rules. Kwakiutl. *Photo by Edward S. Curtis.*

GIVING VOICE TO BEAR

Moving Like A Bear

each a single berry, which they held above their heads as they prayed. In the end, soup was served.[14]

In the eastern part of the continent, where there were no grizzlies, dancers imitated the less imposing black bear, and their dances were less violent then those found in the West, the bears portrayed as less choleric. In a winter bear dance, Cherokee dancers waddled and shuffled clockwise around a fire, swaying their bodies and heads from one side to another to the accompaniment of a drum. The dance leader periodically growled like a bear and shook his gourd rattle. The others grunted in response. At the climax, the dancers, both men and women, lifted their heads and clawed at the air above them. They said that they danced like the black bears who danced in the forest around hemlock trees. They said that the bears left tooth marks on the bark at head height. Sometimes during the dance, the leader imitated the comical antics of black bears.[15]

Bear dancer. Nootka. *Photo by Edward S. Curtis.*

The Iroquois also clowned. In a healing dance, two male singers, one with a small water drum and one with a horn rattle, made music. The patient sat with the two singers on a long bench in the center of the room. A male dance leader and his assistant stood at one end of the bench; two female leaders stood at the other end, facing the patient. All other adult Bear Society members sat along one wall, women on one end, men on the other.

The ritual began with a drum tremolo and three slow chants to call the bear spirit. (The bear spirit was believed to be present throughout the ceremony.) The male leader dropped tobacco into the fire and prayed. His assistant and the two female leaders filled their mouths with berry juice from a birch bark pail and spit it on the patient. To an accelerating drum beat, the singers chanted, "*ooneh jigwiiye*," "Now strip the bushes [of berries]." To this and four or five other songs, the leaders and the society members shuffled bear-like in a long line counterclockwise around the room. At first they moved slowly, almost lazily, with a lumbering waddle. One or two of the dancers left the line and moved into the center of the circle where, clowning, they imitated a bear. When these first songs ended, the dancers made puffing and blowing sounds and drank from the pail of berry juice and ate nuts. They passed a pipe, and everyone, including the patient, smoked and made an offering to the bear spirit. In a while the singing started again and the dances became more animated: dancers hopped and stomped their feet and turned from side to side as they moved. They yelled responses to the singer and took turns clowning, bear-fashion. Eventually the patient joined the dancing. The ritual finally ended with a prayer and a meal of corn soup.[16]

In the West, where both black bears and grizzly bears lived, one of the most popular and famous bear dances of all, the *mammaqunikap*, or Forward-Backward Dance, belonged originally to the Northern and Southern Ute Indians. It spread, however, in the nineteenth century to nearly all the Shoshonean-speaking tribes of the Great Basin.[17] Before it had been influenced much by whites, the Forward-Backward Dance was the most important religious ceremony of the year for the Utes. Later, under the influence of Christianity, it became merely a secular event, a social dance or festival.

In pre-Columbian times, the Utes used rasps and resonators in the *mammaqunikap*, making sounds like thunder to awaken the bears from their winter sleep. (They also believed that bears woke with the first thunder of spring.) They danced, just before they broke-up their winter camps, when their own supplies were low and they were ready to move in search of food, to help the hungry bears find food after their long winter fast. They believed that the ritual helped to bring about the end of the long winter and usher in the spring of the new year. And, because the bear was one of the powerful and dangerous animals of the mountains, they danced so the bear would not attack them. They prayed that the bear would help them

Painting on buckskin that depicts the Ute ceremonial Bear Dance.   *Photo courtesy of the Colorado Historical Society.*

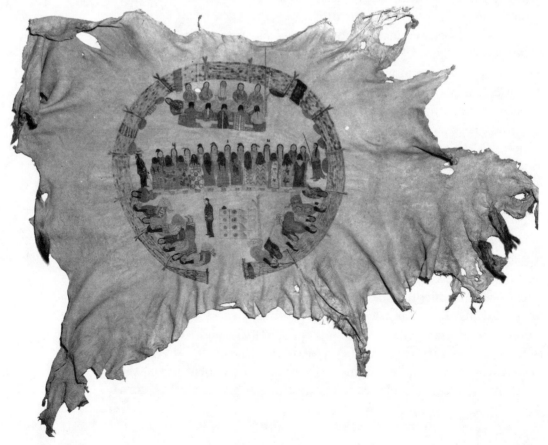

GIVING VOICE TO BEAR

Painting of bears dancing. Ute. *Photo courtesy of the Colorado Historical Society.*

in their quest for meat and berries and would prevent them from getting sick.

> In the fall the snow comes, and the bear has a wickiup in a hole. He stays there all winter, perhaps six moons. In the spring the snow goes, and he comes out. The bear dances up to a big tree on his hind-feet. He dances up and back, back and forth and sings, "Um, um, um, um!" He makes a path up to the tree, embraces it, and goes back again singing, "Um, um, um!" He dances very much, all the time.
>
> Now Indians do it, and call it the Bear Dance. It happens in the spring, and they do not dance in the winter. The bear understands the Bear Dance.[18]

A man who had dreamed of the bear decided on which days to hold the ceremony, but he always chose sometime in February or early March. To dance earlier or later risked angering the bears. This man also led the dance and organized the feast that followed. He had two assistants, each of whom carried cedar sticks painted with red ocher, which they used to prod the dancers. Another man, the dance song leader, took charge of the singing. All the songs used had to have been dreamed. A song served for only one year, so this man was one who had had success in dreaming bear songs. He organized other singers and taught them his songs.

The ceremony took four to eight days. On the morning of the

Moving Like A Bear

first, an old woman came out of her lodge and danced alone around the encampment in the pre-dawn light, imitating a bear. Holding her hands above her head, she stepped back and forth, back and forth. The Utes believed that bears danced this way to trees in the mountains. When she finished, the people came out from their lodges and worked on the dance place (or bear's den), a large, round, roofless brush enclosure about two hundred feet in diameter. The walls, made of cottonwood and birch branches woven between poles, were nine feet high. At one end, opposite the door, the men dug a hole about five feet long, two feet wide and two feet deep, which they covered with a basket or piece of wood. This hole, the Utes said, was "connected to the bears." The singers made booming thunder sounds to accompany their songs by running a stick across a long wood rasp over the hole. On the first day of the dance, the bears heard this "thunder" in their dens and woke up.

The people filed into the brush den. Women sat on the south side, men on the north, and the singers on the west. (The women were not allowed to approach the singers.) The rasps accompanied the songs, which imitated bear sounds. Many of the songs had a strong, monotonous rhythm with a downward glissando.

Women asked men to dance, and the men could not refuse. The women made a sport of capturing men who were hiding outside the enclosure and peeking in through the brush. During the first days, men and women danced facing each other in two long lines, moving first forward and then backward. The dancers occasionally mimicked bears. From time to time, the singers stopped to smoke and make offerings to the bear spirit. In the evening people broke for a short time to eat. As it grew dark, the dance leader built fires that lit up the enclosure, and people danced into the night.

Dancing on the second and third days was much like that on the first. Early, before sunrise, on the morning of the fourth day, two bear impersonators, one male and one female, came into the enclosure. (Among some Ute bands these two were dressed in full bearskin robes). In a drama representing the mating of bears, the woman growled and chased the man. This, the Utes said, is what the female bears do, "They chase their husbands."[19]

After the bear impersonators danced, the regular dancing resumed and went on nonstop all that day and night and into the next morning. The Utes believed that the bears were now out searching for food and might suffer or die if the dancing stopped. At this point, both men and women daubed white clay on their hair. The old men wore eagle feathers, and the women put eagle down in their hair.

During the last day and night, people danced in couples rather than in lines. The women grew more aggressive in their pursuit of the men. On the last morning, the final meal, a celebratory feast of buffalo tongues, waited at the door of the enclosure. The dances continued until someone fell from exhaustion. Then the dance leader, the man who had dreamed of Bear, took a rasp from one of the singers and circled clockwise. He held the rasp against different parts of the man or woman's body, then lifted it to his mouth and blew the evil away. Others who were sick came forward, and the leader treated them similarly. Then the feast began.

Native Americans incarnated the bear in countless rituals. They danced to bring the spring, to heal the sick, to ensure abundant plant foods, to guard themselves against their enemies. By imitating the bear, men and women celebrated and honored the animal and, even more important, the aspect of the sacred that it represented.

The dance of Grizzly Bear in the bow of the canoe. Kwakiutl. *Photo by Edward S. Curtis.*

An Oklahoma Delaware
bearskin suit with its mask,
pouch, cane, and rattle.
*Photo courtesy of the Museum
of the American Indian,
Heye Foundation, New York.*

"I Know Where the Bear is Living"

Twenyucis had a dream. Then she told the chief, about the time of the new moon when we celebrate the feast, "I know where the bear is living. So you call these young men to go and bring the bear."

The chief went and brought Maxkok. The chief told Maxkok, "Twelve men will go with you. All twelve men of the Big House."

Then Twenyucis told Maxkok, "Very near daybreak you will reach there. Then you will see a little creek which runs by. And the tree standing there is an oak. A little hole will be visible. Then the bear's nose will appear as though it comes out of the hole pushed through, his nose icy about the edge. Do not bring him. That is not a good one, it is a smooth bear. You will go on, down past him.

"Then you will see an elm tree leaning toward the east. Then you will look up. You will see a hole. That is the bear's home. Thence you cannot come back. There, accordingly, you stay all night. And then standing by that tree there, you are all standing around. Then you hit that tree. You tell the bear, 'I find you'. Then nothing will be heard. Then also you hit that tree three times. Tell the bear, 'I find you'."

All this the twelve men led by Maxkok did and it happened just as Twenyucis had dreamed it.

So they heard the bear moving about. Once more the tree was hit. He told [the bear], "You we have found." All these men look upward. All saw the bear's head sticking out. Then Maxkok told the bear, "Come down! The chief wants your body."

Then that bear climbed down. Then that bear came down on the ground. Then that bear let his head hang down on the ground. Surely like a dog he was ashamed of something. Maxkok told the bear, "The chief wants your body." Then he told the bear to turn around. Then that bear turned around. Maxkok told this bear, "That's enough." He told him, "Now you take the lead."

The bear went on ahead. Then these men all came behind him. Then they reached the little creek here. Then that bear lay down. Maxkok told him, "What is wrong? Get up!"

Truly that bear did not move. Then Maxkok told these men, "The bear will not come to the Big House." Then Maxkok pointed to one man. He told him, "So you will tell the chief that the bear refuses to come. You will go there yourself."

Then the chief came there. Then Maxkok told him, "The bear will not come to the Big House. So no more will there be a feast dance. Therefore you will have to kill the bear right here."

Then the chief told the bear, "Right here we will have to kill you. We want your body for the Big House."

Then that bear got up. His head was still hanging down on the ground, his eyes were closed. The chief hit him. Then he died. He never kicked. Then these men skinned him. Then that Maxkok picked up the bear skin. He gave it to the chief. Then the chief told these men, "Now will we go to the Big House. You men carry the bear. We, with the dead bear, will take the lead. You will come behind."

Then they reached the Big House. Then they went into the Big House, to the middle of the building. Then they lowered that bear on the ground.

Then that chief untied the old bear hide and put the old bear hide down on the ground. Then he wrapped the new hide around the center post, a little below where these false faces were hanging. Then that chief told the woman and one appointed man, "You cut up that bear. Help these women in the cooking."[1]

So BEGAN, in the words of the Munsee man Nekatcit, the last World Renewal Ceremony of the Munsee-Mahican Delawares. Perhaps the most complex of all bear rites in North America, it brought together in a single ceremony the religious symbols of the hunter with those of the agriculturalist. In so doing, the rite intertwined three symbols of renewal: the Bear, the Moon, and the World Tree. The ritual incorporated many circumpolar bear-hunting practices and juxtaposed the contrasting elements of the universe: sky with earth, male with female, water with land, and life with death.

The rite was actually a blending of two ancient ceremonies, one Mahican and one Munsee. These two tribes, culturally similar although each spoke a distinct eastern Algonquian dialect, originally lived in the Hudson River Valley, the Mahicans to the north in what is now western Vermont, the Munsee immediately south, along the Lower Hudson and Upper Delaware rivers. Another related group, the Unami lived south of the Munsee. Besieged by white civilization, some of the Munsee groups joined with Mahican bands, others affiliated with the Unami. Collectively these various bands were given the political name Delaware. The Munsee-Unami group ended up in Indian Territory (Oklahoma) and are now called Oklahoma Delaware. One of the Munsee-Mahican groups settled in Wisconsin on the Fox River. Another crossed into Ontario, where they joined the Iroquois on the Six Nations Reserve.[2]

This last group, the Canadian Munsee-Mahicans, held a twelve day World Renewal Ceremony at the start of the new year, of which the hunt, just described, is one part. The purpose of the ceremony was to celebrate the unity of all creation and the renewal of the earth. This ceremony, they said, ensured that the cycle of the seasons would be maintained and that the world would never depart from its accustomed ways.[3] The rite reenacted creation and emphasized beginnings: the beginning of a new year and the beginning of a new earth. Delaware mythology taught that the supreme being created the world and all its life anew every day.[4] For them, creation was a continuous, never-ending process. The World Renewal Ceremony guaranteed that it would continue.

The last Munsee-Mahican World Renewal Ceremony occurred in January 1850 on the Six Nations Reserve in Ontario. The description here is based on a 1930s reconstruction by an elder Munsee man, a traditionalist named Nekatcit who had learned the ritual in his youth from his father and other tribal elders. His recollections were recorded by ethnologist Frank Speck in a 1945 paper entitled "The Celestial Bear Comes Down to Earth."[5]

The ritual took place within a sacred space, a large east-west rectangular enclosure called *Xwate'k'an*, literally translated, "The Big House." The frame of this structure was hickory saplings set in the ground in pairs opposite each other and tied together in arches united by horizontal poles. The walls were covered by overlapping sheets of chestnut, elm, or birch bark. The center post was a massive log, a tree trunk, that reached from the floor to the ceiling. At the east and west ends were doors. A long narrow smoke hole ran the length of the roof, and a fire place was situated between each door and the center post. More recent Big Houses, those built after the introduction of metal axes and saws, took the same form but were made of logs and dimension lumber.

This structure, a microcosm of creation, represented the universe. The four walls were the four horizontal directions, the ceiling, the dome of the sky, and the dirt floor, the earth. In the Munsee-Mahican creation story, the supreme being put earth on the back of the Great Turtle. The Great Turtle, facing west, then rose from the waters, and the World Tree grew out of the earth on its back. Where part of the tree touched the earth a woman was created. Where part of it sprouted and grew skyward, a man was created. These, the first woman and the first man, became the parents of all of humanity, and the center floor area of the Big House represented not only the earth but also the back of the Great Turtle and the place of first creation.[6] The center post, actually the trunk of a massive tree, stood not just at the dimensional center of the lodge, but at what the Munsee-Mahicans understood to be the actual center of the world and the place of first creation. The center post was the World Tree, the central axis, reaching from the back of the Great Turtle and the womb of the earth, through the twelve levels of the universe, to the home of the supreme being. As the World Tree, it supported the sky, connected the layers of the universe, regenerated the earth periodically and faithfully, and provided a means of communication with the supreme being. Whoever or whatever climbed the tree became immortal.

Two carved wooden masks the size of a human face hung from this center post. One faced west and was white; the other faced east and was red. Two more masks hung above the doors and faced the center post: a white mask above the east door faced west; a red mask above the west door faced east. Together these four masks, two white ones facing west and two red ones facing east, represented the supreme being, called *Pa'tama'was*, "The Being Prayed To," and to him the Munsee-Mahicans directed the World Renewal Ceremony. They believed that he was there with them throughout the rites, at the top of the World Tree.

During the ceremony, men and women entered opposite doors and sat on opposite ends of the Big House. The women came through the east door and sat on the east side; the white mask and the east fire were theirs. The men entered and sat on the west side, and the red mask above the west door and the fire on that side was theirs. The Munsee-Mahicans associated women with life and plants because women gave birth and tended the plants. They identified the earth with women because all things are born from the earth. They associated men with death and animals and the sky because men hunted and killed animals and fought as warriors, and because the sky was opposite the earth as man is opposite woman. The east, then, belonged to women because that is where the sun rises. The west belonged to men because that is where the sun, turning red, sets or dies. The Munsee said, "The sun and everything else goes toward the west, even the dead when they die." Likewise, men owned the color red; it represented violence and the hunt. White, on the other hand, belonged to women because it represented peace.[7]

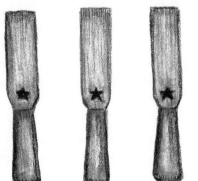

Folded deerhide drum used in the ceremony. The top half (the men's half) is painted red. The lower half belongs to the women and is white. Both the bear and the moon are in black. Below are the prayer sticks used to beat the drum. After a drawing in Speck, *The Celestial Bear. Illustration by Janet McGahan.*

The identification of colors with the sexes may also be related to a tale about the constellation Ursa Major. The sky bear, wounded by a group of celestial hunters, bled over the earth and turned the autumn leaves red. Later its white grease fell as snow. The hunters identified with the color red, and women, who traditionally rendered the grease, with the color white.

During the ceremony, four male singer-drummers sat west of the center post, on the men's side. They sat in two pairs, facing each other, with a drum of folded deerhide between them, resting on their knees. Half of this drum, the west half, was painted red with a black bear at its center. The other half, the woman's half, was white, and in its center was a new moon, also in black. Though it had a male and a female side, the Delaware identified the drum with the men. The singer-drummers beat it with foot-long, red and white, paddle-shaped pieces of wood that the Munsee-Mahicans called prayer sticks. These twelve prayer sticks represented the branches of the World Tree that had dropped from the sky as *Pa'tama'was* climbed through the twelve layers of the universe.

Another instrument used during the ceremony, and identified with the women, was the turtle shell rattle, called simply "shaken instrument." It was made by sewing a few small rocks inside an empty, painted turtle shell. Only the Magical Men, those who recited their visions, used it, and then only during their recitations. It represented the Great Turtle, the cosmic mediator.

As a reflection of the universe and its inherent dualism, the structure of the Big House revealed the opposites of water and earth, of earth and sky, of life and death, and of woman and man. The Great Turtle brought together these contrasting elements. By shaking the turtle shell rattle up and down, the Magical Men united heaven and earth and brought the sky beings in contact with the earth beings and the dead together with the living. When they shook the rattle sideways, they unified men and women and the water with the land.

As their creation mythology suggests, the Delaware considered turtles to be sacred animals. Turtles move easily between land and water. They lay eggs like birds but are four-legged. They eat both meat and plants. The Munsee-Mahicans were also struck by the repeating pattern of twelve or twelve-plus-one in the scales of the turtle's shell.

The number twelve itself was sacred to the Munsee-Mahicans, perhaps because they divided the year into twelve to thirteen lunar periods, and perhaps because of its relationship to the numbers three and four, which were more fundamental and also sacred to the Delaware. At any rate, they believed that twelve realms or layers of sky separated them from *Pa'tama'was*. Their World Renewal Ceremony lasted twelve nights and required twelve prayer sticks and twelve prayer cries. There were twelve Selected Men who escorted the bear from its den and twelve Magical Men who recited visions.

According to Speck, the placement of the instruments and other furnishings in the Big House and the positions occupied by the ceremonial officials corresponded to the positions of the stars forming the constellation Ursa Major. And, he wrote, "The acts and movements of the ritual performers parallel the movements of Ursa major as the events of the annual life cycle of the earth bear symbolically rotate with those of the Sky Bear. Furthermore, the earth bear sacrificed in the ceremony is conceived as a fragment of the celestial bear, and everything done during the ritual is a transcendental reference to him."[8]

(Like Europeans, Native Americans in many parts of North America saw a bear in the constellation known as Ursa Major or the Big Dipper. For the Munsee-Mahicans, the bear was the rectangle of stars that forms the scoop part of the dipper. The three stars making up the handle and stars from the constellation Bootes were hunters in pursuit of the bear. In the spring the bear emerged from its den, the Corona Borealis, and the hunters pursued it all summer long and into the fall, when they finally killed it. But the celestial bear, like earth bears, was immortal; it came to life again every spring to revolve once more around the North Star.)

The spiritual and political leader of the band, the chief, led the World Renewal Ceremony. He sat in a place of honor on a white painted hide or bench between the north wall and the center post, half of his body on the women's side, the other half on the men's. The sacred turtle rattle rested between him and the center post. He oversaw all the activities of the World Renewal Ceremony and ensured that each step of the ritual was done properly.

In Munsee-Mahican society, one woman ranked higher than the chief. She was called the chief-maker and she held the position of ultimate authority in the band. As her title implies, she had the responsibility of appointing the chief and the power of unseating him if she deemed it necessary.

Women held an unusual place of distinction in this culture. Frank Speck attributed it to the Delaware's veneration of the earth as Mother and woman as the source of life. He wrote, "Life begins with woman, so runs the Delaware belief. The life principle of the people as a group, accordingly, dwells in the person of a certain woman, the chief-maker."9

Further, the whole Delaware tribe took the designation of "women" in their relations with the Iroquois, while the entire Iroquois tribe assumed the designation "men." The Delaware were so labeled because of their role as advisors, moderators, and peace-makers. Among both the Delaware and the Iroquois, women held greater social and political powers than men when it came to advisement and peacemaking. Women were considered socially superior to men, and the Delaware therefore considered it an honor to be called women.10

A woman also began the World Renewal Ceremony, when she dreamed the location of a bear in its den and directed the hunters where to find it. It was unusual in native North America for a woman to play this role, because the hunt, even a special ritualized hunt such as this, was normally the province of men.

The twelve men who went out and found the bear and brought it back to the Big House were called Selected Men. During the rest of the year these men served as warriors, advisors, and prophets. It was their responsibility to find the bear that had been dreamed by the woman, call it from its den, and drive it back to the Big House, where it was killed beneath the center post. They also danced the first dance of the ceremony.

Another group of twelve men, the holy men of the tribe, who

were called Magical Men, recited their visions during the ceremony. Some of these men also served as Selected Men, and in the Big House the two groups sat together on the men's side, apart from the other men, facing the center post with their backs to the south wall.

Sweepers, who sat at each door, periodically swept the Big House with turkey or eagle wings to clear away dangerous forces. They also helped people find their places as they entered. The east sweeper handed the turtle-shell rattle to the Magical Men when it came time for them to recite their visions. The turtle rattle then moved east to west from Magical Man to Magical Man until it came finally to the west sweeper, who returned it to the chief.

The World Renewal Ceremony was the first formal sacred rite of the Munsee-Mahican year and began with the new moon of January, the moon they called *Withke'katen*, the "Moon of the New Year." Sometime during the winter, a woman would dream the location of a bear in its den. Apparently the bear was always a male bear; Delaware hunters would not kill female bears.[11] In January, when it came time for the World Renewal Ceremony, she summoned the chief and told him of her dream. He sent for the twelve Selected Men. They gathered, and the woman told them where to find the bear. Following her instructions, they traveled, sometimes for one or two days, and found the tree she described. They camped beneath it that night, and in the morning the leader hit the tree with his ax and called to the bear, saying, "We found you Grandfather! Come down! The chief wants your body!" He badgered the animal by calling to it and hitting the tree until it emerged from the hole and climbed down. Once it was on the ground, the men gathered around it. The leader said, "Grandfather, the chief wants you in the Big House. We will follow you there."

Walking behind and on each side of the bear, the twelve men drove it through the forest and then through the village to the Big House. They guided it through the east door to the base of the center post and circled around it. The chief entered carrying his ax and approached the bear. He killed it with a single blow to the head. As the bear lay beneath the center post, he spoke to its spirit, telling it to climb the center post and report to the sky beings that everything was right on earth, that the ceremony had begun.

Several of the Selected Men skinned the bear, starting at the throat and cutting downward to the tail—opposite the way they skinned other animals. A bearskin from the previous year's bear still hung on the east side of the center post. The chief untied it and took it down, and in its place he tied the new bear's hide so that its nose just touched the chin of the white mask.[12] The two sweepers appointed two men to carry the skinned carcass out of the Big House through the east door. The chief appointed several women and one man to cut it up, supervised by the two sweepers. After the meat was cut, the women washed and boiled it.

That night all the people gathered in the Big House. Everyone entered through the east door on the first night. Every night thereafter, however, the men used the west door, the women, the east. Once everyone was inside, the men divided into two opposing teams for a tug-of-war contest. One team represented the women and lined up on the east side, the other team represented the men and stood on the west side. The spectators placed bets as the two groups pulled on opposite ends of a long pole. The chief stood in the center, with one foot on each side of the line, and told the teams when to start. The team that pulled the other across the center line won. After the contest, the chief gave a speech. He explained the purpose of the ceremony and gave thanks to *Pa'tama'was* and all the sky beings and earth beings of the universe. He welcomed the spirits of departed relatives (they believed that deceased relatives and friends stood side by side with the living throughout the ceremony). He prayed that the world would continue in its "accustomed ways" and that the people would have a good year. The sweepers then ritually served a helping of bear meat to all those gathered in the Big House. After eating, the people went home for the night.

With the exception of the tug-of-war contest, which only happened on the first night, the pattern of the next three nights was the same. On the fifth night the ceremony changed. The moon was at first quarter stage. Early in the evening, the sweepers prepared the Big House. For the first time they placed two red-painted hides or benches just west of the center post where the singer-drummers were to sit. The people came in and took their places, and, for the last time in the ceremony, the chief spoke. When he finished, it was time for the Magical Men to recite their visions, a ritual called *alo'man*. In preparation, the west sweeper took the red and white deerhide drum and the red and white prayersticks from the bag and gave them to the drummer-singers. The east sweeper went to the center post and received the turtle shell rattle from the chief. He took it to the south side of the Big House and placed it on the ground before the easternmost Magical Man. The Magical Man picked it up and began to shake it up and down and sideways, reciting in a singing fashion one of his visions. As he sang he danced across the Big House to the center post, moved around it counterclockwise, and then returned to his seat. He danced with short, shuffling steps, his body erect. When he returned to his seat, the singer-drummers repeated his song while beating their drum. When they finished, he passed the rattle to the next Magical Man, who then recited his vision in the same manner.

The final and largest feast of bear meat also came on the fifth night, after the recitations had ended. As on the previous nights, the two sweepers brought in the cooked bear meat through the east door and placed it at the foot of the center post. They served everyone present, beginning in the east with the women, one sweeper moving down each side of the Big House. On this night the feast continued until all the meat was eaten. When everyone had finished, the sweepers carefully gathered up the bones and burned them in the east fire. In all of the nightly feasts only unsalted bear meat was eaten, and it was taboo to eat any corn foods or other plant foods within the Big House during the ceremony.

After the feast the chief announced three dances. The first was the Man's Dance, which only the young men danced, moving counterclockwise around the center post, accompanied by drumming. Then the men and women danced together in the Mixed Dance. They formed a single line and shuffled counterclockwise around the center post. The last sacred dance was the Woman's Dance and, with the exception of a male singer-drummer who led the dance, it was for women only. It followed the same counterclockwise course as the other dances. These three dances continued until dawn. Just before sunrise, the sweepers quickly put away the instruments, and the people went home to rest until it grew dark again.

The sixth, seventh, and eighth nights of the ceremony were much the same as the fifth night, but without the chief's speech and the feast of bear meat. The holy men continued reciting their visions, and the people danced the three sacred dances. At daybreak following the eighth night, the sweepers put the instruments for the bear ceremony into their hide bag, where they would stay until the next year. During the last four nights of the ceremony, the sweepers brought out the instruments used for social dances and festivities— the water drum and the horn rattles—and the chief called for a series of animal dances, ceremonial games, and masked performances. The mood of the ceremonial leaders and the dancers lightened, and the ritual became a celebration. It ended early on the morning following the twelfth night.

In this ritual, as in the bear hunting ritual of the Cree, the bear was a messenger for the people. The Munsee-Mahicans believed that it revealed its secret location to a woman in her dreams so that it might once again be sacrificed to renew the earth. The Munsee-Mahicans believed that, when the chief killed the bear beneath the center post, it died at the base of the World Tree, or pillar of the

The "shaken instrument" or turtle shell rattle used by the magical men as they recited their visions. *Illustration by Janet McGahan.*

world, and that, over the course of the twelve-day ceremony, its spirit climbed the World Tree through the twelve layers of the heavens to carry the message of the people to the creator. That message, like the message carried by the bear killed in the Cree ceremony, was a prayer that the cycle of the seasons would continue, that there would be abundant plant and animal foods, and that the world would not depart from its ways.

At the time of first contact with white civilization, the neolithic Delaware bands were in a state of transition between a northern gathering-hunting culture and that characteristic of the southern farming tribes. The women grew corn, squash, and beans in riverside garden plots, but they also gathered huge quantities of wild plant foods and shellfish. All winter, the men hunted and fished in family hunting territories. American Indian religions scholar Werner Müller has written that the part played by the bear in the ceremony "belongs to the universal heritage of subarctic peoples; but the dualism characteristic of North American maize-growing tribes is also evident."[13]

When the Munsee-Mahicans killed a bear for food, rather than for the World Renewal Ceremony, the rite was essentially the same as the Cree bear hunting ritual. Like other subarctic and woodland hunting peoples in North America, Europe, and Asia, the Munsee-Mahicans hunted the bear in its den using only an ax or a club. They spoke to the bear before and after they killed it, calling it Grandfather. They held a ritual eat-all feast of bear meat and disposed of the bones in a prescribed manner (by burning).[14] The bear hunt in the World Renewal Ceremony is probably derived from this rite, and so it belonged to the hunters. The rite marked the climax of the hunting season and guaranteed the rebirth of animals killed in the hunt and a continued supply of meat. In climbing the World Tree, the earth bear became immortal, just as the stars and the sky-bear Ursa Major are immortal.

The dualism in the ceremony, which Müller refers to as characteristic of maize growers, includes the male-female division of the Big House, the two colors, the two doors, the two fires, the two faces on the center post, and the ritual tug-of-war between the men and the women, as well as the opposition of earth and sky, land and sea. Annual rites among agrarian societies in North America were generally more complex than the hunting rites of gatherer-hunters. The cultivators sought a new earth, rich and fertile with new life. Their rites came at the end of the old year and the beginning of the new, the time when the earth moves naturally from death to life. From the agricultural point of view, the bear in the ceremony represented the vegetation spirit in animal form, the god that must die to be reborn.[15]

The World Renewal Ceremony was complex and rich in its symbolism, perhaps more so than any other bear ceremony in North America, because it had been created in a culture that was between two distinct modes of living. The psychology of the semi-nomadic gatherer-hunter is, in many ways, opposed to that of the farmer. To a certain extent this opposition was played out in the ceremony, which emphasized the male's role as hunter and the female's as cultivator. Yet, from both the hunter's and the cultivator's perspective, the central theme of the rite was rebirth. In either case the bear was the perfect symbol.

Frank Speck observed among the Oklahoma Delaware a New Year ceremony that also combined hunting rites with agrarian rites. Their annual world renewal ritual, called the Big House Ceremony, differed somewhat from that of the Canadian Delaware. Beginning on the fourth day of the Oklahoma ceremony, some of the men partook in a three-day ritual hunt, but their hunt was for deer, not bear. A bear or a bear-like being did appear in the ritual, however: Just as the hunters gathered to leave the Big House, a dancer, called the Mask Spirit, entered dressed from head to foot in a bearskin and wearing a wooden mask painted half red and half black (the two colors of the Oklahoma Big House). The Mask Spirit was called *Misinghalikun*, or "Living Solid Face," and was associated with the hunt. He was, in fact, the Keeper of the Game or Owner of the Animals, the guardian of all the wild beings of the forest, and the one who released the deer and other animals to the hunters. They said they sometimes saw him in the forest. He rode on the back of a large buck, and he herded the deer. (The Canadian Delaware did not have the Mask Spirit Dance, but the members of their Mask Society, which they borrowed from the Iroquois, wore bearskins.)

As the hunters prepared to leave the Big House, the Masked

Spirit entered and stood near the Center Post. He listened to the instructions that the leader gave to the hunters. He then accompanied the hunters a short distance into the forest and saw them off, while the leader put twelve pinches of tobacco into the fire. The Mask Spirit returned to the Big House a few moments later, to dance and sing while shaking a turtle shell rattle. Although it is said that at one time the Mask Spirit attended all twelve nights of the ritual, he appeared only one time in the ceremonies observed by Speck and other ethnographers.[16]

The Oklahoma Delaware directed one other ceremony to the Mask Spirit, a summertime dance and feast of corn. In this ceremony, the Mask Spirit was both Owner of the Animals and Guardian of the Corn.[17] They performed the ceremony because, they said, if they did not the Mask Spirit would bring disease and misfortune upon the family charged with keeping the mask and bearskin costume.

The bear appeared in other Oklahoma Delaware rituals as well, some associated with the hunt and some with the corn harvest. The bear hunting rites found among all the Delaware bands and the Grease-Drinking Ceremony that Speck described for the Oklahoma Delaware[18] are examples of the kinds of rites one finds among hunting tribes. But the Doll Dance is an example of an agricultural ritual.[19]

The Doll Dance was directed to the Corn Mother but implicated the bear. The foundation myth for this family ritual explains that once, long ago, the Corn Mother unleashed a terrible sickness on the people because they had abused the corn plants. Before she would remove the curse, she demanded that they perform the Doll Dance. In this ceremony, which took place only at night, the Corn Mother, in the form of a doll made from the parts of a corn plant, was fed meat and corn. The people danced twelve dances, one for each lunar month of the year. Then, as Werner Müller explains, "at sunrise, twelve attendants form a line facing east, holding dishes of food in their left hands, in readiness to hand them to the participants in the ceremony. The men at the north and south ends of the row carry large figures baked from maize flour; the northern figure represents the maize mother in woman's shape, the southern one a bear. At a word of command these effigy loaves are cast crosswise among the participants, who take the fragments and go home content."[20]

Along a northern stretch of the eastern coast of North America, centuries before the European invasion, small groups of women with their children kneeled on river banks to tend modest plots of corn and squash and beans. In the fall these same women visited the forest

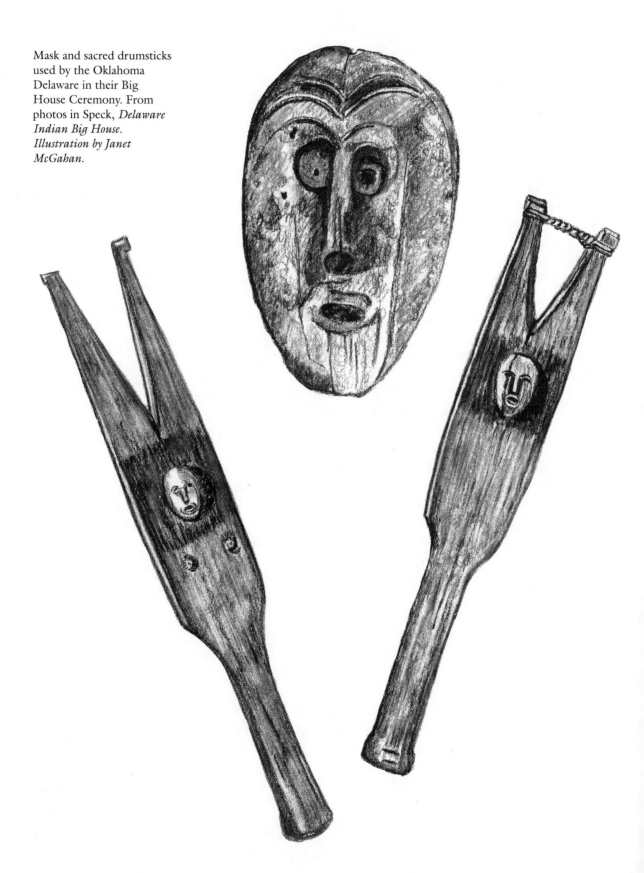

Mask and sacred drumsticks
used by the Oklahoma
Delaware in their Big
House Ceremony. From
photos in Speck, *Delaware
Indian Big House.
Illustration by Janet
McGahan.*

in small groups to gather berries, and at other times they stood ankle deep in tidal pools picking shellfish. And then, when winter came, they moved with their children and husbands inland to ancient family hunting grounds, where the men killed deer and moose and, late in the winter when food was scarce, bear. All winter long these people hunted and tanned hides. They cooked and ate the fresh-killed meat and the dried foods from the previous summer. During the dark evenings they told their stories. From time to time they thought of spring and of summer and their gardens. They watched the night sky, noticed the change in the position of the Bear constellation, and knew that soon it would be time for the Big House again.

It is ironic that, the last time the Munsee-Mahicans held their World Renewal Ceremony, the bear they sacrificed refused to go all the way to the Big House. The twelve Selected Men drove it toward the village for a full day, but to their dismay it stopped at the bend of a small creek, just a few hundred yards from their destination. Maxkok, the leader of the twelve men, tried to prod the bear, but it would not move any closer. Finally in desperation, he sent for the chief. "The bear will not come to the Big House," Maxkok said. "So no more will there be a feast dance." The chief killed the bear there, and they held the ceremony anyway. But it was the last time, and it marked the end of the Delaware's traditional way of life. Within a year many of the ceremonial men, including Maxkok, had converted to Christianity.[21]

Bear feast of the Ainu, a people inhabiting the northernmost islands of Japan. *Photo courtesy of the Smithsonian Institution.*

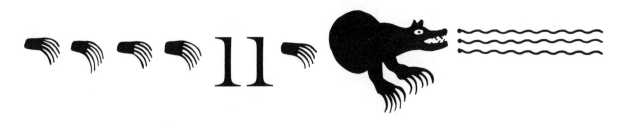

Honey-Paws in the Old World

WHEN OLD VAINAMOINEN   now encountered the bear;
he upset the satiny beds,   overturned the lovely couches;
he says these words,   made this remark:
"Thanks be, God,   be praised, sole Creator,
for having given me bruin as my share,   the gold of the wilderness as booty.
If I set out for bruin's door,   to snub-nose's cattle yard,
to tiny eye's farmyard,   to look at my gold—
the legs are short, the knees bandy—   soft stub-nose,
my bear, my darling,   honey-paws, my beauty
do not get angry without any reason.   I did not lay you low.
You slipped from a shaft-bow,   you misstepped from an evergreen branch,
your wooden pants torn through,   your evergreen shirt ripped across.
'Autumn weather is slippery,   winter days are dark'.
My bear, my darling,   honey-paws, my beauty,
you still have ground to cover,   heath to clamber upon.
Start, splendid one, to go,   glory of the forest, to step along,
blue stockings, to trip along,   nimble of foot, to go
from this little farmyard,   from these narrow trails
to a crowd of people,   a group of men.
There is a storehouse made of old   on silver legs,
on golden posts   where we will take our guest,
transport our treasure.   There no one will ill-treat you,
there one is fed honey,   given fresh mead to drink.
Set out now from here as if you were really setting out   from this little nest,
from your twiggy pillow,   from your piny bed
to a red couch,   a silken bed
under a splendid rooftree,   under a beautiful roof.
Slide quickly on the snow   like a water lily in a pool;
glide lightly on the evergreen bough   like a squirrel on a branch."

179

IN THESE LINES from Rune twenty-eight of Elias Lonnrot's *Old Kalevala*, a collection of traditional Finnish poetry, the hero, Vainamoinen, has killed a bear at its den with his spear. Speaking to the dead animal, addressing its spirit, he invites it to come with him. And in the verses that follow these, he brings it home. He sings loudly and plays music as he goes. When he arrives, the home folk rush out of their cabins and into the courtyard to welcome the bear, calling it Blue-tail and Honey-eater and Glory of the Wilderness. Vainamoinen calls back to them:

The Illustrious is coming,   pride and beauty of the forest,
   'Tis the Master comes among us,   covered with his friendly fur-robe.
   Welcome, Otso, welcome, Light-foot,   Welcome, Loved-one from the Glenwood!

From the courtyard, the home folk welcome the bear into the house. They tell Vainamoinen to lead the animal into the dining hall, and they tell the bear not to fear the young women, the "curly-head-ed virgins." They say:

   Maidens hasten to their chambers   when dear Otso joins their number
      when the hero comes among them.

They then skin and butcher the bear, cook the meat in a copper kettle, and serve it in a great feast.

As they eat they ask Vainamoinen to tell how he killed the bear. He answers that he did not kill it. It fell and stumbled, misstepped, he claims. Dead branches broke its breastbone and twigs slit open the belly. They ask him where the bear was born. "On the shoulders of the Great Bear," he replies, "on the back of the Big Dipper." They devour the bear's meat and drink down its grease and sing and perform small ceremonies while the meat is consumed.

After the feast Vainamoinen takes the skull back to the forest. When he returns he tells the home folk:

   I put it in a fine tree,   in a hundred-branched evergreen,
      on the brushiest branch,   on the broadest leafy spray,
      gums pointing to the east,   aiming at the southwest,
      obliquely due north.   I did not set it in the crown;
      there the wind would destroy it,   the cold spring wind treat it badly.

The verse ends with old Vainamoinen praying that he will kill more bears so that he and his family will have the same good fortune in the future.

In the attitudes of its participants and in specific ceremonial observances, this Finnish hunt resembles the Cree hunt described in chapter 3. The bears were different—the Finns hunted the Eurasian Brown Bear (*Ursus arctos*), whereas the Cree pursued the American Black Bear (*Ursus americanus)*—but fundamentally the rites were the same. And it was not only the Cree and the Finns that shared the tradition. The bear hunting ritual of many northern American hunting tribes—virtually all the northern and northeastern Algonquian-speaking groups and certain northern Athapaskans—was the same as that of the indigenous peoples of northern Europe and Asia.

The correspondences begin with naming the animal. Like subarctic and eastern woodland American Indians, northern Europeans and Asians had an elaborate synonymy for the bear and avoided the generic word (the word equivalent to our word bear). It seems that the most common names, used by almost every group on both continents were Grandfather and Grandmother. But a tribe or band typically had dozens of alternative labels. The Cree used Chief's Son, Black-food, Short-tail, Big-great-food, Angry-one, The One Who Owns the Chin. Others called it The Unmentionable One, That Big Hairy One, and Sticky-mouth. The Koyukon of Alaska, an Athapaskan-speaking tribe, used Black Place, Dark Thing, and, simply, The Animal. Among the many names used for brown bears by the Finns are Apple of the Forest, Pride of the Woodlands, Famous Lightfoot, Blue-tail, and Snub-nose. The Lapps called it The Old Man with the Fur Garment. The Estonians called it Broad-foot. The ancient Hungarians borrowed the Slavic term for bear, *medve*, and thereby avoided using their own word for bear. On the Kolyma lowland of Siberia, the Yukaghir referred to the bear as Owner of the Earth or Great Man. And on Hokkaido, the northern-most island of Japan, the Ainu called it The Divine One Who Rules the Mountains.[1]

As it was among most subarctic and eastern woodland tribes in native North America, the bear hunt in Europe and Asia was a two-stage affair. First the hunter located the den. Second, he returned to the den, usually early in the spring, and killed the bear. And, as in North America, bear hunters in the Old World killed bears with archaic striking or thrusting weapons such as spears, clubs, and axes. Even when guns were available, hunters preferred the older weapons that put them in close range, in hand-to-hand combat with the bear.

Divination was also central to bear hunting in both Europe and Asia. A variety of means were used. Some groups employed the bones of animals, mostly scapulas. Others used a bear hide or a bear's paws. During the bear feast among the Ostyak and Vogul of western Siberia, the man who had killed the bear shot an arrow at the lodge without looking. If it struck a high beam, it meant he would have

good luck and would kill another bear. If he struck a lower beam, he would not fair as well.[2]

Recall the Cree belief that *Memekwesiw*, Spirit Boss of the Bears, told the hunter in a dream where to find a bear's den. In the *Old Kalevala*, Vainamoinen describes how Tapio, the Owner of the Animals, led him to the den. The Siberians also said that the Owner of the Animals showed them where to find bears. All of these people, Eurasians and Native Americans, directed prayers to this supernatural being, the Keeper of the Game. They believed that the bear's spirit went to its owner after the feast and reported how it had been treated by the hunter and his band. If the people treated the bear well, the Owner of the Animals was pleased and released more animals. If for any reason he judged the people unworthy, he withheld game.

When a Cree hunter reached the den, he called to the bear, saying, "Grandfather, I've found you, so come out! Allow yourself to be killed!" Siberian hunters did the same. Ket hunters called the bear out, telling it, "Come out, Old Man! Come out and run like the elk!"[3] Another Siberian tribe, the Lamut, had hunters surround the den and sing, "Grandfather, Old One, Our Grandmother, and the Older sister of yours, Dantra, ordered you saying, Do not frighten us! Die of your own choice!"[4] Siberians and northern Europeans believed, as did the Cree, that the bear gave itself to the hunter. It wanted to be killed by him.

Then the atonement. On both continents hunters made apologies to the animal after they killed it. In northeastern North America a hunter begged the slain animal, saying something like, "I am sorry. Do not be angry! I killed you because I need your skin for my coat and your flesh so that I can eat, because I have nothing to live on." Sometimes he blamed the killing on someone else. The Ojibwa often said that it was an Englishman. Siberians did the same, often apologizing profusely and saying "It was not I Grandfather, it was the Russians who killed you through me. I am grieved, I am truly grieved. Be not angry with me."[5]

On both continents, hunters made offerings to the dead bear. When they brought the carcass into camp, women, especially young women, often left or covered their faces. The people chased dogs away. They decorated the carcass, and sometime later they carefully skinned and butchered and cooked it in a prescribed manner. They reserved certain parts of the animal—almost always the heart and head and very often the entire front half—for the men, saving what was left for the women and children.

Among the Lapps, the women ate separately from the men. After the men's feast was under way, the feast-giver selected two men to

The honoring of a slain bear by the Voguls, a hunting and herding people of the northern Ural mountains. The eyes and the nose of the animal are covered as a protective measure.
Photo by J. A. Kannisto.

carry some meat to the women. As they approached the women's hut they sang a short song: "Here come the men out of Sweden, Poland, England and France." The women answered them by singing, "You men who are come from Sweden, Poland, England and France, we will tie red strings round your legs." When the two came in, the women did tie red strings around their legs.[6]

Often, in Europe and Asia as in America, all of the meat had to be eaten in one meal. In such an eat-all feast, any meat that could not be consumed was burned in the fire. Under no circumstances were dogs allowed to eat bear meat or chew bones or hide.

At the end of the meal the hunter or his wife decorated the skull and hung it in a special tree. They protected other bones as well, and disposed of them in prescribed ways; burning or burying them, returning them to the den, or hanging them in the same tree as the skull.

This bear hunting ritual has, because of its circumpolar distribution (it forms a nearly continuous band from Lapland to Labrador), intrigued explorers and ethnologists for two hundred years. In his monograph on the subject, Irving Hallowell asked the question, "Do the resemblances in customs represent the result of convergent, but historically distinct, developments, or is there any reason to believe that they may have originally sprung from common historical roots?"[7]

Convincingly, Hallowell argued the latter, that the rites diffused from some common point of origin. And he suggested that they were very old, possibly even paleolithic. Largely, he based his argument on the observation that the bear hunting ritual had precisely the same distribution as a number of other material and cultural traits. These other traits, identified by various American, Russian, and Scandinavian ethnographers, include the use of the snowshoe and a companion moccasin, a particular style of clothing, cradle boards, the shaman's hand drum, the birch bark canoe, and the conical lodge or tepee style of dwelling; a characteristic technique of dressing animal skins; certain techniques of divination; certain theories of disease; techniques of driving game; and important myths and tales. In Hallowell's words, the bear hunting ritual "was one of the characteristic features of an ancient Boreal culture, Old World in origin and closely associated with the pursuit of the reindeer."[8] Some of the traits became modified with particular peoples, but the specific correspondences remain striking. That the rite was maintained for so long by so many peoples over such a large geographical area is an indication of the bear's power as a religious symbol.

There is a different explanation for why certain other rites are found both in native North American and in the Old World, rituals that are clearly not related in any historical sense, but which are nevertheless remarkably similar. Unlike the ritual bear hunt, these traditions do not have a common origin. They are examples of analogous rites, of separate groups independently choosing the same symbol to express the same religious concepts.

Recall that before an Ojibwa girl reached puberty she was called *wemukowe*, or "she is going to be a bear." When her menstrual flow started she lived isolated in a hut away from her family and village for several days and was called *mukowe*, "she is a bear."[9]

In classical Greece at Brauron, near Athens, it was required as a precondition of marriage that girls be initiated in a rite called *arkteia*. The tradition required the girls to undergo a period of seclusion outside the city, in the isolated sanctuary of Artemis. During their segregation the girls were called *arktoi*, or "she-bears," and it is said that they behaved like bears. They "neither washed nor cared for themselves in any way, spoke roughly and were called bear cubs."[10] The girls also participated in a feast dedicated to Artemis, when they danced the *arkteuein*, "acting the she-bear."[11] They started the dance wearing orange-yellow robes called *krokoton* (at one time they may have worn bearskins), and they mimicked bears walking on their hind legs. Later they removed their robes and danced nude. Small illustrated pottery jars found in the excavations of the temple show the girls holding torches and wreaths, dancing either naked or wearing the short chiton. The dance is also mentioned in Aristophanes' comedy *Lysistrata*, when the chorus-leader recounts the various sacral duties that she performed as a girl:

> At the age of seven at once I carried the secret objects. Then I was a corn-grinder. At ten for the presiding goddess I was a bear shedding the saffron-robe at the Brauronia, and some time I carried in a basket a bunch of dried figs when I was a fine young girl.[12]

The foundation myth for the ritual explains that at one time a she-bear lived at the temple of the goddess or, in another version, a wild bear entered the temple. Attic youths killed it and unleashed the wrath of the goddess. A terrible pestilence or famine followed. Apollo (Artemis' twin brother) ordered that a girl had to be sacrificed to "the bear Artemis" before the disaster would end. A man named Embaros volunteered to sacrifice his daughter, but instead he hid her in the temple, dressed a goat to look like her, and sacrificed it to the goddess. According to the myth, Artemis accepted the sacrifice, and the epidemic ended. From then on the local people regularly sacrificed a goat to the goddess, and girls, in imitation of Embaros' daughter, hid themselves in the temple and danced as she-bears, imitating the real bear that once visited there.[13]

There are veiled references to other southeastern European bear initiations as well, including rites for males. Herodotus wrote of a Thracian cult centered on Zalmoxis, which included a simulated death—fasting within a "cave-like place"—and a rebirth with the promise of immortality.[14] Greeks living on the Hellespont and the Black Sea told Herodotos that Zalmoxis was a slave of Pythagoras. Others affirmed this, explaining:

> Pythagoras had yet another lad, whom he had got from Thrace, named Zalmoxis because at birth a bear-skin had been thrown over him; for the Thracians call the [bear] skin zalmos.[15]

The cult of Zalmoxis, scholars believe, was a bear cult concerned with death and resurrection and, ultimately, with immortality, just as the Midewiwin Society of the Ojibwa was concerned with immortality. According to the foundation myth for the Thracian rite, Zalmoxis, having been freed from slavery, returned to Thrace to preach that death is not an end. He built a large banquet hall and held great feasts during which he "set forth his doctrine that neither himself nor his guests nor yet their children's children should die, but should come to that very place and there should live forever in enjoyment of every happiness." Then he disappeared beneath the hall into an underground chamber, and his followers mourned him as dead. But after three years underground he reappeared to prove that what he said was true.[16]

The guardian spirit concept in native North America also has a European counterpart. The bear dreamers of the Great Plains tribes were known as great warriors. In battle they led fearless charges. They believed that their helping spirit, the bear, would protect them. They fought like bears and believed they possessed bear power. Often the only weapon they carried was a bear knife. Crow bear men painted their bodies with mud and vowed to storm the enemy's camp, whatever the odds, swearing that they would never retreat in combat.

Among the Germanic peoples of northern Europe there was an elite class of warriors called berserks (ber = bear and serk = skin), who were analogous in certain respects to the bear dreamers of the Great Plains. Berserks fought without armor, sometimes naked or wearing only a bearskin. "They bit their shields and were as strong as bears or boars; they slew men, but neither fire nor iron could hurt them. This is known as 'running berserk'."[17]

Tacitus described a group of berserks who painted their bodies black and attacked their enemies in the darkness of night. "The terrifying shadow of such a fiendish army inspires a mortal panic, for no enemy can stand so strange and devilish a sight."[18]

Berserk warriors worshipped a war god who, they believed, made them immortal. In battle they became wild and frenzied, their ecstasy so complete and their trust in their god and the powers of the bear so strong that they believed themselves to be invulnerable to injury and danger, men "whom the iron bit not." They were feared enough to be treated as an elite class, free from the laws that ruled ordinary members of the society. In the ninth century in Norway they served in the king's bodyguard. They are depicted on ancient Scandinavian helmet plates as half-human, half-bear figures carrying weapons.[19]

Like Native American bear dreamers, berserks were said to be shape-shifters, able to change into bears at will. The legendary warrior Bodvar Bjarki, who served Denmark's King Hrolf, supposedly fought battles in the form of a terrible bear. The story says that Bjarki would suddenly fall into a death-like trance as one of his souls took the form of a bear and left his body. Simultaneously, on the battlefield, a great bear would appear in a horrible rage and kill everyone. After the battle the bear disappeared from the battlefield, and Bjarki reawakened as his bear-soul reentered his body.[20]

The bear's role as a guardian was not limited to berserk warriors. Welsh legend presents King Arthur as a bear,[21] and some say his name comes from the old Celtic *artos*, a word that means bear. If so, the name is related to Artio, the Celtic bear goddess associated with the bears of Berne.[22] And it is accepted that several famous English crests carrying the image of a bear, including those of the Nevilles and the earls of Warwick, originated with a knight of the Round Table, Arthgal, whose emblem was a bear.[23]

The story of a Basque hunter who claimed to have been killed by a bear parallels the initiation experience of certain North American shamans, who saw themselves devoured by a bear spirit and then given new life. Afterward, the hunter said, the bear breathed its own soul into him, and he claimed that his soul was really that of a bear.[24]

Europeans and Siberians also told bear tales similar to those told by Native Americans. In North America one of the most popular stories in the western subarctic is about a girl who marries a bear (chapter 8). The Tungus, a nomadic tribe of central Siberia, tell a variant of the tale (the two are close enough that it is possible for one to have been derived from the other). A girl is kidnapped by a large bear who takes her to his den. They sleep through the winter, the girl receiving nourishment by sucking the bear's paw. Summer comes, and they live together on a mountainside, as husband and wife. One day, while picking berries, the girl encounters her brother-

Artio, the bear goddess, feeds a bear. The inscription reads, "Licinia Sabinilla dedicated this to the Goddess Artio." Found at Berne ("Bear-City"), Switzerland.

in-law, a great shaman, who has been searching for her all winter. Her brother-in-law transforms himself into a bear and fights the real bear. The shaman wins, and the girl returns home with him. Sometime later she gives birth to a boy who has the ears of a bear. They call him Bear-Ear and he becomes the father of all future generations of Tungus.[25]

Tales of women who willingly marry bears or of bears that kidnap and rape women are common in European and Russian folklore. In fact, one of the oldest and most widespread folktales of the Old World, upon which *Beowulf*, *The Odyssey*, and several Old Norse sagas are based, is the bear-son tale. As the tale begins, a woman is stolen by a bear, who becomes her husband. She gives birth to a very large and extraordinarily strong half-human, half-bear child. The bulk of the tale deals with the exploits of this bear-son hero, who overcomes a series of monsters. Beowulf, Odysseus, and the Old Norse heros Hygelac, Grettir, and Bodvar Bjarki are all clones of this supernatural bear-son.[26]

The bear-wife, bear-son legend even found its way into nineteenth century European literature. The French writer Prosper

188

Merimee's novel *Lokis* is based on a variant of the ancient tale. The novel is about a Lithuanian count whose mother was raped by a bear. The count, as a consequence, is half bear and possesses an unmistakable bearish nature: he loves to climb trees, terrifies domestic animals, is prone to sudden acts of savage violence, and embraces the girl he eventually marries with a crushing hug. He murders her on their wedding night; she is found with teeth marks in her throat.

There are other curious correspondences between the continents as well. Many North American tribes identified the bear with thunder, because they believed that bears emerged from their dens with the first thunder of spring. In Europe, in the northern languages, the god of thunder and the bear are synonymous.[27] Even more surprising is the fact that many Native Americans referred to the constellation Ursa Major as the Bear long before Columbus arrived on the continent.

Like Native Americans, Europeans considered the bear to be a curing animal. Apparently, bears in Europe also ate plants that the people used as medicines. Until about two hundred years ago, it was the custom in Europe to parade live bears decorated with bits of colored cloth through towns and villages. People purchased bits of the cloth and snipits of the bear's hair to ward off sickness.[28] Even Socrates is quoted as having encountered Zalmoxis (bearskin) healers who gave him a medicine and a spell to cure headaches.[29]

There were also European rites that corresponded with the World Renewal Ceremony of the Delaware. Until the beginning of this century, in England on the day after Plough Monday (the first Monday after Epiphany on January 6), a procession of young men led a man dressed as a bear from house to house. They called him the Straw-bear because his costume was made of straw, and at each house he danced for money. Likewise in the farming villages of Germany and Czechoslovakia in late February or early March, a man dressed in straw and called the *Fastnachtsbar*, or Shrovetide Bear, was led by a rope from door to door. In some communities he wore a bear-mask, in others he dressed in a bearskin. At each house the straw-bear danced with the women and girls and was given in return food and money. Everyone had to dance on that day if the grain and vegetables and flax of the coming year were to thrive. The harder they danced, they believed, the better their crops would grow. Women plucked straw from the "bear" and put it in the nests of their geese and hens, believing that it would make them lay more eggs.[30]

In England this rite fell on the day after Plough Monday, the first day of plowing for the year. In Germany and Czechoslovakia, the date varied but hovered around middle to late February or early March. Elsewhere it came on the winter solstice, when the days began to lengthen. As with the Delaware World Renewal Ceremony, it marked the end of winter, the end of the dead season. The rite ensured the return of life and the coming of spring.

In both New World and Old the bear was the god of vegetation who suffers, dies, and is reborn. In Sweden the straw bear was replaced by a straw goat. Like the bear, the man acting the goat was led from house to house. But in the end the straw goat was ritually killed. The actor feigned death and came to life again, for the god of vegetation must die to be reborn.

Another ritual drama enacted a wedding ceremony that paralleled the Oklahoma Delaware Doll Dance. The "Sacred Marriage" wed the male god of vegetation, in the shape of a bear, with the earth goddess. Until recently, the town of Arles-sur-Tech, at the base of the Pyrenees in southern France, held the rite on the Sunday following Candlemas. The people built a mock cave in the town square. A young man from the village put on a bearskin and acted like a bear. A woman dressed as the returning spirit of vegetation. As people gathered, the "bear" went through the crowd, scaring all the women as he searched for his bride, Rosetta. When he finally found her he took her back to his den. There the two sat at a huge table covered with cakes and wine. The "wedding celebration" ended with a great feast.[31]

A similar rite survives in contemporary Crete in the cave of Acrotiri near ancient Kydonia, but "Rosetta" has been replaced by the Virgin Mary, and the rite is in her honor. She is known as *Panagia* (Mary) *Arkoudiotissa* ("she of the bear"), and her identification with the rite stems in part from the Christian commemoration of Candlemas as the time when the Virgin Mary came to the temple for purification after the birth of Christ.[32] When this rite was practiced in Greece centuries earlier, the goddess who married the bear was Artemis or Demeter.

Like the male god of vegetation who dies and is reborn, the earth goddess in ancient Greece was also tied to the rebirth of vegetation. Demeter's daughter, Persephone, was the maiden goddess of spring, who each year died and retreated to the underworld, taking with her the growing vegetation. Like a bear, she returned in the spring, bringing with her the lengthening days and abundant fields. Her death and resurrection accounted for the cycle of the seasons. Her reappearance ensured the coming of spring.

Candlemas, on February second, the date of the Sacred Marriage, is also celebrated as the day when Persephone returns from the underworld. It is also considered to be the day when the bears

Terracotta sculpture of the goddess in her animal form with the new born god of vegetation. Vinca Culture. *Photo courtesy of Kosovska Mitrovica, Yugoslavia.*

emerge. In contemporary America, February second is Ground Hog Day, but in Poland, Hungary, and Austria it is still celebrated as Bear's Day, the day when the bear comes fourth from its den to look for its shadow.

Bears have a long association with the agricultural communities of Europe. At neolithic sites in Bulgaria, Romania, Hungary, and Yugoslavia, sites that date back to the sixth and seventh millennia B.C., researchers have found hundreds of clay figurines representing bears. The work of archaeologist Marija Gimbutas and others suggests that they are epiphanies of the ancient mother goddess in her animal form. They depict a bear-headed woman seated on a throne decorated with crescents. Some of the sculptures show the bear holding her left breast, emphasizing her role as nurturing mother. Some are painted with red and black bands. A large number show a bear, or a woman with a bear mask, holding and nursing a cub. Many of the bear women carry bags suspended from ropes over their necks. Gimbutas calls these terracotta sculptures "bear nurses," and she believes that they are images of the goddess protecting the Divine Child, the new born god of vegetation.[33]

The Divine Child, portrayed here as a bear cub, is the goddess's son or fosterling, and her lover. He is the god of vegetation, who suffers, dies, and is born again. He was still worshiped thousands of years later in Greece, western Asia Minor, Crete, and Italy. He was Dionysus and he was the young Cretan Zeus, born in the Cave of Dikte, who was, according to legend, nursed by a bear.[34] He was also Zalmoxis, whose name means "bearskin." Later he was the Strawbear and the Shrovetide Bear. The worship of his female counterpart, the bear nurse, continued as well. She came to be known as Artemis, but she had dozens of local names. Whatever her name, she was the Lady of Wild Nature, present everywhere in the mountains and fields. Her worshipers identified her with the moon, with its cycles of waxing and waning. They associated her with wildlife, as a huntress, but also as a protector of animals, especially the young and innocent. She protected women in childbirth and all little children. A cave at Amnisos, near Cnossus, was consecrated to Artemis *Eileithyia* (childbirth). In Rome, as Diana, they called her "Opener of the Womb."[35]

On her dark side, Artemis was terrifying, a destroyer linked with famine, disease, and death—the devouring Terrible Mother. Her wrath caused women to die in childbirth. At Brauron, she induced madness.[36] She demanded the sacrifice of animals.

> They bring and cast upon the altar living things of all sorts, both edible birds and all manner of victims. . . . And they lay on the altar also the fruits of cultivated trees. Then they set fire to the wood. I saw

indeed a bear and other beasts struggling to get out of the first force of the flames and escaping by sheer strength. But those who threw them in drag them up again on to the fire.[37]

Artemis also ruled the plants and the growth and regeneration of vegetation, and in this capacity she was associated with the cult of Demeter and Persephone. Some scholars consider Persephone and Artemis to be "two sides of the same reality."[38] Artemis also died to be reborn, like her child and lover, the male god of vegetation.

As the Delaware connected the corn mother with the bear, Europeans associated Artemis with the bear. The animal was sacred to her. As Atalanta, she was cared for and nursed in her infancy by a she-bear. In Arcadia, as Kallisto, Zeus changed her into a bear and later immortalized her as the constellation Ursa Major, the Great She-Bear. At Brauron and Munychia, where young girls danced as bears in her honor, she was called Bear. In northern Europe, too, she went by the names of Ursula and Artio, both bear names. The Christian Church later adopted the bear goddess Ursula, transforming her into Saint Ursula. The Virgin Mary, too, became identified with Artemis and the bear. Medieval writers noted that the bear was her animal.[39]

The traditions are fascinating, the correspondences even more so. They are both strange and remarkable because they link, in basic ways, peoples as diverse as one can imagine—the hunting-gathering Cree Indians of James Bay and the reindeer herders of Lapland, the Athenians of classical Greece and eighteenth century Great Lakes Ojibwa, Lakota visionaries and Danish warriors, European peasant farmers and Delaware Indian farmer-hunters.

Some of these traditions, such as the hunt, have a single place of origin and diffused outward. Others, such as the custom of identifying initiates with bears, arose spontaneously in many different places. Both circumstances speak for the bear's enduring power as a religious symbol.

Religious symbols are not the product of an intellectual process. People do not *choose* their symbols, at least not through rational thought. They arise spontaneously and are recognized and comprehended immediately, without reflection. As a religious symbol, the bear has bridged language and culture barriers and conveyed its messages across continents and through millennia. The most potent of those messages is that of its own life cycle.

Seated bear carved out of cedar and painted red and black. Tlingit. *Photo courtesy of the Lowie Museum of Anthropology, University of California at Berkeley.*

12

Beneath is a Bear

I AM WANDERING over a great mountain; the way is lonely, wild, and difficult. A woman comes down from the sky to accompany and help me. She is all bright with light hair and shining eyes. Now and then she vanishes. After going on for some time alone I notice that I have left my stick somewhere, and must turn back to fetch it. To do this I have to pass a terrible monster, an enormous bear. When I came this way the first time I had to pass it, but then the woman from the sky protected me. Just as I am passing the beast and he is about to come at me, she stands beside me again, and at her look, the bear lies down quietly and lets us pass. Then the sky-woman vanishes again.[1]

THESE WORDS DESCRIBE A DREAM of a middle-aged, twentieth-century woman, one of Carl Jung's "normal or slightly neurotic" patients. In his investigations of the unconscious, Jung employed the dreams, fantasies, delusions, and what he called the active imaginations (spontaneous, visual images that arise from concentration on a significant dream-like image) of both normal and insane individuals. The maternally protective goddess of this dream, Jung wrote, is "somehow related to bears, a kind of Diana or the Gallo-Roman Dea Artio." The sky-woman, he believed, is the positive aspect of the goddess, the bear is the negative.[2]

In another Earth Mother dream, also from a middle-aged woman, the goddess is again aligned with the bear:

We go through a door into a tower-like room, where we climb a long flight of steps. On one of the topmost steps I read an inscription: "Vis ut sis" (Will So That You Might Be). The steps end in a temple situated on the crest of a wooded mountain, and there is no other approach. It is the shrine of Ursanna, the bear-goddess and Mother of God in one. The temple is of red stone. Bloody sacrifices are offered there. Animals are standing about the alter. In order to enter the temple precincts one has to be transformed into an animal—a beast of the forest. The temple has the form of a cross with equal arms and a circular space in the middle, which is not roofed, so that one can look straight up at the sky and the constellation of the Bear. On the alter in the middle of the open room there stands the moon-bowl, from which smoke or vapor continually rises. There is also a huge image of the goddess, but it cannot be seen clearly. The worshippers, who have been changed into animals and to whom I also belong, have to touch the goddess's foot with their own foot, where upon the image gives them a sign or an oracular utterance like "Vis ut sis."[3]

In this dream, a primordial or Earth Mother figure emerges as an Artemis-like bear goddess. Called by the dreamer "Ursanna," she dwells in a temple of red stone open to the sky and her constellation, Ursa Major. She is related to the moon and to animal sacrifice.

Another dream, this time from a forty-seven-year-old male, also seems to connect the bear with the goddess. It was collected by Jung's colleague and friend Marie-Louise von Franz.

I am on a platform, and below me I see a huge, black, beautiful she-bear with a rough but well-groomed coat. She is standing on her hind legs, and on a stone slab she is polishing a flat oval black stone, which becomes increasingly shiny. Not far away a lioness and her cub do the same thing, but the stones they are polishing are bigger and round in shape. After a while the she-bear turns into a fat, naked woman with black hair and dark, fiery eyes. I behave in an erotically provocative way toward her, and suddenly she moves nearer in order to catch me. I get frightened and take refuge up on the building of scaffolding where I was before.[4]

In his *Collected Works*, Carl Jung recorded just one other bear dream. In it, the dreamer describes falling into an abyss. At the bottom he encountered a bear whose eyes gleamed alternately in four colors. The bear disappeared, and the dreamer passed into a long, dark tunnel. In Jung's analysis, the bear in this dream represents the chthonic element, a kind of guardian of the underworld, ready to seize and consume the dreamer.

Jung asserted that just as there are mythological motifs, there are typical motifs in dreams—certain situations and types of figures "that repeat themselves frequently and have a corresponding meaning." Among the types of figures, or archetypes, is the Earth Mother, who emerges in two of these dreams as a bear goddess. Based on dreams and images in art, myth, and literature, Jung described the principal characteristics of this Earth Mother figure. She is always related to the

Bear-painted tepee. Sioux.
Illustration by Janet McGahan.

Beneath is a Bear

underworld and is occasionally related to the moon, either through blood-sacrifice or a child sacrifice, or else because she is adorned with the sickle moon. In artistic representations, "the 'Mother' is dark deepening to black, or red (the latter two being her principal colors), and with a primitive or animal expression of face."[5] She is often represented as an animal, commonly a bear. Jung considered the bear to be a "feminine animal," at least in part because of its connection with the goddess.[6]

We know that in their World Renewal Ceremony the Munsee-Mahican Delaware considered the bear to be feminine (regardless of the actual sex of the animal) because they put its hide on the women's side of the Big House and brought its carcass through the women's door. They associated it with the moon (another feminine symbol) because the ceremony began with a new moon, and because an image of a crescent or "sickle" moon appeared on one side of the drum. On the other side of the drum there was a bear image rendered in black against a red background. The ceremonial participants stood in positions that corresponded to the positions of the stars in the constellation Ursa Major. And there was a sacrifice; the bear itself was the victim.

In his discussions of the Earth Mother, Jung did not mention the Delaware ceremony. In all likelihood, he was unaware of the ritual. Nevertheless, there are striking correspondences between elements of the ritual and his characterization of the Earth Mother archetype. Even more remarkable are the correspondences between the symbols of the ritual and those in the dream of the bear-goddess Ursanna. Why would the esoteric symbols of nineteenth-century Delaware Indians appear in the dreams of twentieth-century urban European men and women?

The only plausible explanation is that this bear-goddess imagery arose independently, either out of direct experience with bears or from some second-hand knowledge of bears. The average modern urban European undoubtedly knows much less about bears than did the forest-living Delaware. Jung's dreamers probably did not know much more about bears than what they look like, that they are potentially dangerous, and that they hibernate in dens dug into the earth. It must be this information that gives rise to the shared symbols of the dreams and the ritual. The image of a threatening, human-like animal crawling into a hole in the ground in the fall and emerging again in the spring must be particulary effective at engaging a certain kind of mythological thinking or allegorical interpretation.

Most of the American Indian traditions in which the bear played a role can be considered within the domain of the Earth Mother

A hide shield with visionary designs. Shoshoni. *Photo courtesy of the Milwaukee Public Museum, Milwaukee.*

Beneath is a Bear

archetype. The clearest examples are initiation rites. Tribes that incorporated bears into their initiation rituals probably did so because hibernation resembled an initiation. But the birth symbolism at the heart of the tradition is clearly feminine. Healing rites are another example. In American Indian cultures medicine came from plants. As gatherers, women possessed the knowledge of plants, hence healing, at least healing with plants, fell within the province of the feminine. The bear hunts of northern hunting tribes could also be considered to fall within that category. Among groups such as the Eastern Cree, each bear that was killed became the object of elaborate ceremonial attention principally because it represented the rebirth of animals killed in the hunt. Some groups believed that the bear spirit controlled the supply of all game. The bear's role here might be interpreted as similar to that of Artemis, in Europe, who, as the Lady of Wild Nature, presided over the animals and the hunt.

The Earth Mother archetype also emerges in the myths and tales of American Indians. Two examples are the Grizzly-bear Woman of the Nez Perce and the bear woman with the toothed vagina of the Yavapai and Navajo. Another comes from the Inland Tlingit, the Kaska, the Tagish, and other Indians of western Canada. They believed that, in the beginning, a great mother gave birth to all of the animals. They called her the Animal Mother, but they also referred to her as *xuts tla*, which in Tlingit means "Bear Mother," or as "Strong One Mother" ("Strong One" is one of their names for the grizzly bear). They said that, when the world was new, Bear Mother gave each animal the form it has today. She nursed them and, when one of them cried, she rocked it in a large moosehide hammock stretched between four mountains. As the animals grew, she protected them. She showed them what foods to eat and taught them how to get along with each other. Today, a few of the old people still say they know the location of the den where she gave birth.[7]

*   *   *   *

One April I hiked into the Bitterroot Mountains of Montana. After walking ten or twelve miles on snowshoes, I paused to eat a sandwich and rest. From where I sat I could look either back, out across the long wooded sweep of valley I had just traveled, or ahead, to the steep snow-covered wall where the canyon ended. As I sat in the sun, something on the headwall caught my eye. I thought I had seen something move, and I searched the thousand-foot wall of uninterrupted whiteness. Nothing. It was clean and perfect. Then, six hundred feet above the valley floor, a fleck of darkness appeared where there had been nothing but white. It moved, though barely, then disappeared. A moment later, it appeared again, and grew into the head and forelegs of a bear. It emerged, pushing a pile of snow ahead of it until the snow dropped and slid slowly to the base of the head-wall. The bear pushed out several piles of snow this way, then disappeared back into what must have been its den. I waited and watched until I grew cold from sitting, but the bear did not appear again.

So there she was and there she is. Under the snow. Crawling out of a painting on the side of a tepee. Her skull hanging from a spruce tree in the forests of the Cree, where she mediates between plenty and famine. There with the Pomo, the Dakota, and the Pueblo as they initiate their children into adulthood. There in the visions and stories and dances of Indians throughout ancient America. And here, in our dreams. The Blackfeet danced as bears and sang, *"Beneath is a bear,"* saying, perhaps, that the bear lives within us just as she lives within the earth. The rituals, myths, images, and dreams, give voice to Bear, to this one like us, this One Who Owns the Den.

NOTES

Chapter 1.

1. Osgood, *Ingalik Mental Culture*, 146.
2. Nelson, *Make Prayers to the Raven*.
3. Curtis, *Yakima, Klickitat, Interior Salish and Kootenai*.
4. Grinnell, *Blackfoot Lodge Tales*.
5. McClellan, *An Ethnographic Survey of Southern Yukon Territory*, 130.
6. Barnouw, *Wisconsin Chippewa Myths*, 139.
7. Gifford, "The Southeastern Yavapai," 241.
8. Henderson, *Thresholds of Initiation*, 224.
9. Neumann, *The Great Mother*, 32.
10. Densmore, *Uses of Plants by the Chippewa Indians*.
11. Gayton, *Yokuts and Western Mono Ethnography*.
12. Skinner, *The Mascoutens or Prairie Potawatomi Indians*.
13. Brown, *The Spiritual Legacy of the American Indian*, 38.

Chapter 2.

1. Parsons, *Pueblo Indian Religion*, 2:600.
2. Free, *Discussion Session*, 36.
3. Eliade, *Rites of Initiation*.
4. Eliade, *Myths, Dreams and Mysteries*.
5. Wallis, *The Canadian Dakota*, 64.
6. For a description of this ritual, see Ibid., and Pond, "The Dakotas."
7. McLendon and Lowy, "Western Pomo and Northeastern Pomo."
8. For descriptions of the Pomo initiations, see: Ibid.; Hentze, *Mythes et Symboles*; and Loeb, "Pomo Folkways."
9. Lurie, *Mountain Wolf Woman*, 22.
10. Cruikshank, *The Stolen Women*.
11. Niethammer, *Daughters of the Earth*.
12. Barnouw, *Wisconsin Chippewa Myths*.
13. Landes, *Ojibwa Woman*.
14. St. Clair and Frachtenberg, "Traditions of the Coos Indians."
15. My account is based on the following descriptions of the Midewiwin: Hoffman, *The Midewiwin*; Densmore, *Uses of Plants by the Chippewa Indians*; Johnson, *Ojibwa Heritage*; Vecsey, *Ojibwa Religion*; Landes, *Ojibwa Religion*; Redsky, *Leader of the Ojibway*, Dewdney, *Sacred Scrolls*.

Chapter 3.

1. Flannery and Chambers, "East Cree Belief and Practice," 3-4.
2. For two almost identical accounts of shamans fighting with the bear spirit, see Flannery and Chambers, "East Cree Belief and Practice," 15, and Preston, *Cree Narrative*, 80.
3. Rogers, *The Mistassini Cree.*
4. Speck, *Naskapi*, 180.
5. Tanner, *Religious Ideology of the Mistassini Cree.*
6. For a discussion of the significance of dreams to the Cree, see *Ibid.*; Flannery and Chambers, "East Cree Belief and Practice"; and Preston, *Cree Narrative.*
7. Preston, *Cree Narrative*, 232-4.
8. Flannery and Chambers, "East Cree Belief and Practice," 4.
9. Tanner, *Religious Ideology of the Mistassini Cree.*
10. Preston, *Cree Narrative*, 211.
11. Cree names for the bear can be found in: Hallowell, "Bear Ceremonialism"; Skinner, "Bear Customs"; Speck, *Naskapi*; and Tanner, *Religious Ideology of the Mistassini Cree.*
12. See: Speck, *Naskapi*, and Tanner, *Religious Ideology of the Mistassini Cree.*
13. Flannery and Chambers, "East Cree Belief and Practice," 7.
14. Hunting clothing, tools, charms, and their decorations are described in Ibid., 6-7; Skinner, "Bear Customs"; and Speck and Heye, "Hunting Charms."
15. Flannery and Chambers, "East Cree Belief and Practice," 6.
16. Ibid., 7.
17. Tanner, *Religious Ideology of the Mistassini Cree.*
18. For a thorough discussion of the hunt, see Hallowell, "Bear Ceremonialism."
19. For examples of speeches made to slain bears see: Hallowell, "Bear Ceremonialism." and Flannery and Chambers, "East Cree Belief and Practice."
20. Rogers, *The Mistassini Cree.*
21. Tanner, *Religious Ideology of the Mistassini Cree.*
22. Hallowell, "Bear Ceremonialism."
23. Tanner, *Religious Ideology of the Mistassini Cree.*
24. See: Ibid., and Flannery and Chambers, "East Cree Belief and Practice."
25. Flannery and Chambers, "East Cree Belief and Practice," 8.
26. Ibid., 16.
27. The eat-all feast and the attitude of feast participants is described in Ibid., and Tanner, *Religious Ideology of the Mistassini Cree.*
28. Tanner, *Religious Ideology of the Mistassini Cree*, 163.
29. Flannery and Chambers, "East Cree Belief and Practice," 9.
30. Tanner, *Religious Ideology of the Mistassini Cree*, and Flannery and Chambers, "East Cree Belief and Practice."
31. Flannery and Chambers, "East Cree Belief and Practice."
32. This practice is described in Ibid.; Hallowell, "Bear Ceremonialism"; Rogers, *The Mistassini Cree*; Skinner, *Notes on Eastern Cree*; Idem, "Bear Customs"; and Tanner, *Religious Ideology of the Mistassini Cree.*

33. Flannery and Chambers, "East Cree Belief and Practice," 15.

34. Rogers, *The Mistassini Cree*.

35. Ibid., and Tanner, *Religious Ideology of the Mistassini Cree*.

36. Hallowell, "Bear Ceremonialism."

37. Ibid., and Hallowell, "Bear Ceremonialism Re-examined."

38. For discussions of the Cree attitude toward game, see Preston, *Cree Narrative*; Flannery and Chambers, "East Cree Belief and Practice"; and Tanner, *Religious Ideology of the Mistassini Cree*.

39. Preston, *Cree Narrative*, 215.

40. Tanner, *Religious Ideology of the Mistassini Cree*.

41. Flannery and Chambers, "East Cree Belief and Practice," 8

42. Gunther, "First Salmon Ceremony."

Chapter 4.

1. This narrative is based on an account in Hill, *Methods of the Navajo Indians*.

2. Lamphere, "Symbolic Elements in Navajo Ritual," 291.

3. For a dramatic description of such a healing rite, see Parsons, *Isleta*.

4. Parsons, *Pueblo Indian Religion*, 2:1058.

5. See Russell, *The Pima Indians*, and Bahr et al., *Piman Shamanism*.

6. Nelson, *Make Prayers to the Raven*, 172.

7. Ibid., 175.

8. Mishler, "Northern Athapaskan Men's Riddle Tradition," 61.

9. Ibid., 62.

10. Ibid.

11. Schaeffer, "Bear Ceremonialism," 35.

12. Walker, *Lakota Belief*, 159.

13. Gifford, *The Southeastern Yavapai*.

14. McClellan, *An Ethnographic Survey*, 130.

15. Schaeffer, "Bear Ceremonialism," 35.

16. Nelson, *Make Prayers to the Raven*, 184.

17. Grinnell, *The Cheyenne Indians*.

18. Denig, *Indians of the Upper Missouri*.

19. Hallowell, "Bear Ceremonialism."

20. Parsons, *Pueblo Indian Religion*.

21. Boas, *Religion of the Kwakiutl Indians*, 194.

22. Ray, *Sanpoil and Nespelem*. See also Teit, *Lillooet Indians*, 279; and compare with Boas, *Religion of the Kwakiutl Indians*, 191, and Hallowell, "Bear Ceremonialism," 60.

23. McClellan, *An Ethnographic Survey*, 127.

24. Ibid.

25. Ibid.

26. Ibid., 165.

27. Schaeffer, "Bear Ceremonialism."

28. Dixon, *The Northern Maidu*.

29. Schaeffer, "Bear Ceremonialism."

30. Barnouw, *Wisconsin Chippewa Myths*, 130.

31. Nelson, *Make Prayers to the Raven*.

Chapter 5.

1. McClellan, *An Ethnographic Survey*, 126.

2. Cloutier, *Shaman Songs.*

3. Kroeber, *Indians of California.*

4. Rasmussen, *Caribou Eskimo,* 54-55.

5. Ibid., 52-54

6. Spier, *Klamath Ethnography,* 99.

7. See Eliade, *Shamanism,* and Park, *Shamanism in Western North America.*

8. Kroeber, *Indians of California.*

9. McClellan, *An Ethnographic Survey.*

10. Eliade, *Shamanism,* 59.

11. Ibid., 63.

12. Rasmussen, *Iglulik Eskimos,* 114.

13. Parsons, *Notes on Zuñi.*

14. This story is adapted from a tale in Dorsey, "Teton Folk-lore." There are many variants of it.

15. Barrett, "Pomo Bear Doctors."

16. Dorson, *Folk Traditions of the Upper Peninsula.*

17. Hallowell, "Ojibwa Ontology."

18. Cody, "Pomo Bear Impersonators."

Chapter 6.

1. DeMallie and Parks, *Sioux Indian Religion,* 41.

2. Mandelbaum, "The Plains Cree," 283-84.

3. Goddard, "Hupa Texts," 275-77.

4. Bunzel, *Zuñi Ceremonialism.*

5. Densmore, *Uses of Plants by the Chippewa Indians.*

6. Dorson, *Folk Traditions.*

7. Walker, *Lakota Society.*

8. Densmore, *Teton Sioux Music.*

9. Dr. Joseph Epes Brown, conversation with author, April 1983.

10. Densmore, *Teton Sioux Music,* 196.

11. Ibid., 264.

12. Densmore, *Teton Sioux Music.*

13. Walker, *Lakota Belief,* 157-159.

14. Parsons, *Taos Tales,* 91-92.

15. Parsons, *Pueblo Indian Religion.*

16. Gayton, *Yokuts and Western Mono Ethnography.*

17. Catlin, *North American Indians.*

18. Bunzel, *Zuñi Ceremonialism.*

19. Radin, *The Winnebago Tribe,* 300-301.

20. Kinietz, *Indians of the Great Lakes.*

21. Curtis, *Yakima, Klickitat, Interior Salish and Kootenai.*

22. Swanton, *Beliefs of the Chickasaw.*

23. Russell, *The Pima Indians,* 318-319.

24. Hill, *Methods of the Navajo Indians.*

25. Walker, *Lakota Belief.*

Chapter 7.

1. This story is paraphrased from Pichette, "Mary Sdipp-Shin-Mah."

2. Hultkrantz, *Religions of the American Indian*.
3. Fletcher and La Flesche, *The Omaha Tribe*, 487.
4. Skeels, "Grizzly-Bear Woman."
5. Mishler, "Northern Athapaskan Men's Riddle Tradition."
6. Stefansson, *Stefansson-Anderson Expedition*, 146.
7. Boas, "Current Beliefs of the Kwakiutl," 198.
8. Hultkrantz, *Belief and Worship*, 153.
9. Bowers, *Hidatsa Organization*, 350-351.
10. Wissler, "Blackfoot Indians."
11. Jenness, *The Sarcee*, 90.
12. Ewers, "The Bear Cult."
13. Bowers, *Hidatsa Organization*, 357.
14. Wissler, "Ceremonial Bundles of the Blackfoot," 131.
15. Lowie, *The Crow Indians*.
16. Fletcher, "The Elk Festival."
17. Fortune, *Omaha Secret Societies*, 84.
18. See Boyd, *Kiowa Voices*, and Lowie, "Societies of the Kiowa."
19. Bowers, *Hidatsa Organization*, 355.
20. Landes, *Ojibwa Religion*, 38-39.
21. Hultkrantz, *Religions of the American Indian*.
22. Jones, "Notes of the Fox Indians," 216.
23. Skinner, *Ethnology of the Ioway and Sauk Indians*, 21-22.
24. Radin, *The Winnebago Tribe*.
25. Morice, *Notes on the Western Denes*.
26. Boas, *Religion of the Kwakiutl Indians*, 194-195.

Chapter 8.

1. Preston, *Cree Narrative*.
2. Hymes, "Talk Like a Bear in Takelma," 102
3. Ibid., 103.
4. Preston, *Cree Narrative*.
5. McClellan, *The Girl Who Married the Bear*, 10-11.
6. Adapted from Ibid., 28-33.
7. Bogoras, "Tales from Eastern Siberia."
8. McClellan, *The Girl Who Married the Bear*.
9. Levi-Strauss, *Way of the Masks*.
10. McClellan, *An Ethnographic Survey*, 128.
11. Nelson, *Make Prayers to the Raven*, 179.
12. McClellan, *An Ethnographic Survey*, 125.
13. Ibid., 128.
14. Walker, *Lakota Society*, 141.
15. Byrd, "Of Bears and Women."
16. Walker, *Lakota Belief*, 159.
17. Nelson, *Make Prayers to the Raven*, 187.
18. Gifford, *Yavapai Myths*, 388-390.
19. Ibid.
20. Morris, "Bear Maiden Story," 253.
21. Phinney, *Nez Perce Texts*, 88-112.
22. Skeels, "Grizzly Bear Woman."

23. Jacobs, *Clackamas Chinook Texts.*
24. Ibid., 564-65.
25. Skeels, "Grizzly Bear Woman," 7.
26. Siebert, "Stiff-Legged Bear," 721.
27. Strong, "North American Indian Traditions," 83-84.
28. Lankford, "Pleistocene Animals in Folk Memory."
29. Ibid.
30. Voth, *Traditions of the Hopi.*
31. Frachtenberg, *Coos Texts*, 111-125.
32. Frachtenberg, *Lower Umpqua Texts*, 14-15.
33. Tanner, *Religious Ideology of the Mistassini Cree*, 148-50.
34. Ibid.
35. Dorsey and Kroeber, *Traditions of the Arapaho*, 101-103.
36. Boas, *Tsimshian Mythology*, 87-88.

Chapter 9.

1. Adapted from Hultkrantz, *Belief and Worship*, 149-150.
2. Dorsey, *Traditions of the Skidi Pawnee.*
3. Gayton, *Yokuts and Western Mono Ethnography*, 120-121.
4. Ibid., 120.
5. Ibid., 120-121.
6. Parsons, *Pueblo Indian Religion.*
7. McClintock, *The Old North Trail*, 264-265.
8. Brown, *The Spiritual Legacy*, 72.
9. Gayton, *Yokuts and Western Mono Ethnography*, 120.
10. Ibid., 173.
11. Dixon, "The Northern Maidu."
12. Bunzel, *Zuñi Katchinas*, 1031.
13. See Wissler, "Societies of the Blackfoot," and Mails, *Mystic Warriors of the Plains.*
14. Wissler, "Ceremonial Bundles of the Blackfoot."
15. Speck and Broom, *Cherokee Dance and Drama.*
16. Kurath, "Iroquois Bear Society Ritual."
17. See Densmore, *Northern Ute Music*; Opler, *Jicarilla Holiness Rite*; Schaeffer, "Bear Ceremonialism"; Reagan, "Bear Dance of the Ouray Utes"; Reed, "The Ute Bear Dance"; Jones, *Sun Dance of the Northern Ute*; Steward, "A Uintah Ute Bear Dance"; Lowie, *Notes on Shoshonean Ethnography.*
18. Mason, "Myths of the Uintah Utes," 363.
19. Steward, "A Uintah Ute Bear Dance," 272.

Chapter 10.

1. Speck and Moses, *The Celestial Bear*, 61-62.
2. See Brasser, "Mahican," and Goddard, "Delaware."
3. Speck and Moses, *The Celestial Bear.*
4. Krickeberg, et al., *Pre-Columbian American Religions.*
5. Speck and Moses, *The Celestial Bear.*
6. Miller, "Delaware Big House Rite."
7. On Delaware symbols, see Ibid., and Speck and Moses, *The Celestial Bear.*

8. Speck and Moses, *The Celestial Bear*, 32.

9. Ibid., 6-7, 50.

10. Miller "The Delaware as Women."

11. Wallace, "The Bear in Delaware Society."

12. See Speck and Moses, *The Celestial Bear*, and Krickeberg, et al., *Pre-Columbian American Religions*.

13. Krickeberg, et al., *Pre-Columbian American Religions*, 167.

14. Wallace, "The Bear in Delaware Society."

15. Hultkrantz, *Religions of the American Indian*.

16. Speck, *The Delaware Big House Ceremony*; Harrington, *Ceremonies of the Lenape*; and Speck, "Oklahoma Delaware Ceremonies."

17. Wallace, "The Bear in Delaware Society."

18. Speck, "Oklahoma Delaware Ceremonies."

19. See Ibid.; Krickeberg, et al., *Pre-Columbian American Religions*; and Miller, "The Delaware Doll Dance."

20. Krickeberg, et al., *Pre-Columbian American Religions*, 167-168.

21. Speck and Moses, *The Celestial Bear*.

Chapter 11.

1. Hallowell, "Bear Ceremonialism," 43-53.

2. Hallowell, "Bear Ceremonialism," 94.

3. Alekseenko, "Cult of the Bear," 180.

4. Hallowell, "Bear Ceremonialism," 54.

5. Ibid., 55-58.

6. Ibid., 105.

7. Ibid., 156.

8. Ibid., 161-162.

9. Barnouw, *Wisconsin Chippewa Myths*, 248.

10. von Franz, *Problems of the Feminine*, 53.

11. For descriptions of this ritual feast, see Parke, *Festivals of the Athenians*; Brelich, "Symbol of a Symbol"; Farnell, *Cults of the Greek States*; and Guthrie, *The Greeks and their Gods*.

12. Parke, *Festivals of the Athenians*, 140.

13. Brelich, "Symbol of a Symbol."

14. Carpenter, *Homeric Epics*.

15. Cook, *Zeus*, 227

16. Carpenter, *Homeric Epics*, 113-114.

17. Davidson, *Gods and Myths*, 66.

18. Ibid., 67.

19. Davidson, *Scandinavian Mythology*.

20. See Ibid.; Davidson, *Gods and Myths*; and MacCulloch, *Eddic*.

21. Grimm, *Teutonic Mythology*.

22. MacCulloch, *Religion of the Ancient Celts*, 212-213.

23. Clair, *An Illustrated Bestiary*.

24. Frazer, *The Golden Bough*.

25. Bogoras, *Tales of Eastern Siberia*.

26. See Carpenter, *Homeric Epics*, and Leake, *The Geats of Beowulf*.

27. de Gubernatis, *Zoological Mythology*.

28. Frazer, *The Golden Bough*.

29. Carpenter, *Homeric Epics*.

30. See Ibid.; de Gubernatis, *Zoological Mythology*; and Frazer, *The Golden Bough*.

31. Carpenter, *Homeric Epics*.

32. See Gimbutas, *Gods and Goddesses*.

33. Ibid.

34. Cook, *Zeus*.

35. Gimbutas, *Gods and Goddesses*, 199.

36. Ibid.

37. See Frazer, *Pausanias' Description of Greece*, 8.18.12, or the translation of the same by W. H. S. Jones.

38. See Jung and Kerenyi, *Science of Mythology*, 150, 198.

39. von Franz, *Problems of the Feminine*.

Chapter 12.

1. Jung and Kerenyi, *Science of Mythology*, 234.

2. Ibid., 234-235.

3. Ibid., 235.

4. Jung, *Man and His Symbols*, 204-205.

5. Jung and Kerenyi, *Science of Mythology*, 221-222.

6. Jung, *The Collected Works*, vol. 5.

7. McClellan, *History of the Yukon Indians*, and McClellan, *An Ethnographic Survey*.

BIBLIOGRAPHY

Alekseenko, E. A. 1968. The Cult of the Bear among the Ket (Yenisei Ostyaks). In *Popular Beliefs and Folklore Tradition in Siberia*, edited by V. Dioszegi, 175-191. Bloomington: Indiana University Press.

Bahr, Donald, Juan Gregorio, David Lopez, and Albert Alvarez. 1974. *Piman Shamanism and Staying Sickness*. Tucson: University of Arizona Press.

Barnouw, Victor. 1977. *Wisconsin Chippewa Myths and Tales and their Relation to Chippewa Life*. Madison: University of Wisconsin Press.

Barrett, S. A. 1917. Pomo Bear Doctors. *University of California Publications in American Archaeology and Ethnology* 12(11): 443-65.

Boas, Franz. 1916. *Tsimshian Mythology*. Bureau of American Ethnology Annual Report no. 31:29-979.

———1930. *The Religion of the Kwakiutl*. Columbia University Contributions to Anthropology, vol. 10, pts. 1 and 2. New York: Columbia University Press.

———1932. Current Beliefs of the Kwakiutl Indians. *Journal of American Folklore* 45:177-260.

Bogoras, Waldemar. 1918. Tales of Eastern Siberia. *Anthropological Papers*, 20(1). New York: American Museum of Natural History.

Bowers, Alfred W. 1965. *Hidatsa Social and Ceremonial Organization*. Bureau of American Ethnology Bulletin no. 194.

Boyd, Maurice. 1983. *Kiowa Voices*. Fort Worth: Texas Christian University Press.

Brasser, T. J. 1978. Mahican. In *Handbook of North American Indians* vol. 15: *Northeast*, edited by Bruce Trigger, 198-212. Washington, D. C.: Smithsonian Institution.

Brelich, Angelo. 1969. Symbol of a Symbol. In *Myths and Symbols: Studies in Honor or Mircea Eliade*, edited by Joseph M. Kitagawa and Charles H. Long, 195-207. Chicago: University of Chicago Press.

Brown, Joseph Epes. 1982. *The Spiritual Legacy of the American Indian*. New York: Crossroad Publishing Co.

Bunzel, Ruth L. 1930. *Introduction to Zuñi Ceremonialism*. Bureau of American Ethnology Annual Report no. 47:467-544.

———1930. *Zuñi Katchinas*. Bureau of American Ethnology Annual Report no. 47:837-1086.

Byrd, Carolyn. 1988. Of Bears and Women: Investigating the Hypothesis that Menstruation Attracts Bears. Masters thesis, University of Montana.

Carpenter, Rhys. 1956. *Folktale, Fiction and Saga in the Homeric Epics*. Berkeley: University of California Press.

Catlin, George. [1841] 1973. *Letters and Notes on the Manners, Customs and Condition of the North American Indians*, 2 Vols. Reprint. New York: Dover Publications.

Clair, Colin. 1967. *Unnatural History: An Illustrated Bestiary.* London: Abelard-Schuman.

Cloutier, David. 1973. Spirit, *Spirit: Shaman Songs and Incantations.* Providence, RI: Copper Beach Press.

Cody, Bertha Parker. 1940. Pomo Bear Impersonators. *The Masterkey* 14(1): 132-36.

Cook, Arthur B. 1914. *Zeus: A Study in Ancient Religion*, 2 vols. London: Cambridge University Press.

Craighead, Frank. 1979. *Track of the Grizzly.* San Francisco: Sierra Club Books.

Cruikshank, Julie. 1983. *The Stolen Women: Female Journeys in Tagish and Tutchone.* National Museum of Man, Mercury Series, Canadian Ethnology Service Paper no. 87. Ottawa: National Museums of Canada.

Curtis, Edward S. 1911. *The North American Indian.* Vol. 7, *Yakima, Klickitat, Interior Salish and Kootenai.* Norwood, CT: Plimton Press.

Cushing, Frank H. *Zuñi Fetishes.* Bureau of American Ethnology Annual Report no. 2:9-45.

Davidson, H. R. Ellis. 1964. *Gods and Myths of Northern Europe.* New York: Penguin Books.

Davidson, H. R. Ellis. 1986. *Scandinavian Mythology.* New York: Paul Hamlyn Publishers.

de Gubernatis, Angelo. 1872. *Zoological Mythology or The Legends of Animals.* 2 vols. London: Trubner and Co.

DeMallie, Raymond J., and Douglas R. Parks, eds. 1987. *Sioux Indian Religion: Tradition and Innovation.* Norman: University of Oklahoma Press.

Denig, Edwin T. 1930. *Indian Tribes of the Upper Missouri.* Edited by J. N. B. Hewitt. Bureau of American Ethnology Annual Report no. 46:375-628.

Densmore, Frances. 1918. *Teton Sioux Music.* Bureau of American Ethnology Bulletin no. 61.

_____ 1922. *Northern Ute Music.* Bureau of American Ethnology Bulletin no. 75.

_____ 1927. *Uses of Plants by the Chippewa Indians.* Bureau of American Ethnology Annual Report no. 44:275-397.

Dewdney, Selwyn. 1974. *The Sacred Scrolls of the Southern Ojibway.* Toronto: University of Toronto Press.

Dixon, Roland B. 1905. The Northern Maidu. *Bulletin of the American Museum of Natural History* 17:119-346.

Dorsey, J. O. 1889. Teton Folk-Lore Notes. *Journal of American Folklore* 2:133-39.

Dorsey, G. A. 1904. *Traditions of the Skidi Pawnee.* Memoirs of the American Folklore Society, vol. 8. New York: American Folklore Society.

Dorsey, G. A., and A. L. Kroeber. 1903. *Traditions of the Arapaho.* Anthropological Series, vol. 5. Chicago: Field Museum of Natural History.

Dorson, Richard M. 1971. *Bloodstoppers and Bearwalkers: Folk Traditions of the Upper Peninsula.* Cambridge, MA: Harvard University Press.

Eliade, Mircea. 1958. *Rites and Symbols of Initiation: The Mysteries of Birth and Rebirth*. New York: Harper and Row.

———— 1960. *Myths, Dreams and Mysteries*. New York: Harper and Row.

———— 1964. *Shamanism: Archaic Techniques of Ecstasy*. Translated from the French by Willard R. Trask. New York: Pantheon Books.

———— 1969. *The Two and the One*. New York: Harper and Row.

Ewers, John C. 1955. The Bear Cult Among the Assiniboin and Their Neighbors of the Northern Plains. *Southwestern Journal of Anthropology* 11(1): 1-13.

Farnell, L. R. 1971. *The Cults of the Greek States*. Chicago: Aegaean Press.

Flannery, Regina, and Mary Elizabeth Chambers. 1985. Each Man has his own Friends: The Role of Dream Visitors in Traditional East Cree Belief and Practice. *Arctic Anthropology* 22(1): 1-22.

Fletcher, Alice C. 1883. The Elk Mystery or Festival. *Peabody Museum of American Archaeology and Ethnology* no. 16-17:276-88.

Fletcher, Alice C., and Francis La Flesche. 1911. *The Omaha Tribe*. Bureau of American Ethnology Annual Report no. 27:17-654.

Frachtenberg, L. J. 1913. *Coos Texts*. Columbia University Contributions to Anthropology, vol. 1. New York: Columbia University Press.

———— 1914. *Lower Umpqua Texts and Notes on Kusan Dialects*. Columbia University Contributions to Anthropology, vol. 4. New York: Columbia University Press.

Frazer, James George. 1913. *Pausanias' Description of Greece*. London: Macmillan and Company.

———— 1935. *The Golden Bough*. New York: Macmillan.

Free, Stuart. 1968. "Discussion Session of the International Conference on Bear Research and Management." Session at the annual meeting of the Bear Biology Association. Fairbanks, Alaska.

Jacobs, M., A. S. Gatschet, and L. J. Frachtenberg. 1945. Kalapuya Texts. *University of Washington Publications in Anthropology* 11.

Gayton, A. H. 1948. *Yokuts and Western Mono Ethnography*. Anthropological Records, vol. 10, nos. 1 and 2. Berkeley: University of California Press.

Gifford, E. W. 1933. Northeastern and Western Yavapai Myths. *Journal of American Folklore* 46:347-415.

———— 1933. The Southeastern Yavapai. *University of California Publications in American Archaeology and Ethnology* 29(3): 117-252.

Gimbutas, Marija. 1974. *The Gods and Goddesses of Old Europe 7000 to 3500 BC: Myths and Legends and Cult Images*. Berkeley: University of California Press.

Goddard, P. E. 1904. Hupa Texts. *University of California Publications in American Archaeology and Ethnology* 1(2): 89-368.

Goddard, Sergius. 1978. Delaware. In *Handbook of North American Indians* vol. 15: *Northeast*, edited by Bruce Trigger, 213-238. Washington, D. C.: Smithsonian Institution.

Grant, Campbell. 1981. *Rock Art of the American Indian*. Grand Junction, CO: Outbooks.

Grimm, Jacob. 1883. *Teutonic Mythology*. London: George Bell and Sons.

Grinnell, George Bird. 1972. *Blackfoot Lodge Tales*. Williamstown, MA: Corner House Publishers.

——— 1972. *The Cheyenne Indians.* Lincoln: University of Nebraska Press.

Gunther, Erna. 1928. A Further Analysis of the First Salmon Ceremony. *University of Washington Publications in Anthropology* 2(5): 129-73.

Guthrie, W. K. C. 1954. *The Greeks and their Gods.* Boston: Beacon Press.

Hallowell, Irving A. 1926. Bear Ceremonialism in the Northern Hemisphere. *American Anthropologist* 28:1-175.

——— 1960. Ojibwa Ontology, Behavior and Worldview. In *Culture in History: Essays in Honor of Paul Radin,* edited by Stanley Diamond, 49-82. New York: Columbia University Press.

——— 1968. Bear Ceremonialism in the Northern Hemisphere Re-examined. Paper presented to graduate seminar conducted at Bryn Mawr by Dr. Fredrica de Laguna.

Harrington, Mark R. 1921. *Religion and Ceremonies of the Lenape.* Notes and Monographs no. 19. New York: Museum of the American Indian.

Henderson, Joseph L. 1967. *Thresholds of Initiation.* Hanover, NH: Wesleyan University Press.

Hentze, Carl. 1932. *Mythes et Symboles Lunaires (Chine Ancienne, Civilisations Anciennes De L'asie, Peuples Limitrophes du Pacifique).* Anvers, France: De Sikkel.

Hill, W. W. 1938. *The Agricultural and Hunting Methods of the Navajo Indians.* Yale University Publications in Anthropology no. 18. New Haven, CT: Yale University Press.

Hoffman, W. J. 1886. *The Midewiwin or "Grand Medicine Society" of the Ojibwa.* Bureau of American Ethnology Annual Report no. 7:143-300.

Hultkrantz, Ake. 1980. *The Religions of the American Indians.* Berkeley: University of California Press.

——— 1981. *Belief and Worship in Native North America.* Syracuse, NY: Syracuse University Press.

Hymes, Dell. 1979. How to Talk Like a Bear in Takelma. *International Journal of American Linguistics* 45(2): 101-6.

Jacobs, Melville. 1959. *Clackamas Chinook Texts.* Indiana University Publications in Anthropology, Folklore, and Linguistics no. 8, Pts. 1 and 2. Bloomington: Indiana University.

——— 1960. *The People are Coming Soon: Analyses of Clackamas Chinook Myths and Tales.* Seattle: University of Washington Press.

James, E. O. 1959. *The Cult of the Mother Goddess.* New York: F. A. Praeger.

Jenness, Diamond. 1938. *The Sarcee Indians of Alberta.* National Museum of Canada, Department of Mines and Resources, Bulletin no. 90 Anthropological Series no. 23.

Johnston, Basil. 1976. *Ojibwa Heritage.* New York: Columbia University Press.

Jones, J. A. 1955. *The Sun Dance of the Northern Ute.* Bureau of American Ethnology Bulletin no. 157, Anthropological Papers no. 47.

Jones, W. 1911. Notes on the Fox Indians. *Journal of American Folklore* 24:209-37.

Jung, C. G. 1956. *The Collected Works.* Vol. 5, *Symbols of Transformation.* New York: Pantheon Books.

——— 1964. *Man and His Symbols.* New York: Doubleday.

Jung, C. G., and C. Kerenyi. 1949. *Essays on a Science of Mythology*. New York: Pantheon Books.

Kinietz, W. Vernon. 1940. *The Indians of the Western Great Lakes 1615-1760*. University of Michigan Museum of Anthropology Occasional Contributions no. 10. Ann Arbor: University of Michigan Press.

Krickeberg, Walter, Hermann Trimborn, Werner Müller, and Otto Zerries. 1968. *Pre-Columbian American Religions*. New York: Holt, Rinehart and Winston.

Kroeber, Alfred L. 1925. *Handbook of the Indians of California*. Bureau of American Ethnology Bulletin no. 78.

Kurath, Gertrude. The Iroquois Bear Society Ritual Drama. *American Indian Tradition* 8(2): 84-5.

Lamphere, Louise. 1969. Symbolic Elements in Navajo Ritual. *Southwestern Journal of Anthropology* 25:279-305.

Landes, Ruth. 1968. *Ojibwa Religion and the Midewiwin*. Madison: University of Wisconsin Press.

———. 1971. *Ojibwa Woman*. New York: Norton.

Lankford, George E. 1980. Pleistocene Animals in Folk Memory. *Journal of American Folklore* 93:293-304.

Leake, Jane Acomb. 1967. *The Geats of Beowulf*. Madison: University of Wisconsin Press.

Levi-Strauss, Claude. 1988. *The Way of the Masks*. Seattle: University of Washington Press.

Loeb, Edwin M. 1926. Pomo Folkways. *University of California Publications in American Archaeology and Ethnology* 19(2): 149-405.

Lommel, Andreas. 1967. *Shamanism: the Beginnings of Art*. New York: McGraw Hill.

Lonnrot, Elias. 1969. *The Old Kalevala and Certain Antecedents*. Cambridge, MA: Harvard University Press.

Lowie, R. H. 1916. Societies of the Kiowa. *Anthropological Papers* 11:837-51. New York: American Museum of Natural History.

———. 1924. Notes on Shoshonean Ethnography. *Anthropological Papers* 20:185-314. New York: American Museum of Natural History.

———. 1956. *The Crow Indians*. New York: Holt, Rinehart and Winston.

Lurie, Nancy Oestreich. 1961. *Mountain Wolf Woman, Sister of Crashing Thunder: The Autobiography of a Winnebago Indian*. Ann Arbor: University of Michigan Press.

McClellan, Catharine. 1970. *The Girl Who Married the Bear*. National Museum of Man, Publications in Ethnology no. 2. Ottawa: National Museums of Canada.

———. 1975. *My Old People Say: An Ethnographic Survey of Southern Yukon Territory*. National Museum of Man, Publications in Ethnology no. 6. Ottawa: National Museums of Canada.

———. 1987. *Part of the Land Part of the Water: A History of the Yukon Indians*. Vancouver, BC: Douglas and McIntyre.

McClintock, Walter. 1910. *The Old North Trail*. Lincoln: University of Nebraska Press.

MacCulloch, J. A. 1930. *Mythology of All Races*, vol. 2. *Eddic*. Boston: Marshall Jones.

———1930. *Mythology of All Races*, vol. 3. *The Religion of the Ancient Celts*. Boston: Marshall Jones.

McLendon, Sally and Michael Lowy. 1978. Western Pomo and Northeastern Pomo. In *Handbook of American Indians* vol. 8: *California*, edited by Robert F. Heizer, 306-322. Washington, D.C.: Smithsonian Institution.

Mails, Thomas E. 1972. *Mystic Warriors of the Plains*. New York: Doubleday.

Mandelbaum, David G. 1941. The Plains Cree. *Anthropological Papers* 37(2): 155-316. New York: American Museum of Natural History.

Mason, J. A. 1910. Myths of the Uintah Utes. *Journal of American Folklore* 23:299-263.

Miller, Jay. 1974. The Delaware as Women: A Symbolic Solution. *American Ethnologist* 1(3): 507-14.

———1976. The Delaware Doll Dance. *Man in the Northeast* 12:80-4.

———1980. A Structuralist Analysis of the Delaware Big House Rite. *University of Oklahoma Publications in Anthropology* 21(2): 107-33.

Mishler, Craig. 1984. Telling About Bear: A Northern Athapaskan Men's Riddle Tradition. *Journal of American Folklore* 97(383): 61-8.

Morice, Rev. Father A. G. 1893. *Notes, Archaeological, Industrial and Sociological on the Western Denes*. Transactions of the Royal Canadian Institute no. 4, pt. 1. Toronto: Royal Canadian Institute.

Morris, C. Patrick. 1976. Bears, Juniper Trees, and Deer, The Metaphors of Domestic Life: An Analysis of a Yavapai Variant of the Bear Maiden Story. *Journal of Anthropological Research* 32(3): 246-54.

Nelson, Richard K. 1983. *Make Prayers to the Raven*. Chicago: University of Chicago Press.

Neumann, Erich. 1955. *The Great Mother*. Princeton, NJ: Princeton University Press.

Niethammer, Carolyn. 1977. *Daughters of the Earth*. New York: Macmillan.

Opler, Morris Edward. 1943. *Character and Derivation of the Jicarilla Holiness Rite*. Anthropological Series Bulletin, vol. 4, no. 2. Albuquerque: University of New Mexico.

Osgood, Cornelius. 1959. *Ingalik Mental Culture*. Yale University Publications in Anthropology no. 56. New Haven, CT: Yale University Press.

Parke, H. W. 1977. *Festivals of the Athenians*. Ithaca: Cornell University Press.

Park, Willard. 1938. *Shamanism in Western North America: a study in cultural relationships*. Northwestern University Studies in the Social Sciences, vol. 2. Evanston and Chicago: Northwestern University Press.

Parsons, Elsie Clews. 1917. Notes on Zuñi. *Memoirs of the American Anthropological Association* 4:151-327.

———1930. *Isleta*. Bureau of American Ethnology, Annual Report no. 47:193-466.

———1939. *Pueblo Indian Religion*, 2 vols. Chicago: University of Chicago Press.

———1940. *Taos Tales*. Memoirs of the American Folklore Society, vol. 34.

Phinney, Archie. Letter to Franz Boas dated 20 November 1929. Franz Boas Collection of American Indian Linguistics. American Philosophical Society Library, Philadelphia, PA.

_____ 1934. *Nez Perce Texts*. Columbia University Contributions to Anthropology, vol. 25. New York: Columbia University Press.

Pichette, Pierre. 1947. Story of Mary Sdipp-Shin-Mah. Full Blood Flathead Indian Montana Study Group. University of Montana. Photocopy.

Pond, Rev. Samuel William. 1908. The Dakotas or Sioux in Minnesota as they were in 1834. *Collections of the Minnesota Historical Society* 12:319-501.

Preston, Richard J. 1975. *Cree Narrative: Expressing the Personal Meanings of Events*. National Museum of Man, Mercury Series, Canadian Ethnology Service Paper no.30. Ottawa: National Museums of Canada.

Radin, Paul. 1916. *The Winnebago Tribe*. Bureau of American Ethnology Annual Report no. 37:33-550.

Rasmussen, Knud. 1929. Intellectual Culture of the Iglulik Eskimos. *Report of the Fifth Thule Expedition*. 7(1): 1-304. Copenhagen: Gyldendalske Boghandel.

_____ 1930. Observations on the Intellectual Culture of the Caribou Eskimo. *Report of the Fifth Thule Expedition*. 7(2): 1-114. Copenhagen: Gyldendalske Boghandel.

Ray, Verne F. 1932. *The Sanpoil and Nespelem*. University of Washington Publications in Anthropology, vol. 5. Seattle: University of Washington Press.

Reagan, A. B. 1929. The Bear Dance of the Ouray Utes. *Wisconsin Archaeologist* 9:148-50.

Redsky, James. 1972. *Great Leader of the Ojibway: Mis-quona-queb*. Edited by James R. Stevens. Toronto: McClelland and Stewart.

Reed, V. H. 1896. The Ute Bear Dance. *American Anthropologist* 9:237-44.

Rogers, Edward S. 1973. *The Quest for Food and Furs: The Mistassini Cree, 1953-1954*. National Museum of Man, Publications in Ethnology no. 5. Ottawa: National Museums of Canada.

Russell, F. 1908. *The Pima Indians*. Bureau of American Ethnology Annual Report no. 26:3-390.

St. Clair, H. H., and Leo Frachtenberg. 1909. Traditions of the Coos Indians of Oregon. *Journal of American Folklore* 22:25-41.

Schaeffer, Claude E. 1966. Bear Ceremonialism of the Kutenai Indians. Museum of the Plains Indian. *Studies in Plains Anthropology and History* 4:1-54. Browning, MT: Museum of the Plains Indian (U.S. Department of the Interior Indian Arts and Crafts Board).

Siebert, F. T. 1937. Mammoth or "Stiff-legged Bear." *American Anthropologist* 39:721-725.

Skeels, Dell. 1969. Grizzly-Bear Woman in Nez Perce Indian Mythology. *Northwest Folklore* 3(2): 1-9.

Skinner, Alanson. 1910. Notes on the Eastern Cree and Northern Salteaux. *Anthropological Papers* 9: 1-116. New York: American Museum of Natural History.

_____ 1914. Bear Customs of the Cree and other Algonkin Indians of Northern Ontario. *Papers and Records* 12:203-9. Ottawa: Ontario Historical Society.

_____ 1924-1927. *The Mascoutens or Prairie Potawatomi Indians*. Bulletin of the Public Museum of Milwaukee vol. 6.

_____ 1925. *Observations on the Ethnology of the Ioway Indians and Sauk Indians*. Bulletin of the Public Museum of Milwaukee vol. 5.

Speck, Frank G. 1931. *A Study of the Delaware Big House Ceremony*. Harrisburg, PA: Publications of the Pennsylvania Historical Commission no. 2.

———— 1935. *Naskapi: Savage Hunters of the Labrador Peninsula*. Norman: University of Oklahoma Press.

———— 1937. *Oklahoma Delaware Ceremonies, Feasts and Dances*. Memoirs of the American Philosophical Society no. 7.

Speck, Frank G., and George G. Heye. 1921. Hunting Charms of the Montagnais and the Mistassini. *Indian Notes and Monographs*, misc. series 13(1): 5-19.

Speck, Frank G., and Jesse Moses. 1945. *The Celestial Bear Comes Down to Earth*. Reading, PA: Reading Public Museum and Art Gallery, Scientific Publication no. 7.

Speck, Frank, and Leonard Broom. 1951. *Cherokee Dance and Drama*. Berkeley: University of California Press.

Spier, Leslie. 1930. Klamath Ethnography. *University of California Publications in Archaeology and Ethnography* 30. Berkeley: University of California Press.

Stefansson, V. 1914. Stefansson-Anderson Arctic Expedition. *Anthropological Papers* 14. New York: American Museum of Natural History.

Steward, Julian H. 1932. A Uintah Ute Bear Dance. *American Anthropologist* 34:263-273.

Strong, W. D. 1934. North American Indian Traditions Suggesting a Knowledge of the Mammoth. *American Anthropologist* 36:81-4.

Swanton, J. R. 1928. *Social and Religious Beliefs and Usages of the Chickasaw*. Bureau of American Ethnology Annual Report no. 44:169-273.

Tanner, Adrian. 1979. *Bringing Home the Animals: Religious Ideology and Mode of Production of the Mistassini Cree Hunters*. New York: St. Martin's Press.

Teit, J. A. 1906. The Lillooet Indians. *Memoirs of the American Museum of Natural History* 4:193-300.

Vecsey, Christopher. 1983. *Traditional Ojibwa Religion and its Historical Changes*. Memoirs Series, vol. 150. Philadelphia: American Philosophical Society.

von Franz, M. L. 1972. *Problems of the Feminine in Fairytales*. Dallas: Spring Publications Inc.

Voth, H. R. 1905. *The Traditions of the Hopi*. Anthropological Series, vol. 8. Chicago: Field Museum of Natural History.

Walker, James. 1980. *Lakota Society*. Edited by Raymond J. DeMallie. Lincoln: University of Nebraska Press.

———— 1983. *Lakota Belief and Ritual*. Edited by Raymond DeMallie and Elaine Jahner. Lincoln: University of Nebraska Press.

Wallace, Anthony F. C. 1949. The Role of the Bear in Delaware Society. *Pennsylvania Archaeologist* 19(1-2): 37-46.

Wallis, Wilson D. 1947. The Canadian Dakota. *Anthropological Papers* 41(1) 64-5. New York: American Museum of Natural History.

Wissler, Clark. 1912. Ceremonial Bundles of the Blackfoot Indians. *Anthropological Papers* 7:65-289. New York: American Museum of Natural History.

_____ 1912. Social Organization and Ritualistic Ceremonies of the Blackfoot Indians. *Anthropological Papers* 7(2): 1-64. New York: American Museum of Natural History.

_____ 1913. Societies and Dance Associations of the Blackfoot Indians. *Anthropological Papers* 11:359-460. New York: American Museum of Natural History.

INDEX

Italicized numbers indicate illustrations.

Acrotiri, Cave of, 190
Active imagination, 195
Acoma Pueblo, *11*
Adams Lake Indian Band, *15*
Afraid-of-Bear, *106*
Aincekoko (Zuni), bear kachina, 152-54, *153*
Ainu, 181, *178*
Algonquian Indians, northern, 41, 45, 48-49, 181; tale of woman and her bear lover, 125. *See also* individual tribes
Algonquian language, 26, 115
Alo'man (Delaware), vision reciting ritual, 171-72
Alsea Indians, 137
Amnisos, Cave of, 192
Animal Mother, 200. *See also* Earth Mother
Animals: as models to be emulated, 5-6; Owners of the, 26, 174-75, 183; spiritually more powerful than humans 95; supply of, associated with the bear, 26, 57, 174-75; as symbols, 5-7
Apache Indians: bear sickness, 89; tale of Fox and Bear, 70; tales of bears stealing women, 125
Apollo, 185
Apology to slain bear, 35-36, 183
Arapaho Indians, 71, 99; refusal to eat bear meat, 55; tale of Bloodclot Boy, 136; tale of Coyote and the bear women, 140-43
Arikara Indians, *149*, *150*
Aristophanes, 185
Arkteia (Greek), initiation rite, 185
Arkteuein (Greek), acting the she-bear, 185
Arktoi (Greek), she-bear, 185
Arles-sur-Tech, 190
Artemis, 185, 190, 192-93, 200; as a bear, 185, 192-93; *Eileithyia*, 192; girls dancing for, 185; as goddess of vegetation, 190-93; marriage of, to bear, 190; as protector of animals, 192, 200; as Terrible Mother, 192. *See also* Earth Mother
Arthgal, 187
Artio, 187, 193, 195, *188*
Artos (Celtic), bear, 187
Assiniboin Indians, 54-55, 71, 90; bear dance of, 149; bear society of, 99-103, *101*; treating slain bear as enemy, 56
Atalanta, 193
Atco naxeti (Navajo), it may change into anything, 47
Athapaskan Indians, 48-49, 52, 95, 116, 125. *See also* Athapaskan Indians, Northern; individual tribes
Athapaskan Indians, northern, 121; bear hunts, 2, 45, 48-49, 52-53; beliefs about bears, 52; riddle traditions, 53;

women avoiding grizzly bears as guardian spirits, 95; women and fear of bears, 123-25. *See also* individual tribes
Ayanyan, Chief *90*

Bad-horn, 100
Bear, black, 181; dances mimicking, 157, 158; differences between attitude toward, and grizzly, 55-56, 95; hibernation of, 10; in shamanic initiation, 68; as a spirit guardian, 55, 95
Bear, Eurasian brown, 181
Bear, grizzly: bundle, 105; considered half human, 2, 55, 121; differences between attitude toward, and black bears, 55-56, 95; hat, *50*; hibernation of, 10; impersonation of, 13-14 (*see also* Dances, bear); power from meat of, 110; as spirit guardians, 91-92, 95-96; in tales, 114-15. *See also* Grizzly-bear Woman
Bear carving, Tlingit, *194*
Bear claw, *82*; necklace, *3*, *74*, *91*, *101*, *141*
Bear dance. *See* Dances, bear
Bear Dreamers Society. *See* Bear societies
Bear fat, 38, *36*
Bear goddess, 195-98, *191*. *See also* Artemis; Artio; Ursanna; Ursula
Bear grease, 167; bladder sac for, *33*; ceremonial use of, 25, 29, 37-38, 60; general uses of, 38, 60
Bear Head, 1
Bear knife: of Assiniboin, 100, 103; of Blackfeet, *97*; of Sarcee, 99; transfer of, bundle, 97-99
Bear-Looks-Back, *106*
Bear medicine men, 75, 78; Lakota rituals of, 78-82, 103. *See also* Bear societies
Bear nurse, 192, *191*
Bear pole, *41*
Bear's Arm, 96
Bear's chin, as charm, *40*, *43*
Bear's Day, 192
Bear sickness, 50-51, 87-89
Bearskins: ritual treatment of, 40, 60; uses of, 60; in World Renewal Ceremony, 164, 170; worn by shaman, *62*
Bear skull, painted, 25, 39-40, 49, *24*, *41*, *42*
Bear societies: as curing societies, 78-82, 103-5; dances of, 81-82, 147, 151, 154; feast of, 100; female, 105; among Great Plains tribes, 78-82, 99-105; Iroquois, 157; rituals of, 81-82, 157; warriors of, 100-103, 186-87, *101*
Bear-Stops, The-, *106*
Bear tongue as charm, *31*, *43*
Bearwalk, 72-73, 78, *72*
Bear-With-White-Paw, *74*

Beaver Indians, 63
Beowulf, 188
Berne, Switzerland, 187, *188*
Berserks, 73, 186-87
Big Dipper. *See* Ursa Major
Big House, 164, 165; construction of, 165; dualism symbolized in, 174; symbolism of, 165-66. *See also* World Renewal Ceremony
Big House Ceremony of Oklahoma Delaware, 174-75, *176*
Bijosh yeda'a' (Navajo), the overwhelming vagina, 128
Bison, 5-6
Bitterroot Mountains, 200-201
Bjarki, Bodvar, 187-88
Black-bear, 97-99
Black bear. *See* Bear, black
Black Elk, 78
Blackfeet Indians, 2, 71; bear dances, 150-51, 154-55, 201; bear knife of, *97*; bear-knife bundle transfer ceremony, 97-99; bear society, 103, 154; Bloodclot Boy tale, 136; healing rite, 84-86, *85*; taboo against killing bears, 55; women avoiding bear hides, 55; word for bear, 55
Blackfoot. *See* Blackfeet Indians
Black Grizzly Bear,
Blood, bears associated with, 133
Blood, Indians, *99*
Boas, Franz, 115
Bones, beliefs about, 68, 69-70
Bones, ritual treatment of bear, 28, 39-40, 49, 69, 180, 181, 184, *24*, *41*, *42*
Brauronia, 185, 192-93
Brown, Joseph Epes, 6, 151
Brown Bear, 114
Brown bear. *See* Bear, grizzly
Bulgaria, 192

Caddo Indians, 136
Camas, 1, 136-37
Candlemas, 190-91
Carcass, ritual treatment of bear, 36-37, 41, 47-48, 48-49, 56, 116, 119, 123, 170, 150, 180, 183
Caribou: East Cree hunters' attitudes toward, 42-43; Owner of the, 26
Carrier Indians: bear hunts of, 60; bear as totem animal among, 109; initiation of, youth, 109
Carrying line, 34, *28*; draped on bear, 35, 36
Catlin, George, 84, *85*
Celestial Bear Comes Down to Earth, The (Frank Speck), 165
Cherokee Indians: bear dance, 157; bear pipe, *x*, *xi*; winter ceremony, 75
Cheyenne Indians, xv, 71; bear hunting,

55; beliefs about bears, 75; counting coup on bears, 56; use of plant medicines, 76-77; women avoiding bear hides, 55

Chickasaw Indians, 89

Chief George, 107

Chief-maker of the Delaware, 169

Chukchansi Indians, 64

Cicenapew (Cree), Owner of the Caribou, 26

Clackamas Indians, 132-33

Clans, bear, 6, 107-9, 147

Comb case, birch bark, 27

Conjurers, 26-28

Coos Indians: tale of girl who became a bear, 17-18; tale of Night-rainbow and Grizzly Bear, 136-37

Corn Mother, 175, 193

Coyote tale, 140-43

Cree Indians. *See* Cree Indians, East; Cree Indians, Mistassini; Cree Indians, Plains

Cree Indians, East, 7, 71, 200; attitude of the successful hunter, 36-37; bear hunt of, 25-45; bear hunting charm of, *40, 43*; bear pole of, *41*; beliefs about bear hunting, 42-45; carrying line of, *28*; division of space in lodges of, 37; names for bear, 33, 35, 41, 181; relation of bear hunt to other hunts, 43-44; ritual treatment of carcass, 35-37, 41; ritual treatment of skull, 25, 39-40, 49, *24, 41, 42*; story telling of, 114; tale of Nenimis, 39; Twins tale, 136. *See also* Cree Indians, Mistassini; Naskapi Indians

Cree Indians, Mistassini, 137-40

Cree Indians, Plains, 55, 99; bear dance of, 149; healing powers of bear among, 75-76

Creek Indians, 89

Cross-legged, 96

Crow Indians: Big Dog Society, 103; man imitating bear, 105-7; use of plant medicines, 77

Crow Bull, 96

Culture hero, 128, 137

Curer. *See* Healer, bear as

Czechoslovakia, 189-90

Dakota Indians, 12-13, 99, 136, *106*

Dances, bear, 147-61, *146, 149, 150, 155, 156, 158, 159 161*; costumes for, 152-54; reasons for, 149-50, 161, 185. *See also* individual tribes

Dancing, wild bears, 147-49, 157, *159*, 160

Deadfall, 59, *58*

Delaware Indians, 7, 149, 163-77, *167, 173*; bear hunt of, 163-64, 170, 173; tale of Ursa Major, 167, 168-69. *See also* Munsee-Mahican.

Delaware Indians, Oklahoma, 165; Doll Dance of, 175; mask and drumsticks used in Big House *176*; Mask Spirit, *162*; New-year's Ceremony of, 174

Demeter, 190, 193

Den, bear 1, 9-10, 63, 109, 200-201; checking during hunt, 32, 58; in initiation and dance rituals, 12, 14, 17, 18, 22-23, 86-87 150-51, 154; in tales, 1, 17, 154, 159, 118, 137-39; on tepee cover, *22*

Denmark, 187

Devouring female, bear as, 126-29, 129-33, 192-93

Diana, 192, 195

Dikte, Cave of, 192

Dionysus, 192

Diet, Indian, 5

Divination: bear bones used for, 28; dreams used for, 28-32; role of, in the bear hunt, 26-32, 43-45, 181-83; shaking tent used for, 26-28

Divine Child, 192

Djakabish, 134-36

Dogs, bear hunting, 59, 119-21

Dorset culture, *122*

Dreams: bear, of contemporary Europeans, 195-98; bear hunting, 25, 28-32, 32, 40; dance songs from, 159; designs and songs used in the hunt from, 29, 33, 34, *27, 28*; and divination, 25, 28-32; Indian beliefs about, 28-29; interpretation of, 29; role of, in Delaware hunt, 163, 169, 170; *taawpwaataakan* and use of charms to bring, 25, 29, 40

Dressing slain bears, 36, 37, 47-48, 170-71

Drum, Delaware, *167*

Eagle Shield, 79-81, *79, 80, 82*

Earth Mother, 195-200; archetype of, 196-98. *See also* Animal Mother; Mother Goddess

Eat-all feast, 37-39, 41, 173, 183-84; division of meat in, 37, 183-84; feast-giver's role, 37-39; importance of, to East Cree, 38; sealing the lodge, 37; similarities to shaman's initiation, 69. *See also* Feast

Eliade, Mircea, 68

Embaros, 185

England, 189

Eskimo, 68, 69, 75, 95-96, *66-67*,

Estonians, 181

Etap, Charlie, 137

Exogamy, 122

Fastnachtsbar (German), Shrovetide Bear, 189

Fear of bears, 2, 51-52, 123-25, 132-33, 135-37

Feast, bear: Ainu, *178*; Finnish, 180; Lapp 183-84; in World Renewal Ceremony, 171, 172. *See also* Eat-all feast

Feather Head, 99

Feminine, bear as a symbol of, 128, 132-33, 195-200

Fetish, Zuni bear, *xi, xiv*

Figurine, bear, 192, *15, 62, 66, 67, 191*

Finland, 179-81

First fruits ritual, 148

Flathead Indians. *See* Salish Indians, Inland

Foods, bear, 76-77

Fool Bull, *3*

Fox Indians, 71; bear claw necklace, *141*; bear as totem animal for, 107; practice of scalping bears, 56; Twins tale, 136

Free, Stuart, 10

Gatherer, bear as, 76

Gayton, Anne, 148

Geese, Owner of the, 26

Gentes, bear, 107-8

Germany, 189-90

Gifford, Edward, 126

Gimbutas, Marija, 192

Girls: imitating bears, 185; initiation of, 14-18, 185. *See also* Women

Great Bear. *See* Ursa Major

Great Turtle, 165, 168

Grettir, 188

Grizzly bear. *See* Bear, grizzly

Grizzly-bear Woman, 95, 129-34, 200; characteristics of, 132-33; in Nez Perce tale, 129-32; in Talkema tale, 114

Gros Ventre Indians, 97, 136

Ground Hog Day, 190-92

Guardian spirit, 91-111; born with, 96; in Europe, 186-87; general concept, 92-95; inherited, 96-97; medicine bundles for, 95, 97; person's body inhabited by, 72, 107, 130; purchase of, 97-99. *See also* Athapaskan, northern; Nez Perce; Spirit helper

Gunther, Erna, 44-45

Gwizhii ideegwidlii (Kutchin), wisdom that is performed, 53

Gwizhii ideeridlii (Kutchin), wisdom that is told, 53

Haida Indians, *107*

Hallowell, Irving, 41, 184

Hat, grizzly bear, *51*

Headdress, bear, *1*

Healing animal, bear as, 66, 71-72, 75-89, 103-5, 147, 157, 189, *76*

Hellespont, 186

Henderson, Joseph, 4

Herodotus, 186

Hibernation, 9-10, 12; associated with initiation, 10-23

Hidatsa Indians: bear society, 100; shield of, *ii*; vision quest, 96; wife acquiring grizzly spirit through husband, 105

High-Bear, *106*

Hokkaido, 181

Hopewell Culture, *62*

Hopi Indians, 136

Hultkrantz, Ake, 147

Hungarians, 181, 192

Hunting, bear, 25-61, 179-84; charms, 41, 61, *30, 40, 43*; circumpolar, tradition, 41-42, 173, 181-84; equated with war, 56-57; failed hunt, *54*; petroglyph depicting, *46, 49*; speeches made to bear, 35-36, 41, 47, 56-57, 179, 183; taboos governing women, 36, 37, 60 180, 183-84; two phases of, 32, 181; weapons, 35, 44, *46*, 48, *49, 54, 58-59*, 51, 64, 181. *See also* individual tribes

Hupa Indians, 77

Huron Indians, 71; bear dance, 87

Hygelac, 188

Hymes, Dell, 114-15

Igjugarjuk, 66-67

Iktomi (Lakota), 78

Imitation of bears, 6; during agricultural rites, 189-90; in bear societies, 100-106; among berserks, 186-87; during bundle transfer, 98; during healing rites, 81-82, 85-86, 87, *84, 85*; during initiation rites, 12, 13-14, 22, 109, 185-86. *See also* Dances, bear

Immortality, bear as a symbol of, 22-23, 44-45, 186

Indians, correspondences with bears, 2, 4, 5, 76-77. *See also* individual tribes.

Ingalik Indians, 1

Initiation: of Acoma Pueblo youth, *11*, of Carrier youth, 109; of Coast Pomo youth, 13-14; correspondences with hibernation, 10-12, 17, 22-23, 66-67; of Dakota boys, 12-13; of Eastern Pomo boys, 14; general, 10-12; of Greek girls, 185; of Midewiwin Society, 18-22, *19, 20, 21*; of Ojibwa girls, 14-17, 185; of Pueblo boys, 9, *11*; of secret societies, 18

Iowa Indians, 71, 99, 136

Iroquois bear dance, 157

Isleta Pueblo, 9

Ivory carving of bear and woman, *122*

Jacobs, Melville, 132

James Bay, 29, 32

Jemez Pueblo, 56

Johns, Maria, 116

Jolly, Anderson, 39

Jung, Carl, 195-98

Kachina, bear, 152-54, *153*,

Kallisto, 193

Kanatiwat, Charlie, 29-31

Kaska Indians, 200

Katebetuk, William, 31-32

Keepers of the Game. *See* Animals; Owners of the Animals

Ket, 183

King Arthur, 187

King Hrolf (king of Denmark), 187

Kinnikinnick, 76-77

Kiowa Indians: Bear Woman Society, 105; tale of Bloodclot Boy, 136; tepee cover, *22, 93*

Klamath Indians, 68

Kootenai Indians, 2, 55, 87-88; bear dance, 149

Koyukon Indians: bear-telling riddles of, 53; grizzly bears and, 55-56; names for bear, 181; treatment of bearskins, 60; women and fear of bears, 123-25; women showing genitals to bears, 123

Krokoton (Greek), robe worn during Arkteuein, 185

Kuksu (Pomo), mythological First Man, 13-14

Kutchin Indians, bear-telling riddles of, 53

Kwakiutl Indians: bear and neophyte carving, *8*; beliefs about bears, 96; eating bear meat to gain power, 110-11; grizzly bear dancer, *155, 161*; hunter's speech to bear, 56

Kyaio (Blackfeet), black bear, 55

Kydonia, 190

Lakota Indians, 71; bear dance, 81-82, 149; bear doctor's necklace, *74*; bear medicine men, 75, 78-82, *79, 80, 82*; bear society, 78, 99, 103; emergence myth, 78; shield, *102*; tale of man transformed into bear, 71-72; winter count, *124*; women avoiding bear hides, 55, 125

Lamut, 183

Lankford, George, 136

Lapps, 181, 183

Levi-Strauss, Claude, 122

Lithuania, 189

Little Priest, 86-87

Lokis (Prosper Merimee), 188-89

Lone Chief, 93

Lonnrot, Elias, 180

Lysistrata (Aristophanes), 185

McClellan, Catharine, 116, 121, 122, 123

Magical Men, 168, 170, 171-72

Mahchsi-Karehde (Flying Eagle), *91*

Mahican Indians, 164. *See also* Munsee-Mahican

Maidu Indians: bear dance, 149, 152; bear hunt, 59-60

Make Prayers to the Raven (Nelson), 53

Mammaqunikap (Ute), Forward-Backward Dance, 158-61, *158, 159*

Man associated with death and animals, 166-67

Mandan Indians, 71, 99

Map of select tribes, *vi*

Mask: black bear, *7*; Delaware, *162, 166, 174, 176*

Mask Spirit: as Guardian of the Corn, 175; as Owner of the Animals, 174-75

Maternal devotion, bear as a symbol of, 4

Mato wan winsan manu (Lakota), A bear came to steal a virgin, 124

Maxkok, 163-64, 177

Medicine bag, bear paw, *20*

Medicines, bear as guardian of first, 76

Memekwesiw (Cree), Owner of the Bears, 39, 42, 183; in divination rites, 26-28, 32; fighting with shamans, 26-28; in name for bear, 33; offerings and

prayers to, 34, 36, 37, 38; as Owner of the Animals, 26. *See also* Owner of the Animals; Owner of the Bears

Menomini Indians, 136

Menstruation: bears associated with, 14, 16-18, 55, 125, 109, 125, 133, 185; Indian beliefs regarding, 14-16; initiation at time of first, 14

Merimee, Prosper, 188-89

Miami Indians, 75

Micmac, 136

Midewiwin lodge, *19*

Midewiwin Society, 18; bear paw medicine bag of, *20*; concern with immortality, 18, 21-22, 186; evil bear of, *21*; initiations of, 18-22, *19*; plant knowledge of members, 78

Mimbres pottery images, *5, 52*

Misinghalikun (Delaware), Living Solid Face, 174, *162*

Moon, 9; associated with goddess, 192, 196-97; crescents on bear nurse, 192; in World Renewal Ceremony, 164, 167, 168, 170, 171, 198

Morris, C. Patrick, 128

Mother goddess, 195-98; epiphanies of, 192. *See also* individual goddesses

Mountainway Ceremony, *88*

Mountain Wolf Woman, 14

Mukowe (Ojibwa), she is a bear, 16, 185

Mu'kwa (Winnebago), 107

Muller, Werner, 173, 174, 175

Munsee Indians, 164. *See also* Munsee-Mahican

Munsee-Mahican Indians, 164-74, 175-77, 198. *See also* Delaware Indians

Munychia, 193

Mural, bear, *11*

Names, Indian bear, 109, *106*

Names for bear, 2, 33, 35, 41, 49, 55, 123, 181

Nane (Kwakiutl), Grizzly bear dancer, *155*

Naskapi Indians, 134, *24, 27, 30, 33*

Native American. *See* Indian; individual tribes

Nature, bear as a symbol of wild, 128-29, 137. *See also* Earth Mother.

Navajo Indians: bear hunt, 47-51; bear sickness, 50-51, 89, *88*; painting, *88*; reasons for killing bears, 49-50; bear tales of, 128, 200

Necklace. *See* Bear claw necklace

Nekatcit, 164, 165

Nelson, Richard, 53, 55, 125

Neumann, Erich, 4

Nevilles, crest of, 187

Nez Perce Indians: Grizzly-bear woman, 129-33, 200; problems with translating tales of, 115; women avoiding grizzly bear as guardian spirit, 95

Night-rainbow, 136

Nitakyaio (Kootenai), real bear or grizzly bear, 55

No Ears, *124*

Nootka Indians, *156*

Odyssey, The (Homer), 188
Ojibwa Indians, 2, 71; apology to slain bear, 183; belief in bearwalks, 72-73, *72*; girls identified with bears, 14-17, 185; initiation of girls, 14-17; Midewiwin Society, 18-22; miniature bears residing in people, 107; tales, telling of, 113-14; Twins tale, 136; use of plant medicines, 77, 78. *See also* Ojibwa Indians, Plains
Ojibwa Indians, Plains, 55
Okiciko, 26
Old Kalevala, The (Elias Lonnrot), 179-80, 183
Omaha Indians: bear societies, 99; grizzly bear doctor, 103
Ostyak, 181
Otter-chief, 105
Owner of the Animals: bear as, 26, 41, 57, 174; Cree beliefs about, 26, 43, 45; Finn conception of, 183; Oklahoma Delaware conception of, 174; shaman's journey to, 70-71
Owner of the Bears, 26, 70. *See also* Mask Spirit; *Memekwesiw*; Owner of the Animals

Panagia Arkoudiotissa (Cretan), Mary, She of the Bear, 190
yPa'nongkasi (Maidu), bear dance, 152
Parsnip root, 97, 98
Passamaquoddy Indians, *54*
Pa'tama'was (Delaware), The Being Prayed To, 166, 167, 168, 171
Pawnee Indians, 71; bear dance, 147; guardian spirit concept of, 96; pipe, *69, 139*; tale of Bloodclot Boy, 136
People of the Myth (painting), *89*
Perqanaq, 66-67
Persephone, 190, 193
Petroglyph, *4, 46, 49, 70, 71*
Phinney, Archie, 115, 129
Pictograph, *113*
Piegan Indians. *See* Blackfeet Indians
Pima Indians, 51, 89
Pinjiz, 96
Pipe, bear: Cherokee, *x, xi*; Pawnee, *69, 139*
Plants as medicine, 76-84
Plenty-bear, 106-7
Plenty Coups, 110
Plough Monday, 189
Pohot, Joe, 151
Polar bear hunt, 29-31
Pomo Indians: bear shamans, 68; initiation of youth, 13-14; Kuksu, 13-14
Pomo Indians, Coast, 14
Pomo Indians, Eastern, 13-14
Ponca Indians, 71, 99, 136
Potawatomi, 71
Prairie Potawatomi Indians, 6; use of plant medicines, 77
Prayer sticks, 167
Preston, Richard, 29
Pueblo Indians: bear sickness, 51, 89; beliefs about bears, 51, 89; doctors as

bears, 71, 82-83, *84*; guardian spirit, concept of, 96; plant medicines of, 83; treatment of slain bear, 56; winter solstice ceremony, 149. *See also* individual pueblos
Puhagant (Shoshoni), medicine man, 147
Pythagoras, 186

Radin, Paul, 86
Rasmussen, Knud, 66, 69
Raven tale, 143-45
Red Cloud, *106*
Religious symbol, bear as, 6, 184, 193. *See also* Symbol
Renewal, bear as a symbol of, 7, 45, 89, 148, 172-73
Riddles, bear-telling, 53
Romania, 192
Rosetta (bear's bride), 190

Sacred Marriage, 190
Salish Indians, Inland: pit-roasted bears, 60; vision quest, 91-92.
Salmon, 1, 44-45
Sapir, Edward, 115
Sarcee Indians, 99
Sate-tsow-hee, 105
Sauk Indians, 107-9, 136, *141*
Schultz, James W., 55
Sculptures, terracotta, of bears, 192, *191*
Sdipp-Shin-Mah, 91-92
Selected Men, 168, 169, 170
Selmo, Sapiel, *54*
Seneca Indians, 136
Shakes, Chief, *108*
Shaking Tent, 26-28, 44
Shaman: Basque, 187; bear as, 63-64, 123; charm, *65, 66, 67*; fights with the bear spirit, 26-28, 64, 137-40, 187-88; as healer, 71-72, 84-86, *85*; and the hunt, 26-28; initiation of, 66-69; initiatory vision of, 68; mystical flights of, 70-71; role of, in society 66, 70-72; trance, 70
Shamanism compared with guardian spirit concept, 92-93
Shield: Hidatsa, *ii*; Lakota, *102*; Shoshoni, *199*; Upper Missouri, *94*; Zuni, *104*
Shoshoni Indians, 96, 147
Shrovetide bear, 189, 192
Sia Pueblo, *84*
Siberia, 183; central, 187; Kolyma lowland, 181; western, 181-82. *See also* individual groups
Sioux Indians: bear dance of, *146*; bear painted tepee, *144, 197*; Fool Bull, *3*; headdress of, *1*; names, *106*. *See also* Dakota Indians; Lakota Indians
Skeels, Dell, 132-33
Skeletonized bears, *66, 67*
Snares, 58-59, *59*
Socrates, 189
Song: bear hunt, 33, 47-48; to call a spirit guardian, 95; to cure bear sickness, 51, 89; dance, 148, 150, 157,

159, 160; for medicine plants, 78-79; shaman's, 64, 137-38; sung by bears, 83, 147
Speck, Frank, 165, 168, 169, 174, 175
Spirit helper, bear as, *84*. *See also* Guardian spirit
Spiritual Legacy of the American Indian, The (Brown), 6
Spring as season for hunt, 32, 41, 181
Stacey, Jim, 126
Story telling, 113-15
Straw-bear, 189, 190, 192
Sun Dance, 147
Sweat bath: in Midewiwin initiations, 19; as preparation for bear hunt, 33-34; as preparation for bundle transfer, 97-98
Sweden, 190
Symbol, 151. *See also* Religious symbol

Taawpwaataakan (Cree), that which brings dreams, 25, 29, 40
Tacitus, 186
Tagish Indians, 200; tale of girl who marries a bear, 116, 121, 123
Takelma Indians, 114-15
Tale: Bear Old Man Digs for Medicine, 82-83; bear-son, 188; bear-wife, 116-25, 129, 187-88; Bear Woman with the Snapping Vagina, The, 126-29, 200; Bloodclot Boy, 136; Boy Who was Kept by a Bear, The, 137-40; Coyote and the Bear Women, 140-43; culture-hero, 126-29, 134-37; devouring grizzly bear, 129-34, 136-37; European and Russian bear, 187-89; Girl Who Became a Bear, The, 17-18; Girl Who Married the Bear, The, 116-25; Greek, of Ursa Major, 193; Grizzly-bear Woman, 95, 129-33, 200; of man who became a bear, 71; of man who slept in den, 1; marriage to bear, 117, 116-29, *122*, 187-89; Medicine for Pregnant Women, 77; of Nenimis, 39; Night-rainbow and Grizzly Bear 136-37; Norse, 186-87, 188; of the One Who Owns the Chin, 41; of the One Who Owns the Feast, 39; Raven Kills Grizzly Bear, 143-45; of sacred lake, 68; Stiff-legged Bear, 134-37; telling of, 113-15; trickster-bear, 140-45; Twins, 136; Ugly Boy Slays Monster Bear, 136; Ursa Major, 167, 168-69, 189, 193; Wali'ms and the Grizzly-bear Women 129-33
Tanner, Adrian, 137
Taos Pueblo, 83
Tapio, 183
Tapisikakan (Cree), chest-hanging cloth, 34, 36
Tattoo, bear, *107*
Tepee, bear, *100*; Assiniboin, *90*; Blood, *99*; Kiowa, *22, 93*; Sioux, *144, 197*
Thrace, 186
Thunder, bear associated with, 150-51, 154, 158, 160, 189

Thunderbird, 150-51
Tlingit Indians, 2, 200; bear carving of, *194*; bear as helping spirit among, 64; bear hunter's face paint, *120*; bear hunts with dogs, 59; beliefs about bear, 64; first menstruation, 16; grizzly bear song, 64; grizzly bear viewed as half human among, 55, 56; men avoiding grizzly bear as guardian spirit, 96; shaman's charm, *65*; tale of girl who married the bear, 116-25; totemism, *108*
Tobacco offering to bear spirit, 25, 34, 35, 36-37, 40, 43, 86, 157
Totemism, 107-9, *107*, *108*
Transformation into bear, 64, 71-73, 121, 131, 133, 139, 151, 187
Transformed human, bear considered, 51, 55
Traps, bear, *58*, *59*
Trickster tales, 140-43
Tritt, Abel, 53
Tsimshian Indians, 143
Tug-of-war contest, 171
Tungus, 187
Turtle (as sacred animal), 168
Turtle shell rattle: of Oklahoma Delaware, 175; in World Renewal Ceremony, 168, 170, 171, *173*,
Tutchone Indians, 121, 123-24
Twenyucis, 163
Tyon, Thomas, 81

Unami Indians, 164-64. *See also* Delaware Indians, Oklahoma
Ursa Major, 167, 168-69, 189, 193 195-96
Ursanna, 195-96, 198
Ursula, 193
Ursula, Saint, 193
Ute bear dance, 158-61, *158*, *159*

Vainamoinen, 179-80, 183
Vegetation, bear as God of, 174, 190, 192
Vegetation spirit, bear as, 174
Virgin Mary, 190, 193
Vision quest, 91-95, 96. *See also* Guardian spirit
Voguls, 181, *182*
von Franz, Marie-Louise, 196

Wakan (Lakota), 75, 81
Wali'ms, 129-34
Warwick, earls of, 187
Way of the Masks, The (Levi-Strauss), 122
Wayilatpu, 129
Wedge, Dora Austin, 116
Wemukowe (Ojibwa), going to be a bear, 16, 185
White Man, Chief, *93*
Wichita Indians, 136
Wikhegan (Passamaquoddy), storied mark on birch bark, 54
Wilson, Maggie, 107
Winnebago Indians, 71, 100; bear clan, 109; bear dance, 86-87, 89; beliefs

about menstruation, 14
Wita'mumpsi (Klamath), Black Bear's Place, 68
Withke'katen (Delaware), Moon of the New Year, 170
Wolf, 5, *113*
Women: addressing bears, 123-25; associated with bears, 14-15, 17-18, 119; associated with life and plants, 166; avoided bears, 55, 119, 123-25; as bears, 17-18, 121, 126-29, 129-33, 192; bears attracted to, 123-25, 188-89; exposing genitals to bears, 123; and fear of bears, 125; marriage to bear, 116-25, 188-89; menstruating, and bears, 14-15, 17-18, 55, 109, 125, 133; place held in Delaware culture, 169; taboos governing, 36, 37, 60 180, 183-84; transformed by marriage, 122. *See also* Girl; Grizzly-bear Woman; menstruation
World Renewal Ceremony (Big House Ceremony), 163-74; dances, 171-72; dualism in, 173, 174; number twelve in, 168; role of bear in, 163-64, 168-69, 170-71, 172, 174
World Tree, 165-66; *167*, 172

Xuts tla (Tlingit), Bear Mother, 200
Xwate'k'an (Delaware), The Big House, 165. *See also* Big House

Yanktonai Indians, 71
Yarrow, 76
Yavapai Indians, 4-6; avoided bear hunting, 55; bear as shaman among, 63; snapping vagina tale, 126-29, 200
Yokuts Indians: dance of, 6, 147-49; man transformed into bear, 151; shaman Supana, 84
Yuchi Indians, 107
Yugoslavia, 192
Yukaghir, 181

Zalmoxis, 186, 189, 192
Zeus, 192, 193
Zuni: bear kachina, 152-54 *153*; bear fetish, *ix, xiv*; doctors called bears, 71, 86; initiations, 9; man transformed into bear, 71; Mixed Dance, 154; plant knowledge of healers, 78; shield, *104*; Winter Solstice Ceremony, 86